A MEMOIR OF CHRIST

A Student of A Course in Miracles Awakens

Elizabeth Cronkhite

Copyright © 2021 Elizabeth Cronkhite

All rights reserved

No part of this book may be reproduced, or stored in a retrieval system, or transmitted in any form or by any means, electronic, mechanical, photocopying, recording, or otherwise, without express written permission of the publisher (author).

ISBN: 9798544858317

Library of Congress Control Number: 2018675309
Printed in the United States of America

CONTACT LIZ

To contact Liz for interviews, life coaching, or Joining in Christ, or for information about her books, both nonfiction and fiction, go to www.LizCronkhite.net.

OTHER BOOKS BY LIZ CRONKHITE

<u>Spiritual Nonfiction</u>

The Plain Language *A Course in Miracles*:

The Message of A Course in Miracles*: A translation of the Text in Plain Language*

Practicing A Course in Miracles/*The Way of* A Course in Miracles*: A translation of the Workbook and Manual for Teachers in Plain Language*

Volumes 1, 2, 3 of The ACIM Mentor Articles: Answers for students of *A Course in Miracles* and *4 Habits for Inner Peace*

4 Habits for Inner Peace

Releasing Guilt for Inner Peace: A Companion to *4 Habits for Inner Peace*

<u>Non Spiritual Fiction</u>

A Good Woman

Towing the Moon

TABLE OF CONTENTS

How to read notations for *A Course in Miracles* and this memoir...IX

What is *A Course in Miracles*?...XI

Preface...XV

Introduction...1

Prologue...7

Life I: Split-mind (Christ Unconscious)...9

  One: Undoing...10
  Two: Sorting Out...50
  Three: Relinquishment...98
  Four: Settling...123

Life II: One Mind (Christ Consciousness)...160

  Introduction...162
  A. End Game...164
  B. The Holy Relationship...190
  C. The Terrible Conflict...232
  D. The Dismantling...258
  E. New Life, New Love, New Land...279
  F. Closure...313

Afterword: The Path to (Six) Achievement...364

Ontology of *A Course in Miracles*...372

Glossary of Terms...377

Glossary of Significant Events in Liz's Experience...383

Acknowledgments

HOW TO READ REFERENCE NOTATIONS FOR A COURSE IN MIRACLES AND THIS MEMOIR

Quotes for *A Course in Miracles* throughout this book are in italics and followed by a reference notation in parentheses. Here is how to decipher the references:

T-1.II.3 Text, chapter 1, subsection II, paragraph 3

W-1.2 Workbook, lesson 1, paragraph 2

M-1.2 Manual for Teachers, question 1, paragraph 2

C-1.2 Clarification of Terms, term 1, paragraph 2

Here is how to decipher reference notations to other passages in this memoir:

LI-Two.3 Life 1, chapter Two, subsection 3

LII-C.4 Life II, part C, subsection 4

WHAT IS *A COURSE IN MIRACLES*?

This memoir describes my spiritual path, which was *A Course in Miracles*. As markers along my path, I use the periods a student of *A Course in Miracles* can expect to go through to achieve inner peace (*Development of Trust*, M-4.I.A). As not everyone who reads this book will be familiar with the *Course*, I introduce it here.

Certainly, if you are a student of the *Course*, you do not need this introduction and can go right to the Preface. If you are on a similar nondualistic (one Truth) path, you also may wish to get started at the Preface and perhaps return here if you find you need to understand something specific about the *Course*. But if you are not familiar with the *Course* or nonduality, be prepared that what the *Course* teaches may seem radical. This may make you curious about my story or it may turn you off. Either way, so be it. However, you, too, may wish to dive in at the Preface and return here later if you find you need to understand what the *Course* is.

One of the first challenges a student of the *Course* faces is how to describe it to others. It took me many years before I came up with a succinct description: *A self-study course for inner peace.*

It is, as it says, one of many thousands of paths to the same goal. If you feel moved to find inner peace (you may put it a different way - find fulfillment, answers, love, happiness, etc.), a path that will lead you to it will show up. That may or may not be *A Course in Miracles* as

> *A universal theology is impossible, but a universal experience is not only possible but necessary.* (C-in.2)

In my experience as a teacher and life coach for students

of the *Course*, I found that some use it to make for themselves a more harmonious life in the world. It offers many tools for this. Others, however, feel pulled to Truth and find in the *Course* a path to awaken to their Reality in God (the Transcendent and Only Reality; limitless, timeless, formless).

Nothing real can be threatened. Nothing unreal exists. Herein lies the peace of God. (T-Intro)

The *Course* teaches that only God is real. Consciousness, or existence, is an illusion. You cannot deny you experience consciousness; in fact, to do so would denigrate the power of your mind. Instead, you can discover the Bridge to God in consciousness, Christ (or Spirit) within your mind, to lead you to an awareness of Reality, God.

There are only two possible experiences in consciousness, Love (Spirit) and fear (ego), and they are completely different experiences of existence. Love comes from God and reflects your Wholeness in Truth (God). Fear is opposed to Love (God) and is a false state of lack.

In ego-identification, you have only one problem, the belief that you are separate from God. This is known as the "authority problem", or the belief that you are what you make of yourself (a person), rather than as God created you (Christ/Spirit). This puts you in perceived conflict with God, which is reflected in your conflicts within yourself and with others. As others are the mirror in which you see yourself, the *Course* uses your relationships with others as the means to heal yourself.

Using Christian symbols, but uniquely blending timeless and universal spiritual and psychological truths, the *Course* leads you to the awareness of the part of you that is Part of God (Christ), healing your conflict with yourself, leading to inner peace.

The *Course* offers a two-pronged approach: As you grow your awareness of God within (Christ), you face the guilt and fear that block your awareness of God. With Spirit (the teaching aspect of Christ in your mind), you undo your belief in these obstacles, so you are willing to accept yourself as God created you.

There are three "tools" for gaining inner peace in the *Course:* The Holy Spirit, the holy instant, and the holy relationship. Spirit is your Inner Teacher and comes from Christ, the part of every mind that is Part of God. The holy instant is any moment you choose to be still and turn inward to your Christ Mind. And the holy relationship is the expression of the holy instant in your awareness of Christ in you mirrored in your awareness of what seems like another.

The *Course* consists of three books: Text, Workbook, and Manual for Teachers. The Text lays out the theory of the *Course,* the Workbook is a year of practice, and the Manual for Teachers outlines the path by answering questions likely to arise for students. There are also three supplements, *Clarification of Terms*, which is attached to the Manual for Teachers; and *Psychotherapy: Purpose, Process, Practice* and *Song of Prayer: Prayer, Forgiveness, Healing*, which came later. All these books and supplements can now be found in one volume.

It is not required that students share with or teach the *Course* to others. The Manual for Teachers is for students, whom the *Course* calls *teachers of God.*

Everyone teaches all the time, and they only teach themselves. By choosing the perceptions of either ego or Spirit in your mind, you teach yourself every moment what you believe you are. All you are responsible for is "accepting the Atonement" *for yourself*. This means accepting correction of the perception that you are separate from God.

The *Course* was "scribed" by Dr. Helen Schucman, a child psychologist, and a colleague, Dr. Bill Thetford, in the late 1960s and early 1970s. An agnostic, Dr. Schucman was surprised to hear an internal Voice she understood to be Jesus speaking to her. She took down the *Course* in her own shorthand and read her notes to Dr. Thetford, who typed it out.

The *Course* came through Helen and Bill's holy relationship. This and Helen's specific obstacles to inner peace proved the context for the *Course.* You can read their story in the book, *Journey Without Distance*, by Robert Skutch.

As it is a self-study path, there is no overarching organization for disseminating *A Course in Miracles*. In fact, the *Course's* goal is for you to be guided by your own Internal Teacher, Spirit. Any guidance you receive from other teachers should come through the guidance of Spirit. Many teachers and some independent organizations have sprung up to share and teach the *Course,* and there are hundreds of informal *Course* study groups around the world. It has been translated into all major and many minor languages.

At the end of this book, you will find the *Course's* ontology, or theory of existence, as it was given to me, as well as a glossary of terms.

PREFACE

[Christ] is the only part of you that has reality in truth. The rest is dreams. (W-pII.6.3)

Imagine sleeping and dreaming and learning in the dream that you are dreaming. But you go on for a long while feeling the dream is real. Then, suddenly, you are aware of the dream *as* a dream and the dream shifts to reflect your awakened state.

This is what happened to me. Only, I wasn't sleeping.

Sleeping and dreaming are metaphors for consciousness, or the experience of existence in a material world. As one can only be said to be fully *Awake* in God, when one's consciousness shifts toward God, it is to an awakened dream that reflects the Wholeness (Oneness) of God.

The substance of consciousness has not changed for me. There is still a material world before me. But my experience of existence has changed, and with it my experience of myself and the material world. In a moment I call *The Break*, I awoke to my reality as God's Extension, Christ, and I now know, not merely intellectually, but truly, that all of consciousness is indeed no more real than a dream.

As a teacher of *A Course in Miracles*, I taught for eighteen years that the experience of being a person in a world was a dream or illusion. But, despite glimpses of Reality now and then in miracles or Revelation, I had not realized this in an ongoing way. And I had it all backwards anyway. I thought the life that I was living as a spiritually aware person would lead to my awakening. What I did not understand was that my experience as a spiritually aware person was an effect, not a cause. That life did not lead to the awareness I am Christ. Christ was the Source of that life's spiritual process. Christ was all that was real in that life.

If this new experience of existence is *as* Christ, the life I dreamt before was *with* Christ. What emerged in my spiritual awakening was What inspired my spiritual practice in my former life. At the very least that life was, in the limited context of ego-consciousness, a good life because it was with Christ. I had as much peace as I could have. I mastered being a Spirit-centered person before it fell away.

Months after The Break, on a walk along a gum tree lined country road in summer in Elleker, Western Australia, I experienced myself as Christ. I wondered about the life that had gone before and saw it was insignificant, not dismissively, but factually. It had nothing to do with What I truly am. I did not become or attain Christ through that life. Christ was always here. The journey I seemed to take with and to Christ was a dream. It was about Christ because Christ was there in my awareness to varying degrees. But ego-consciousness could never be Spirit-consciousness. Ego did not transform; it fell away as my reality. That experience of existence met its natural end where, for this mind, existence as Spirit began.

Is [Jesus] the Christ? O yes, along with you. (C-5.5)

A day or so after The Experience as My Self (Christ) in Elleker, it came to me I would go forward with the message, "I am Christ, like Jesus, and so are you." *Oh, no, no, no, no, no.* I did not use the term *Christ* much in my teaching or writing. It is too identified with a man who lived in western Asia two thousand years ago. But this initial resistance did not matter. It faded, as did the term *Christ* (but not my Self as Christ), until a year later when, back in the US, the prologue to this book came to me. And then some of the introduction. And, finally, the title. I found I was no longer uncomfortable saying *I am Christ*. It is simply true.

[Christ] is the Self we share, uniting us with one another, and

with God as well. (W-pII.6.1)

If you think there is anything special about me or this story, it can only be ego that tells you this. The Christ in me is the Christ in you, so my memoir is yours as your memoir of Christ would be mine.

The *Course* has been published for forty-six years, so only about two generations. There has not been time for many students to offer their experience for others on the same or similar nondualistic paths. And I know many spiritual teachers who have shifted consciousness do not share their previous life, and students find this frustrating. My former life truly does not matter, but from here, where it is over. I realize that for the spiritual student, however, there is interest because it can be reassuring and validating to read of a life as unremarkable as their own, lived with Christ, and which ended as Christ in Spirit-consciousness. You should know that you do not need special qualities for this to occur.

So, I share my story, both as a Spirit-centered person in ego-consciousness and in my shift to Spirit-consciousness, as honestly as I can, and to the best of my ability to understand as I am still in transition as this is written.

Some things I share may feel too personal to the reader, but I feel an honest record of the experience of awakening can be helpful to those who follow, as we will have many of the same experiences. Keep in mind, however, that there is no *typical* way the path unfolds for *Course* students. We each embark on a process that is generally similar but unfolds uniquely for each of us. So, my former life and my shift in consciousness do not indicate how things will unfold for you, and are not templates to follow.

I cannot teach you how to awaken. That may or may not be your part to play. It is not your choice apart from the whole. But I can teach you how to find Christ within and live in relative peace, as I did in my previous life. And if your desire for Truth is a signal that you, too, will shift consciousness, then I hope the story of my transition will help you with yours.

Las Vegas, Nevada, US
2021

INTRODUCTION

At recess one morning in high school when I was fifteen, my friends were discussing Buddha and Jesus. I lived on Oahu, in Hawaii, and our school buildings opened to the outdoors. We were sitting on a bench on a hill not far outside the school library. I did not join in the conversation because I considered myself an atheist. So, I looked at the scenery and watched other students nearby. But their discussion baffled me, as they were claiming the same attributes for Buddha and Jesus but were stating that Jesus was the real deal and Buddha was not.

The bell rang for class, and as I walked away, I suddenly knew with clarity and certainty that everyone could be what Jesus was. "Why don't you become that?" a quiet, clear Voice in my mind asked.

"Because I'm not so ambitious," I answered, and shut my mind on the unidentified Voice as hard as I could.

But it was too late. Spirit had come into my conscious awareness as an insight and Voice, and although I would not think about this experience for years, my life's direction was revealed in that moment. It was only five years later that I was introduced to *A Course in Miracles* and consciously set out on a spiritual path.

This is a memoir of a mind that began almost wholly ego-identified, learned to trust Spirit within, dropped its illusion of itself as a person in a world, and awoke to itself as Christ.

God is beyond consciousness (existence), but Christ is God's Extension in consciousness, bridging consciousness and God. Christ is the part of every mind that is Part of God, so Christ is universal, not special. As only Christ in every mind is eternal, only Christ in every mind is real.

So do not mistake the person—body and personality—of Liz for Christ. The details of my former life, which was ordinary, are not the life of Christ. Instead, the trajectory and meaning of that life was Christ. It fell away when it was over, leaving only Christ. My former experience of existence was as a person. Now I exist as Christ. But Christ is not the person, whose life remains ordinary. Christ is a state of consciousness or existence. *I See* as Christ rather than *am seen as* Christ.

Identity is different as Christ than it was as a person. As a person, identity was *who* I was. As Christ, identity is *What* I am. *Who* was specific and was made; *What* is universal and given by God. The person remains, but not as my identity.

Both too much and too little is made of Christ. On one hand, Christ is exalted as a sacred and powerful state of awareness far out of reach of an ordinary mind. It is limited to Jesus, and maybe other teachers, despite their teaching It is universal. On the other hand, Christ is sometimes referred to as merely a different way to look at things, without acknowledging the complete shift in consciousness required to See as Christ.

This mind did not accept this shift in consciousness easily. I was already in the process of ego death before Christ rose as my new consciousness in an event I call *The Break*. In that moment, the existence I had known was gone and with it the life I had led. This is not a detailed story of that life, as all that was significant in it was Christ. It is an account of a student of *A Course in Miracles*' development of trust in Spirit through and to the end of one life and the beginning of her new life as Christ.

I understand now that what was to happen in my material life was to happen (and what was not to happen was never going to happen), and that any motivations I attributed to my actions (or inactions) were stories I told myself to build or reinforce an identity. But I share those stories here as I experienced them to flesh out the person I felt I was, and after the person was gone, to impart my full experience.

My message is, "I am Christ, as Jesus was, and so are you." I am aware of what ego does with a message like this, so I want to make clear that it is not intended to start a religion or to encourage a culture in which we go around calling each other *Christ*. Again, no *person* is Christ. My message is intended to inspire you to find Christ in your mind. If you take away anything else, you miss my message.

I label the significant experiences preceding and following my shift in consciousness (as in *The Break*) with tongue firmly in cheek because of how dramatically I experienced them at the time. These labels also make for easy reference. I do not intend for them to be significant markers for anyone else.

This book is written in the context of the six stages laid out in the *Development of Trust* (M-4.I.A) in the Manual for Teachers that a student of the *Course* can expect to go through as they advance. The descriptions of each stage, offered here at the beginning of each chapter, can seem rather vague. It is my belief that these descriptions are deliberately imprecise because each student will pass through them in their own unique way. They are meant to offer a *general* idea of what to expect.

The *Course* teaches that there are only two experiences of consciousness, Love and fear. Love reflects God and is an experience of abundance, wholeness, happiness, peace, and security. In the *Course* this is called *Christ* or *Holy Spirit*. Any other experience is fear, or *ego*, and is false because it seems to set you apart from God. For the purposes of this book, I use *ego-consciousness* to refer to the *state* of fear and *ego* for its manifestation in an individual mind. I use the term *Spirit-consciousness* for the state that occurs when ego no longer blocks one's awareness that God is their Source and Spirit (Christ) is their Identity.

Because *ego* is defined in different ways in different disciplines, I clarify here how I use the term as I understand it from the *Course*. As part of the material world, a body and personality—*person* in this book, but just *body* in the *Course*—are neutral expressions of consciousness, like a flower or a table or a cat; whether beautiful or ugly, strong or weak, healthy or disabled or disordered. While a person is your undeniable experience of consciousness, it is not your true identity. That is Christ (Spirit). When you identify with a person, it seems to set you apart from God, and you identify with fear (lack, limitation) and *that* is ego.

In ego, you constantly define and defend your person to set yourself apart to make yourself special, which you think will make you feel whole—or at least lack less. You attack others for not appreciating your specialness or for demanding that you appreciate theirs over your own. And you project onto others the guilt you feel for seeming to make yourself not as God created you. So, you are in constant conflict with others, with only moments of respite when ego's needs are temporarily met.

If you shift to Spirit-consciousness, ego falls away as the context of your experience. But it remains in your awareness, diminishing as your identity and defining experience. At minimum, it remains in your awareness in those around you. As you are whole in Spirit, you no longer need to make yourself special and you no longer project guilt, so you accept others as they are, and your relationships are harmonious.

The *Course* says the gap between ego and God is too wide for a mind to leap without going into shock. Spirit-consciousness reflects God's Glory to bridge ego and Truth.

While in ego-consciousness, you can choose Spirit to be the thought system that replaces ego for you as you make your way in the world. You can call on It to do so more and more. If you do, eventually you will become aware of the split in your mind between Truth and illusion. You will feel you have two realities, the world and Spirit. Your awareness of Spirit will mitigate the pains of seeming to live in the world. This describes the Spirit-centered existence I share in the first part of this book.

And if it is your part to play, you will shift to Spirit-consciousness. You will See as Spirit Sees, a world of Light, what the *Course* calls the *real world*. You will no longer repurpose the material world for a split-mind but see it as the mere appearance it is. I share how this happened for me in the second part of this book.

I certainly found the shift from ego- to Spirit-consciousness shocking enough! But in hindsight, I see I was prepared. It was often difficult, but it was never intolerable. Looking back—but certainly not always *during* it—I see Spirit gently emerging in this mind. The violence this mind seemed to experience was not due to Spirit, but rather the false boundaries of ego breaking down.

Christ is the Source of Spirit and the Inspiration of Spirit-consciousness. For me, *Spirit-consciousness* is an ongoing lighthearted sense of wholeness and en-joy-ment, and *Christ* is a Golden Light in my mind and Unity I experience in holy relationships where I recognize my Self. I feel Spirit bridges ego and Christ, and Christ bridges consciousness and God. It is because of this difference that I make a distinction between *Spirit* and *Christ*, but it is a fine distinction, and I may not always adhere to it in these pages.

As consciousness (not-God) is to Knowledge (God) as sleeping is to awake, it is my view that only in Knowledge can one be said to be *Awake*. So, consciousness is a state of sleep, or dreaming, whether one is in ego-consciousness or Spirit-consciousness. Ego-consciousness is a state of deep sleep and Spirit-consciousness is a state of *awakened dreaming* (or *enlightenment*), a light sleep where dreaming is recognized as such and is left behind more and more until such time as "God takes the last step" and lifts a mind to Knowledge.

Everyone has their part to play in the Atonement and they will do so perfectly. Some will be what I call *manifest undoers*, those who are aware of God to some degree. How this shows up and how each walks their path is unique to their mind. If your role to play is for ego to die to you and your reality as Christ to rise to your awareness, you will be ready. If you experience any difficulty around this, it will come to an end, as it did for me. Wherever you are on the path, I hope my story validates yours and helps you to understand and face the challenges of any stage as you watch it pass.

PROLOGUE

AUGUST 2014

My little cairn terrier was sick. Ginny had thrown up a couple of times that week. I did not think much of it; dogs throw up a lot and she was only four years old and healthy. Both times it was in the middle of the night and just bile. We had had many dogs, and this was nothing I hadn't seen dozens of times.

But my wife, Jessie (pseudonym), was concerned and wanted me to take her to the vet. I went over with her why she didn't have to worry. And I didn't want to make something of nothing. Only the month before, we had put down our beloved, joyous Pomeranian, Paavo, after a lifetime of health issues that had me, at the end of his fourteen years, at the vet seemingly every week. I still grieved him and wondered at a sense that a huge part of me was gone, too. I just could not believe something was wrong with Ginny. But a few days later Ginny's appetite diminished and, finally, she became lethargic.

I brought Ginny to the vet and felt validated as Dr. M was unconcerned. Ginny was young and healthy after all. She ordered blood tests and I brought Ginny home. But first thing the next morning my phone rang, and the caller ID showed it was the vet's office. I knew that could not be good. Dr. G was shocked: Ginny's liver was shot. I needed to bring her in right away for more tests and to start treatment.

Here we go again, I thought. Another dog with chronic health issues. I was destined to be on familiar terms with the staff at the vet's office. But it turned out Ginny didn't have liver disease. The damage was acute. She must have eaten something toxic. What, we would never know. She was dead within a week.

It was an awful time. My pain that week was keen and like nothing I had felt before. I was nearly overwhelmed, which I had never experienced. I realized Ginny was sick and at risk of dying right after Paavo. But Paavo's end had been sweet and inevitable, and my grief for him was gentle. This seemed like more than compound grief.

And I was certainly familiar with compound grief. At the turn of the millennium, my family went through a rough four-year period of deaths and illnesses. So, I knew how to recognize and process grief.

I *did* sense that week that we were going to lose Ginny, although I did not admit this to myself and grasped at every bit of hope the doctors offered. Unlike our other dogs, all rescues, we got Ginny as a puppy. She was my baby as no other had been. I had a special relationship with her.

But that did not seem to explain to me how deep and raw the pain was. I was in perimenopause. Was that it? I was used to hormones exaggerating my negative feelings and making me irrational, but this was *anguish* rather than disproportionate emotions. But what else could it be? That had to be it.

In the middle of that awful time a quiet thought came to me: *I am done with pain.* I did not feel this with rancor or resistance. It was a simple statement of fact.

But, done with pain or not, I was still feeling it.

What I did not know yet was that Ginny's death signaled my entry into ego death.

LIFE I: SPLIT-MIND (CHRIST UNCONSCIOUS)

ONE: UNDOING

First, they must go through what might be called "a period of undoing." This need not be painful, but it usually is so experienced. It seems as if things are being taken away, and it is rarely understood initially that their lack of value is merely being recognized. How can lack of value be perceived unless the perceiver is in a position where he must see things in a different light? He is not yet at a point at which he can make the shift entirely internally. And so the plan will sometimes call for changes in what seem to be external circumstances. These changes are always helpful. When the teacher of God has learned that much, he goes on to the second stage. (M-4.I.A.3)

<u>1</u>

What stood out for me when I began *A Course in Miracles* was how deeply familiar it felt. It was as though I had written it. It seemed to come from within me rather than the book in front of me. Of course, I had not written it. Helen Schucman had it dictated to her by a Voice in her mind that she identified as Jesus. For me, however, I knew from the start that the Voice I heard as I read it was the universal Christ. Right out of the gate the *Course* brought my Self to mind. It was my first holy relationship.

It was the middle of 1984 and I was twenty years old. Like many at that age, my life was full of new experiences, but I was not aware until I looked back much later that, for me, they were mere housekeeping and preparation for experiences that were out of the ordinary.

Only three years before, just after graduating high

school, I had come out to myself as a lesbian. This was significant for me for more than the usual psycho-emotional reasons. The moment I came out to myself I heard the Voice I would later identify as the Holy Spirit—the teaching aspect of Christ in my mind.

I had, yet again, a crush on a woman and thought, "You know this means you're a lesbian."

And the Voice answered reassuringly, "Yes, I know."

I felt joyful recognition as it seemed a curtain behind which I had been hidden was pulled back to reveal me to myself. Because of the Source of the response, I knew I was okay with God, despite living in a culture at the time that considered homosexuality a sin or disease. This only had significance for me later, however, because at the time I was too caught up in what I had just acknowledged about my personal identity to give any thought to What else I had just recognized in my mind.

Besides, I was an atheist.

It was two years before I ventured out into the lesbian community and began the process of coming out to others. Those two years were dark and full of anxiety. I had spent my teen years in fantasies of the future rather than in plans for it. I expected to marry a man and have children, just as I read in romance novels. I set this up as my salvation, not in those words, but in effect. This was supposed to be the source of my happiness.

As for a career, my mother had always told me that, no matter the limitations society put on women at that time, I could do anything I wanted. I had grown up in the second wave of feminism in the US telling me the same thing. I knew this and felt it to be true. I considered becoming a psychologist as, like my mother, I loved and had a natural aptitude for psychology. But I struggled with math and science in high school, and, despite my mother and feminism, I accepted the common fallacy that most women lacked an aptitude for math and science. So, I felt college would be an uphill battle and, although my father would help defray the costs of community college to start, I would also have to work. I simply did not want anything bad enough to work that hard.

My priority anyway was love and marriage.

After coming out to myself I had no real issue switching my fantasies of a life partner to a woman. I knew that women made less money than men and, without thinking about it consciously, I knew I was less likely to find a partner who would support me and want a housewife. So, I did expect that I would have to work outside the home all my life. However, I still felt, although I did not articulate to myself, that I wanted my personal life settled as my foundation before I would look to expressing myself through a career.

But while my fantasies adjusted easily to my reality, I still grieved the loss of who I thought I was. I discovered I had developed a false persona as a heterosexual to hide me from myself, as well as everyone else. Though false, it had been a big part of my young life. So, coming out to myself was joyous and liberating, but also difficult. While the false identity began to be undone right away, for a long time I was to run into self-concepts, habits, and expectations that did not fit.

Of course, being so young, I had no template or model for a shift on that scale. I had had a stable, structured upbringing and, although my family was not perfect, it was, for me (although not for all my siblings) happy and functional. I was the youngest of five and was loved and nurtured by everyone. But I was also shy and sensitive and easily anxious. I did not like change. Even when change was positive, I was aware of what was lost, and the smallest transitions would come with at least a spasm of grief.

This huge shift in my personal identity followed right on the heels of my first major life transition, graduating high school, for which I had also been unprepared.

Until I left high school, the only grief I had experienced was when two of my siblings left for the military. But I always knew, as the youngest, that those losses would come. I did not expect the grief that crept up on me as graduation approached. I did not ever notice my siblings grieving graduating. School was all I had ever known. I was not social outside of school, and not much in school either, so it was what community I had. Some kids I had known since kindergarten.

My classmates and I sometimes wept, but most of them seemed to have exciting plans that drew them forward out of the loss. I was excited, too, because I had always wanted to be an adult and free. But grief seemed to pass over my friends easier than it did me. I compared my insides to their outsides. I was embarrassed by emotions at that time of my life and felt them to be a weakness. I did not talk to anyone about it.

A month later I was to start hotel management courses at a one-year private business college my father insisted I attend. He was afraid I would not find a decent job without something more than a high school diploma. I did not particularly want this. But I did not want anything else, either, except my fantasies. I knew I had to do *something*.

When I was about ten I one day said to my mother, "I'm strong, aren't I?" I did not mean physically strong. I was aware of an inner strength that I discovered comparing myself to others. I was not boasting when I asked this question. It struck me as a fact. She answered yes. But, in fact, nothing tested this awareness until I was seventeen. I was grieving leaving high school and anxious about starting business college and life in general. And suddenly experiencing a huge shift in self-identification.

I felt out of control, not just of my life, but of myself. How could I have been in such *denial*? Looking back, it was obvious that I had always loved women. I plunged into a deep depression that terrified me. I feared if I became any more depressed, I would be suicidal.

My mother was aware I was depressed and was concerned, but I did not tell her why. I would not have been able to say why. I did not yet know my own mind. I only suspected my depression was related to coming out. I had never had to process anything like it, and I felt emotions without identifying them.

When my siblings grew up and moved away, I learned that anyone could leave for their own good reasons. Frankly, anyone could die. I realized the only one I had to go through life with was me. I decided I had better be happy with me because I was stuck with me. But during this episode I one day said to my parents, "What is terrifying in life is you can get away from anyone but yourself." My father was baffled. "Why would you want to get away from yourself?" My mother grew more anxious for me.

I did not intend to be in the closet for the rest of my life. In fact, I expected to live wholly out, no matter the consequences. But at that time, I could not see past my present depression and was not yet ready to come out to others. I told only my sister, E, who was still living at home, that I was gay. (She was not surprised). But I did not discuss my anxiety and depression with her.

One day, after business college, as I rode the city bus to an office job that I found miserable—which only added to my depression—an older man got on. His face was beaming as he passed out leaflets that declared the ten steps to happiness. I do not remember what they were, except that they had to do with being Love and extending Love. I also do not know if his joy and light were genuine or if he was mentally ill or high. But wherever he was coming from, I felt a flicker of recognition and stirring of joy in my heart over what he wrote. And quickly extinguished them in a hateful rage. I did not want that Light. I felt it would make me foolish and vulnerable. It threatened my sense of self-control.

I decided the man was clearly stoned, a goody-two-shoes, or delusional. I threw the leaflet in the trash as soon as I got off the bus.

I finally hit bottom one day and made an appointment at a community mental health center. A therapist there told me I was going through the coming out process and gave me the number for the gay community center in Honolulu. I was relieved to learn I was in a predictable process. I also felt, for the first time, that my self-awareness was validated. I was right about what I was going through. This was my first step in being with, looking into, and understanding my own mind.

I called the gay community center from a pay phone at school. I wish I could adequately convey what it is like for a gay person to connect with another gay person *as a gay person* for the first time. I did not have to explain a thing. All I did was ask for a referral to a therapist and I knew that the guy on the other end of the line *knew*. He knew why I had tears in my voice. He knew my experience; he had had it himself. He saw me in a way no one else did. I was not alone; he was my tribe.

After a very rough couple of years, this was a turning point. I contacted the recommended therapist, and I surprised her when, after only one session, I was out in the lesbian community for the first time.

Can I convey what it was like to walk into a room full of women for the first time and know that they all felt for women what I felt for women without questions or explanations? It felt like a miracle.

2

What followed was a period of intense personal growth. Hiding my true nature had stunted my emotional and social development in many ways. My sexual orientation was an integral part of my personal identity, after all. It was as fundamental as being female because it was the kind of female I was. And in order to not reveal this to myself, much less anyone else, I had held myself back in just about every way.

In the next two years I came into myself. I was not on the outside who I had *expected* to be, but I was now living who I *was*. I was getting to know myself and I felt strong. I felt coming out had been so shattering and difficult that, having come through that process, there was nothing else in life I could not face. But, despite this, I was still anxious and seeking control over my life. I wanted to know that there was nothing else hidden in me that would require such a shattering transformation to realize. I began to have panic attacks that seemed to come out of nowhere and only increased my anxiety. More than ever, I wanted to get a grip on fear.

So, I sought the "ultimate Liz"—the fundamental *me* that would not change. After all, I was stuck with me! I began reading self-help books. But looking inward I sensed something terrifying: My personal identity was insubstantial.

Oh, I did not want to see *that*! This was so frightening; I consciously chose to not think about it. But unconsciously, I slipped into reading books that blended psychology and spirituality. They told me there *was* Something in me that was permanent, and I sensed this to be true. It simply was not what I had hoped! But I was intrigued and hungry for the Truth *because it was the Truth*. I figured there had to be security in knowing the Truth, even if it was something I did not like.

Approaching Truth through psychology flowed naturally for me, given my intuitive understanding of it. Christian fundamentalism was growing in voice and power in American politics, turning me off Christianity more than ever. It was certainly no place for a self-respecting lesbian. Living among mostly Asian cultures in Hawaii, Buddhism was all around, but I seemed to feel its approach would be too foreign for me. Anyway, when I glanced at it, it said terrifying things like I would have to give up ego. No matter I felt liberation whenever I read this—that was no way for me. I did not realize Buddhism taught what I did not get from Christianity but did from the psycho-spiritual books that resonated deeply with me: Truth was to be found within me.

Whatever term those books used to refer to Truth within—God, Spirit, Divinity, Self, Higher Self, Christ Consciousness—this felt like something I knew, although I could not remember hearing it before.

So, I was again aware of something that put me at odds with most of the world. But I was used to being an outsider, and that meant I felt free to find what was true as I had nothing to lose. Besides, this awareness pulled at me like nothing else ever had. Nothing else had ever rung *true*. I found myself in the awareness that "the Kingdom of Heaven is within you." (A quote from the Bible. Why didn't Christians say this?)

3

I was not raised with a religion. My father grew up in a small rural town in Montana. The only church was Presbyterian, and the minister gave long, boring discourses comparing classic mythology with Christianity. This did not work to draw Dad in. Later he joined the Catholic Church for his first wife, G. But he hated the Church and stopped going when she died.

My mother's mother, who had come to the US from Sicily as an infant, was raised Catholic, but left the Church when the priest told her she had to stay with an abusive husband. She divorced him and never went back to the Church, eventually marrying and divorcing my mother's father, and, finally, marrying the man I knew as my grandfather. But each Sunday my mother went with her sister, P, to any one of various churches in their neighborhood. She seemed to have stopped as an adult, however. Church attendance never came up with us.

The Methodist church owned the house across the street from our home in Aiea, on Oahu, where I grew up. The minister lived there with his family. His son was for a time my best friend, but I never had an interest in their church, and they never pushed it. Two of my siblings attended it briefly but stopped when they realized they would have to donate to the church's coffers from their allowances.

My mother felt one's spirituality was private, so while I was aware of hers, I did not know the details. If I asked, both my parents would say that they believed in God. They seemed to identify as Christian in a vaguely cultural way, but neither spoke about it or engaged in any religious or spiritual practice. My mother knew the Bible backward and forward, but it seemed to me she used this knowledge mostly for doing crossword puzzles. If we had a Bible, it was in the attic.

To provoke Mom, I sometimes played at being a defiant non-believer, as I knew she had a quiet but firm faith in her god. I now recognize that my defiance was my attraction to her faith. Once I asked her, if there was a god, where was he? I couldn't see him. She smiled and spread her hands and said, "Everywhere." This was not the first time I heard something like this. But I could not fathom what it meant. My understanding of a god was as a *maker*, and you are not what you make.

Mom was the first to teach me about projection, so she no doubt understood that behind my defiance was attraction. She was always patient when expressing her beliefs and let them lie there for me to pick up or not. But I was secretly afraid that there *was* a god (which she no doubt knew, too) and I felt guilty for not being particularly interested. The only time I hoped he existed and called upon him was when I was on the toilet with horrible cramps and diarrhea. But when that passed, so did my interest in a god.

However, my non-beliefs and fears were quite apart from a handful of experiences I had playing quietly by myself. On these rare occasions, I was aware of a reassuring Presence in the quiet. In fact, these exceptional experiences reinforced my love of solitude. Alone did not mean *lonely* to me, even if those experiences were not common.

One of these events stands out, perhaps because it was more powerful than my earlier, subtle experiences of Presence. I was probably nine or ten years old and playing by myself in the garage of our home. I had turned my bicycle upside down so I could pretend I was at the helm of a ship as I looked out over the driveway, which stood in for the ocean ahead. The front wheel was for steering the ship and I spun the back wheel with the pedal to power the engine. As I played at this, I felt the Presence, and although I had no Vision, it was as if I could place It off to the left in the distance in the driveway. From It, I felt that everything would always be okay.

Like any child, I took all experiences as they came as natural, not having had enough of life to make comparisons. So, I took these mystical experiences for granted, too. They came and went, and I guess were not remarkable enough to think of sharing with anyone. I did not think about them until I was an adult and embarked on a spiritual path.

(In writing the second part of this memoir, I remembered an episode of Light and reactionary darkness when I was seven or eight years old. Fifty years later, something about it seemed to be coming to fruition. It was not a time I had totally forgotten, but throughout my former life if something brought it to mind, I felt only vague guilt. I was never sure why but had theories that had nothing to do with spirituality. As it seems I did not take anything away from this episode as a child —at least not consciously—I leave description of and theories about it for the second part of this book [LII-F.48].)

In my adolescence, and maybe even younger, I did have times when I sensed a Light in Christianity that was warm and comforting. But the Light was lost for me in doctrine and dogma and my interest in Christianity, but not the Light, would wane. However, I did not know how to find the Light without religion.

When very young, I asked Catholic kids why we were all sinful and they said it was because our parents had sex to have us. But that's how babies are made! How could God say be fruitful and multiply, but then punish us for having sex? It made no sense—or God was cruel and I wanted nothing to do with Him.

In high school, my friends dragged me along to an interdenominational Christian organization for Christian teens,

Campus Crusade. The pastor was young and energetic and glowed with his faith. I was drawn to his glow even as I disparaged it in my mind, because it seemed to me that to accept the Light, I also had to accept my sin. I had done nothing wrong! Why should I be punished for what Adam and Eve did? And how could God killing his own son release me from it? This seemed to heap guilt upon guilt.

But as a teenager I became aware of a sort of therapist and guide within me that I later recognized as Spirit. I thought of It as an older version of me, like an "inner adult" the way adults have "inner children." I do not remember when or how I got the idea to turn inward for guidance or answers. I suspect in a quiet moment with some question burning in me, I simply found one day I was answered. I had only a vague sense of It as something spiritual. But although I always found comfort in It, I rarely turned to It, usually only when feeling conflicted and guilty about sex. It never occurred to me that these experiences had anything to do with God. They were loving and positive, not judgmental and condemning. So, I considered myself an atheist.

Which is why I was startled when the awareness that I wrote of in the introduction came to me at fifteen: We are all what Jesus was. I was not Christian and was not interested in Christianity. I certainly did not realize I had a context for this awareness in the comforting experiences I already had. Christianity was, for me, about guilt, and Jesus symbolized that.

4

When *A Course in Miracles* came into my awareness, I was immersed in an intense period of self-discovery and personal growth and the recognition of a spiritual truth that I felt I was willingly choosing as my life's purpose. I was also in love with my first girlfriend, Michele, and she was leaving soon, so

I faced my first heartbreak. I was in my first real job as a clerk at a ground handler for Japanese tourists. And I would soon be taking over Michele's basement apartment in an older home in the Honolulu neighborhood of Makiki, my first home away from my family.

It was through Michele that I learned of the *Course.* We were both reading psycho-spiritual themed books and she had ordered the *Course* from the mainland. To introduce me to it, she loaned me a copy of Jerry Jampolsky's *Love is Letting Go of Fear.* As I was an anxious person, the title was appealing. It was from the *Course*, as were the ideas in the book. It seemed a step up, but a natural progression from, the books I had been reading. It stoked my interest in the *Course.*

Not long before she left, Michele received the three blue hardback books that made up the *Course* back then. Flipping through them, I was instantly interested. She took me to a *Course* study group that was held at a Unity church at the base of Diamond Head. I intended to order the books and attend the meetings when she was gone.

Before Michele left for law school in San Francisco, we had dinner with her three closest friends at The Old Spaghetti Factory in Honolulu near the harbor. I had met one of them, her best friend. The other two I had only seen in a photograph.

Michele and I arrived at the restaurant first, and while waiting a young woman walked in and the Voice in my mind said, "There's Emily." I recognized Emily, but not from the picture Michele had shown me. This recognition was something new. But I had no room for that in the moment as all I could think about was Michele's leaving. I merely registered that Emily was cute, warm, and funny and I liked her. She occasionally attended the *Course* study group to which Michele had taken me, and we discussed meeting there sometime.

I knew when I became involved with Michele on St. Patrick's Day that the relationship was going to be brief as she was leaving in June. I was conflicted, and I briefly broke it off before I accepted the circumstances. I grieved on and off throughout the relationship. I felt she had the easy part, as she was off to new vistas and I would be left behind with memories. But I tried to keep my sadness out of Michele's sight, as it made her uncomfortable. Our relationship was an intense class in living at choice and in the moment. I learned about the value of open, honest communication as well, although I did not practice this as thoroughly in this relationship as I could have. I made the judgment that some issues were just not worth bringing up in the short time we had. It would be different if our relationship were open ended.

Michele left, I moved into her basement apartment, and I ordered the *Course*. I began it as soon as it arrived, in June of 1984.

The *Course* is three books, Text, Workbook, and Manual for Teachers. I read the Text and Manual for Teachers as I felt moved, which was often, and did the daily lessons in the Workbook. But hungry for it as I was, no matter the time of day, I dozed off. I intuitively understood this was resistance, as I was twenty years old and healthy and nothing else I read put me to sleep. It was frustrating.

The *Course* said all we need is a little willingness and I must have had it because I somehow got past this dozing form of resistance. But my study was still slow going. In a single paragraph, I could find several new or mind-blowing ideas, and I would have to put the book down to absorb and process the implications of what I read before I could go on.

The *Course* validated what I had been reading and feeling, which was that God was within, not a powerful external father figure who sat in judgment on me. But it went further, saying *only* Christ, or God-within, was my reality. My one problem, it said, was my sense of separation from God in a false identification with a person (body and personality—but only *body* in the *Course*) through an ego. All conflict could be traced back to this misidentification.

In fact, it said *only God is real*. God is Knowledge and wholly different from consciousness, which is an illusion. (The

Course uses *perception* for *consciousness*. You could also use *awareness, existence, material experience, not-God, etc.*) Christ is the Source of Spirit, the truest experience in consciousness, bridging Truth (God) and illusion (consciousness).

I recognized right away that the Holy Spirit was the Voice I heard when I came out to myself and felt was my "inner adult" as a teenager. It was the Voice I heard as I read the *Course*. And It could replace ego whenever I chose. It would be my thought system if ego fell completely away.

The world is a harsh place, so either God is Love *or* God made the world—it could not be both. So, it made sense to me and was a relief to learn God—Reality— did not create the world. In the *Course, Creation* is God's *Extension* of God, Christ. Ego and its material world were *made* by the *Son of God* (the part of God's mind where the idea of not-God abides—see the ontology at the end of this book) and are miscreations. But the material world is neutral and open to interpretation and can be used by Spirit to lead one back to God. All this means there is no sin. My sense of separation from God was a mistake, not a fact. I never left God. The *Course* likened my seeming existence apart from God to a dream:

You are at home in God, dreaming of exile but perfectly capable of awakening to reality. (T-10.I.2)

The central practice of the *Course* is *forgiveness*, by which it means recognizing that only God is real. It said my only responsibility was to *accept the Atonement for myself*. This meant accepting *correction of my perception of separation from God*. This is done through the practice of forgiveness, or remembering that only God is real.

Guilt and fear, the chief experiences of ego, were my obstacles to being aware of God. The *Course* takes common religious and other symbols and redefines them in ways to undo guilt and fear, as it does with *forgiveness* and *Atonement*. It corrects the errors of Christianity while imparting, beneath the heavy Christian language, universal nondualistic truths. I felt it blended western psychology and eastern religious philosophy in Christian language.

(The *Course* is a *nondualistic* path, like most eastern religions and some pre-Christian western [Greek] philosophies. Nondualism teaches there is only one reality so, for example, there is no divide between nonmaterial Spirit [God] and the material experience. Nonduality takes two approaches [ironically]: God is the nonmaterial Reality underpinning everything, including matter, making everything one in fact if not in appearance or experience; or, as the *Course* teaches, only God is real, so the material experience is an illusory appearance. Both approaches are derived from the mystical *experience* of One Reality and a subsequent *intellectual* [ego] desire to explain the continued appearance and experience of the material world. So, in the end, the answer one chooses does not matter, as the *experience* of Oneness reveals Truth and transforms consciousness, and the rest is arrogance.)

All of this was radically different from anything I had read or heard before, but I felt the truth and liberation in it. I was also terrified. I understood from the start that the *Course* was leading me to undo my identification with what felt like me, exactly the source of liberation and fear I felt when I glanced at Buddhism. I was going to face ego's fear of nonexistence after all. But Truth pulled me like no illusion of myself ever could.

I took comfort in the *Course* saying that I *did* exist, just as Something Else. I am Spirit, one with God, immortal and eternal. But as wonderful as that sounded, it was just an idea to me. It was not my experience.

This is not a course in the play of ideas, but in their practical application. (T-11.VIII.5)

One reason the *Course* appealed to me was because it emphasized practical experience over intellectual understanding, despite its long, theoretical, mind-blowing Text. I knew ideas were not enough to shift my consciousness and therefore my experience. I had to *experience* Truth to shift to It.

But, oh how I wished this were not so! If only it *were* a matter of merely accepting ideas. I felt the "cost" the shift in consciousness would entail. Often as I studied, I heard ego in my mind, "You are killing yourself." I fully understood my resistance to the *Course*. It brought a fundamental conflict I was not aware of to my conscious awareness.

For someone who was anxious and seeking a way out of anxiety, finding the conflict underpinning all forms of anxiety only increased it for me, because I felt the "cost" of its resolution. I had to give up what I thought I was for what I am but was alien to me.

But I also knew that resolving this fundamental conflict was the only way to lasting peace. This quickly became my life's purpose. What could be more important than realizing Truth? It was, after all, **_Truth_**! In good moments I described the *Course* as a Love letter from my Self to me.

Initially for a *Course* student, practical application is done through the Workbook, which provides a lesson a day for a year. Each lesson has meditations, thoughts, and exercises to apply throughout the day. The instructions said to do a lesson whether I liked it or not, whether I understood it or not, and whether I was resistant to it or not. Some lessons I found beautiful; others were incomprehensible to me. Some brought me joyous relief; most increased my guilt and fear. I was frankly so terrified it is as though I never looked at the Workbook directly but read it out of the corner of my eye.

I was determined to do the lessons, though, even if in my fear I would not give them more than the minimum attention necessary to say I had done them. My meditations were often just going through the motions. Despite writing each day's lesson on three-by-five cards and carrying them in my pocket, I forgot to do them. The lessons I was to apply every half hour or hour I was lucky to remember to do twice a day.

I did the lessons lamely while I read the other two books hungrily because, as much as I knew a shift was needed and I wanted it, I was terrified of it. The Workbook brought the theory and path laid out in the other books to life. It threatened *change*. It felt safer to focus on *understanding*.

You retain thousands of little scraps of fear that prevent the Holy One from entering. Light cannot penetrate through the walls you make to block it, and it is forever unwilling to destroy what you have made. No one can see through a wall, but I can step around it. (T-4.III.7)

Ah, but I let Spirit in anyway, just in a way I did not recognize. Eventually I read the *Course* to the exclusion of anything else, whenever I had a free moment, and even carried all three heavy hard bound books in a backpack wherever I went. Only much later did I understand why: I *felt* the Holy Spirit when I read it. Despite reading guilt into much of the *Course* at that time, overall I felt comfort and familiarity and recognition of Spirit beyond the words. *This* drew me back again and again. Study was, for the time being, my primary practice, because the way I felt when I studied was all the Love I could accept at the time.

It was in these early days that I soon had what I thought of for a long time as my first miracle, not realizing that all those earlier experiences of Spirit (Presence), the sense of liberation and joy and light around Buddhism and the old man on the bus, and recognizing the *Course* were miracles.

The travel agency I worked at was on the third floor of a four-story building in Honolulu. I did not like elevators, always fearing I would get stuck in one, so I usually took the stairs. But one morning the elevator was open as I stepped into the building and I decided to take it. As the doors shut and I felt the familiar spasm of anxiety, I suddenly shifted consciousness. I knew I was no different inside the elevator than outside of it. But this experience did not take in just my immediate circumstances. It was a completely different experience of existence. I fully understood outer circumstances did not dictate my internal state. I knew I was whole and unchangeable, always. This was Spirit-consciousness.

My other miracles seemed to come to me from something outside of me. This was my first conscious experience as their Source.

5

After I came out, I was immersed in my small group of lesbian friends. It was difficult for me to be around what we then called *straight* people—cis heterosexuals. Among them I was not seen, as they assumed I was like them. If I let their assumptions pass, I felt skuzzy, like I was hiding, and if I corrected them, it was generally awkward. It was the mid-1980s. Even liberals would often say something well-meaning, but ultimately condescending, to show how open minded they were.

My generation rejected the closet occupied by generations of sexual minorities before us and, simply by living openly, paved the way for the openness, rights, and freedoms of today. But it was a process and exhausting because of the sheer amount of educating we had to do, even with supportive people. There were many misconceptions about homosexuality in general and lesbians in specific. Sexual minorities were still considered by many to be ill. Conservative Christians were spreading misinformation. Gay men were dying of AIDS in droves. So, except when I had to be around cis heterosexuals at work and in my family, I only wanted to be with my own kind.

But while acclimating to my lesbian identity, I was now pulled in a new direction, one which I thought of as the *ultimate coming out*. I immediately saw the parallels between coming out as a lesbian and coming out as, well, Christ. I did not use that label, however. I thought of It more as my *True*

Self. I felt, in fact, that I had an advantage having gone through one coming out process already. It served as a template. I was ready for the discomfort and disorientation, which I understood would be to a greater degree, as this would be a shift in *what* rather than *who* I am.

I attended the *A Course in Miracles* study group to which Michele had introduced me. We met once a week in the front of the chapel of the Unity church at the base of Diamond Head. It was led by a minister from the Metropolitan Community Church. The core of the group was middle aged men and women, most in their fifties and sixties, all white (unusual in Hawaii) and economically well off. Many of them were Lutherans who attended the same church. They were all familiar with the concepts and practice of the *Course*. There were also several irregular attendees, and those who came once or twice, never to be seen again. They were more diverse than the core, and ranged in age from their late twenties to eighty, so at twenty I was the youngest by far.

I met up with Emily at the study group and we bonded and developed a friendship over our spirituality. I felt much more attuned with her than I had felt with Michele.

When I had been living on my own for only three months, one morning as I turned to lock my door as I left my apartment I heard in my mind as clear as a bell, "It's time to live with people."

I froze. It was rare for me to hear Spirit as a *Voice*. I was used to intuitions and insights; to unformed thoughts rising to my conscious awareness. I put those thoughts into my own words until they lined up with what I felt. This was how I was used to "hearing" Spirit.

Right away a house in lush, green Manoa Valley, near the University of Hawaii, came to mind. It was currently occupied by several of my acquaintances in the lesbian community, most, but not all, students. (I felt I was a student, too, just not at the university.) It was privately owned, six bedrooms and three bathrooms, built dormitory style to rent to university students. I knew they were about to have a vacancy and the owner allowed current occupants to choose their roommates.

I was excited to have heard the Voice so clearly. I shared it, but carefully. Certainly, in the *Course* study group, where it would be understood. But not with my family or with all my friends, just those I thought might be open to such a thing occurring. A nurse friend of mine—a recovering Catholic and religious skeptic—asked, "Was the Voice inside or outside your mind?" I assured her It was inside my mind. I was not psychotic. I thanked her for her concern.

But when I looked into renting the room in Manoa it had just been filled. There was mutual disappointment, as those I knew in the house liked me and thought I would be a good fit. I figured I must have been wrong about *where* I was going. I was confused and I doubted what I heard—or really *that* I'd heard. I had no option but to stay open to further guidance, if such it was.

Then suddenly the applicant who was to move into the house in Manoa fell through and I was offered the room, which I readily took. This was my first experience of hearing guidance from Spirit, sensing the outcome, and having it come to fruition despite seeming obstacles. This was the bare beginning of trust.

Soon after moving in, I had what I thought of as *The Week With No Time*. For several days I felt completely present and had no sense of time passing. I acted as I was moved to act, with no thought and no planning. Life went on as usual and everything that needed to get done was done, but I never left the moment I was in.

I was not to experience anything similar for decades.

6

One night the *Course* study group was not in the chapel

as usual, but in an upstairs classroom in an adjacent building. I have a recollection of being a little out of sorts. I was tired after working all day. I was falling in love with Emily and did not like something about the way she greeted me. I did not like the space in which we were meeting and missed the chapel.

I do not remember if my mood changed as the meeting went on or what the topic was.

After the meeting everyone hugged everyone else, as usual. It was the leader's way to murmur loving things as he wrapped someone in an earnest hug. I was used to this as we embraced that night.

And then I was gone.

As I came back, I felt that I was cradled in the Arms of God, like a child in a parent's lap. And then I was back in the classroom, and the minister and I were stepping apart.

I found myself walking down the stairs with Emily, somewhat dazed. I knew something greatly significant had happened, but I could not think about it. My mind would not go there.

It was a few weeks before I "remembered" what occurred when I was "gone" during that hug. I apparently needed distance from it before I could let it into my conscious awareness. I also had the sense that, even though I could pinpoint when it seemed to happen to me, it had not occurred in time. I had been outside of time, in Timelessness or Eternity. I had a direct Revelation of God. And I was shattered.

My miraculous experiences of liberation and joy, Spirit, and Spirit-consciousness on the elevator occurred in consciousness. They were, to varying degrees, episodes of *awareness* of God. But none of them were *only-God*, or *Revelation*. The *Course* calls this *Knowledge*, to distinguish God apart from consciousness, even God-consciousness (Spirit/Christ).

What most people think of as existence is fear, or ego-consciousness. It is lack and limitation, occasionally off-set by inconsistent and unreliable human love and kindness and fleeting happiness and contentment. It feels dependent on the material world as its source and the source of its supply.

But if you have ever had or read of an experience of Spirit-consciousness, you know it is a completely different experience of existence. You are limitless, abundant, whole, happy, peaceful, secure, and immortal. You are nonmaterial Spirit, an Extension of God, your Source. You overlook the material world because it is nothing.

In consciousness there is always subject and object. You *and* the world; you *and* others. As you advance in spiritual awareness, there is still a subject *seeing* an object, even if they are recognized as one and the same. *Awareness aware of awareness* is how it is sometimes described. Sometimes it is described as *Spirit* Sees *Spirit* or *Christ* Sees *Christ*. Consciousness is always split, even if it is "corrected" to the Oneness of Spirit-consciousness.

But in Knowledge, or God, there is no split, no subject and object. God does not need to *see* Itself as there is never a time when God does not *Know* Itself. (There is no time in God.) God goes only inward to God. So, the Oneness of consciousness is not the *Onlyness* of God. It only *reflects* God's Onlyness.

So, what *is* God? God is not like anything with which you are familiar in the experience of consciousness or existence. The Glory of God surpasses anything that can be conceived in consciousness. It cannot be described.

After Revelation, I would say God is Wholeness, but It surpasses any notion of wholeness in consciousness, as all we know of wholeness in consciousness contrasts with lack. The wholeness of Spirit-consciousness is understood in contrast to the lack of ego-consciousness. And consciousness can never get entirely away from duality because it is a state split-off from True Wholeness, or God. Even at its highest, Christ Consciousness, there is still (if only barely) consciousness *and* God, but in God, there is only God.

God is Life, but not life as we know it in the world. Certainly, God is not biological life. God is the Source of the immortality experienced in Spirit-consciousness. So, it could be said that the only thing conveyable in consciousness about God is the experience of Eternal (Timeless) Life in Spirit-consciousness.

God's Glory inspires Love—Spirit-consciousness—so it is not a mistake to say *God is Love*. It is just that Love falls far short of the Reality of God. God is Love's Source the way the sun is the source of sunlight. And how different is the sun from the sunlight extending from it onto your head? The churning mass of hot plasma that is the sun is so different from the relatively gentle light that reaches earth they hardly seem related. Sunlight gives life as you know life. But if you went into the sun what you know of life would burn up and only the sun would be left.

God is nonexistence. God is no-consciousness. God is no-experience. God is no-state. God is Glorious, but relative to what I thought I knew, God was a great Void, because nothing familiar to me in ego was in God. And so, Revelation shattered me, and I had to have some distance from it to even think about it.

Once I acknowledged the Revelation consciously, I was in shock. My mind felt blown into a million pieces. Sometimes I felt I could hardly hold myself together. I was not certain I would maintain my sanity. But I was able to function. I don't remember how long this lasted. More than a few days. Somehow the recollection eased off, my mind seemed to reform, and I got on with life.

I would have other Revelations, so my experience of feeling cradled by God after this Revelation I would later recognize as a typical experience of higher consciousness after Revelation. I would "come back" out of Revelation (God-only) and slowly "descend" to a *consciousness* of God (Spirit) and then to ego-consciousness.

It never occurred to me to share this Revelation with anyone. On the surface, it could appear I was afraid they would think I was crazy, as I certainly had those thoughts myself. But frankly, I was never moved to speak of it. It did not seem like anything to share. In a very real way, it left me speechless. It was so out of the realm of what *could* be conveyed. This is probably why I never felt moved to try.

I did not feel special because I had Revelation, even though I was certain it was rare. I knew it could happen to anyone. It was also almost impossible to tolerate, which is why it was rare. The only reason I could think it happened to me was somehow I was open, ready, and able to tolerate it. But only just. It came close to completely undoing me.

What I thought I knew on a day-to-day basis was so far from What I Knew in Revelation It was not something I could hold in my mind for long. My mind sprang back to former beliefs of God as Love, which was grossly imprecise and better applied to Spirit. But, then again, this is what Spirit is for. It is God-in-consciousness.

No one in the study group ever shared anything remotely like Revelation. As with most spiritual teachings, the *Course* can be read on two levels, the mundane and the mystical. The mundane approach is to use the awareness of spiritual truths to improve your life in the world. In other words, to mitigate the pain of ego-consciousness. By far, this is what the study group seemed concerned with. Right or wrong, I felt my mystical experience went beyond their experiences and interests. It pulled me away from the world.

I was too new to the *Course* and spiritual ideas in general to be aware of these two approaches. After Revelation, however, I began to discern them. And there were more mystical experiences to come. It would turn out I was thrown right into the truth of the *Course* just as I began to study it.

7

Occasionally on my path I became aware of something without there being a dawning moment to which to point. It was this way with my mystical holy relationship with Emily.

To explain the significance of the holy relationship I first need to discuss specialness, extension and projection, special relationships, and the holy instant, as described in the *Course*.

The *Course* points out that there are only two experiences you can have in consciousness: Love or fear. These are diametrically opposed experiences of existence. They never intersect.

Love-consciousness (Spirit-consciousness) is consciousness without ego. It reflects the Wholeness of God, as I described earlier. In Love-consciousness you are whole, so you have nothing to seek from the world.

Ego-consciousness is the direct opposite of Love-consciousness. It is a state of lack, represented by your identification with a person (body and personality). The person is the experience of consciousness, so it is not limited to ego. But *identifying* with it is. In Love-consciousness, the person is simply the setting in which you find yourself.

Since ego-consciousness is a state of lack, before even asking the world to supply its lack, you cling to the little you feel you have. And that is the person's unique expression. In fact, the unique expression of the person is neutral and has no meaning in itself. But in ego, your *specialness* is the instrument you wield to supply your sense of lack. Since it is all you have, you define it to others and expect them to recognize how special you are. And you defend it against their attacks, which occur to defend their own sense of specialness.

Consciousness cannot get away from the fundamental "laws" of God, even in illusion. And the primary law of God is God's Onlyness. Another way to say this is God *extends* God infinitely—God is All-that-is.

The reason Spirit-consciousness is the "truer" consciousness is that, although still an illusion, its Oneness reflects God's Law of Extension, or Onlyness. As God knows only God, Spirit Sees (extension-in-consciousness) only Spirit. And Seeing only its Self, Spirit knows it is the source of what it sees.

This, in fact, is its wholeness—Spirit is the Seer, the Seeing, and the Seen.

Ego-consciousness cannot undo the Law of Extension, but it opposes it through *projection*, which is *extension plus denial*. In projection, your mind denies its wholeness by seeing what is not like itself and denying it is the source of this seeing. This makes it seem a world outside of it causes it. For example, in ego it seems your fear is caused by forces outside of you—others, your circumstances, world events, etc.—when in fact the only cause of fear is the consciousness of fear (ego).

A *special relationship* is based on projection. There are two kinds of special relationships. *Special love* and *special hate*. In special love relationships, you see others (or an object or situation) as the source of your wholeness. In special hate relationships, you feel powerless over someone or a situation that is an ongoing source of pain for you.

Ego-consciousness will never change. As long as you are in it, you will define and defend your specialness, project, and seek special love and experience special hate. All you can do while ego is your experience is learn to recognize it and detach from it. For this, beside Spirit as your guide and teacher, the *Course* offers the *holy instant*.

As pointed out in the ontology at the end of this book, time is the illusion on which all other illusions rest. Time makes it seem you will realize God in some indefinite future when, really, you have never left God. To counteract this illusion, the *Course* suggests practicing the holy instant.

Revelation is the ultimate holy instant. But in consciousness, there are many expressions of the miracle of a holy instant. This can be anything from hearing or feeling the Presence of Spirit up to a *higher miracle* (my term) in which you are aware of yourself as Spirit or you see illusion as illusion or both. *Practicing* the holy instant means inviting these experiences. You turn inward in meditation or even for brief moments throughout the day and open yourself to Truth.

You choose to open to a holy instant, but the experience

that comes is not up to you. You will receive what is needed, either for yourself or the greater unfolding Atonement. Sometimes you will not feel anything in the moment, but the invitation is as if you opened a door, and the needed experience will walk through in its own time. This may be an answer you have been seeking, unexpected guidance, peace descending on you—anything up to Revelation.

A *holy relationship* is an ongoing expression of the experience of the holy instant. Just as practicing the holy instant does not always result in a mystical experience, neither does practicing a holy relationship. Based on my experiences, I teach that there are two types of holy relationship, the *practical* (consciously chosen) and the *mystical* (Spirit's Vision). (The *Course* does not make this distinction).

In a practical holy relationship, you and another consciously choose to join over some common cause. This invites Spirit, whether you or the other is aware of this. (Helen Schucman and Bill Thetford merely decided to seek together for a "better way" to work with each other and their colleagues in a competitive and conflicted work environment. Both were agnostics, but their decision to join together invited Spirit—and *A Course in Miracles*. The holy relationship written about in the *Course* describes their "special function" of bringing the *Course* into the world.)

In a consciously chosen practical holy relationship, such as a *Course* student might practice, Spirit becomes your primary relationship and your relationship with the other is an extension of this relationship. In essence, the holy relationship is with Spirit, or to put it another way, your relationship with each other is Spirit.

Many *Course* students choose to make all of their relationships practical holy relationships by using their relationships as classrooms in which to learn of Spirit. This does not require others to be aware of their choice or Spirit.

The best way for me to describe a *mystical* holy relationship is to describe what I experienced in my relationship with

Emily.

At some point it seeped into my awareness that she and I were one and the same. For me to even think of Emily was to experience the kind of deep recognition I would feel looking in a mirror. There was no difference between us. We were One. I recognized her as my Self.

This was spiritual *Vision*, not seeing with the body's eyes, as physically we looked different. Nor was it seeing the same traits in her personality as I had in my personality. I saw beyond her person, so I saw from beyond mine. I saw our shared Spirit, so I saw *as* Spirit. I *extended* my Self.

This is important: We did not *become* One. What was revealed to me was that we *are* One. Or, more correctly, that Oneness *is*. Because although I saw this only with her, I knew Oneness was not limited to us. This was not an experience of "twin souls." In fact, it was past "us." Our persons were merely symbols, or insubstantial frames, as the One Self beyond them was All. We could have been any two minds. Our persons were irrelevant.

So, the holy relationship did not *make* us whole, as special relationships are meant to do. It showed me we were already whole in our Self.

Oh, the joy of this Vision! It filled my mind with a blazing Light of Love. It lifted me from the world I was used to into another, nonmaterial world of Light—what is called the *real world* in the *Course*. In fact, once after playing board games with Emily for hours, when I recalled the day, I remembered only Light sitting across the table from me.

Although it had crept quietly into my conscious awareness, unlike Revelation the holy relationship was an ongoing awareness. It was not in my conscious awareness as intensely as when I thought of Emily. The blazing Light of those moments blinded me to the material world and would have made it impossible for me to get anything done. But it was with me in an ongoing awareness of Love and lightheartedness. I was in Spirit-consciousness and I only had to think of Emily to be in

Light and Oneness again.

I was barely familiar with the *Course* when I had this experience. The holy relationship is not introduced in the Text until Chapter 17. I do not remember when I first read about it. The study group was ahead of my reading of the Text, so perhaps I first learned about it there. But I knew I was experiencing a holy relationship—what I would later call a *mystical* holy relationship. My experience was well described in the *Course*.

Although Christ was the Light I saw with Emily and recognized as my Self, I did not label It *Christ* at the time. I simply and joyfully rode the experiences. I did think about them, but they were so new and stunning that I could not catch my breath and assimilate them. How shocking to learn so quickly that the radical ideas in the *Course* were true! I had not even had time to study the *Course* as mere theory.

I did not tell Emily about my experiences. I shared the Light-across-the-table experience, but not the most profound aspect of Vision, seeing my Self in her. I assumed she must have had experiences, too. I did not think, from what I read in the *Course*, that these things were one sided. (It was not until much later that I fully understood that the holy relationship described in the *Course* was specific to Helen and Bill.) But I was conflicted. I was both afraid she would validate my experiences and that she would not validate them. The Visions were beautiful, and I valued them beyond measure. But they terrified me, as they revealed what I thought was reality was not.

Our relationship had not gone beyond friendship, although I wanted it to, and we seemed to be inching that way. And I interpreted my experiences of Oneness with her to mean we were meant to be together. But not mentioning these experiences to her signaled my doubt about this.

Emily said things I latched onto as possibly indicating she was having the same experiences, but, like me, was afraid to talk about. Once she told me she had never been attracted to someone in every way—spiritually, emotionally, intellectually, and physically—as she was to me. I thought this might be her way of describing the holy relationship, although it was not an apt description of my experience. But I did not have the language to describe the *completion* I experienced in the Visions, either.

However, I was also confused by other statements she made, like not wanting a partner. Despite having already learned with Michele how open, honest communication deepens a relationship, I sensed I would send Emily running if I pressed her about our relationship, mystical experiences aside. This was a step backward in my maturing process, I knew, but I did not want to lose her. I told myself that there was no rush for us to define our relationship, which was true. But it also created tension within me because I knew I put holding onto her above valuing myself.

Oh, I was a mess of conflicts, most deeply in ego, which was directly threatened by the holy relationship. In fact, it is wiped out by it. There is no lack in a mystical holy relationship. There is no need for specialness or special relationships. As wonderous and joyous as was Seeing and Vision, I felt how in Spirit-consciousness I would lose what felt like me and all I had valued to supply me.

In fact, for the first time I was aware of ego as a thought system in my mind rather than as *me*, as it martialed obvious defenses against the holy relationship. Sometimes I would hear in my mind about Emily, "Get away from her!" in a distinct voice I recognized was not speaking for me. This was not accompanied by a feeling that I would get hurt emotionally if she did not return my feelings. That was a separate anxiety. Here, in its desperation, ego was not even pretending concern for me. It was too threatened to care if it exposed itself. But the result of this exposure was the beginning of detachment from ego for me.

It sounds here as though ego was an autonomous being in my mind, almost like Satan, a myth modelled on ego by ego. It *was* an idea of a will opposed to God, but it was in no way a power equal to God. In fact, it was not a power at all, as the power behind it was my own belief in it (which *was* the Power of God). But I was not in touch with this yet, so when it attacked, it *seemed* like a power apart from me in my mind.

And for a long while it would still seem like me. I did not discern it apart from me, but for those moments of open attack. It would take *years* to sort it out from me. But I had just become aware of it, as I became aware of my Self, Spirit, through Vision. I was in touch with the split in my mind, ego and Spirit. Ego's ending had just begun. It was terrified and vicious. And I was terrified and under attack.

Despite my anxiety, this stage was, overall, a joyful passage. I would later think of it as *The Young Golden Time*. Many others refer to early adulthood as a golden time, when they do not have many responsibilities, but a lot of possibilities as everything seems ahead of them. But for me, it was not just youth. The Golden Light of Love had broken into my conscious awareness and I was to experience Its glow for a while. Before It, I had not known such joy was possible.

8

I had entered a relationship with Michele with open eyes and an open heart and accepted the bouts of grief that came with it. I simply wanted to love her in the time we had. So, when she told me it was hard for her to look at me sometimes because my eyes blazed with such love for her, I found this painful for both of us. For me because I felt my love deflected. For her because, although she may have thought it was that she did not want me to be hurt when she left, she clearly did not feel worthy of such love.

Emily, too, sometimes repelled my love. Around the holidays, our relationship became physical. We both spoke of love. But occasionally when I told her I loved her she used a quick, cute phrase to say I was seeing the Love in me in her. I felt she was using spiritual truth to avoid the human experience. (Not uncommon for *Course* students!)

Was I just too intense for these women? I do not know if my love scared her off. I do not know if she also experienced the holy relationship and that scared her. Maybe she simply did not want a partner at that time, as she had once said. We drew closer than ever. Our relationship peaked. And sometime after the New Year she drifted away.

Emily lived on the west side of the island, in Mililani. Traffic was already an issue on Oahu, and it was a long drive to her job and friends in Honolulu. I had a moped for getting around the city but could not use it on the freeway. So, when she did not want to come to Honolulu, we spoke on the phone and even wrote letters because we both enjoyed it. We were in touch almost daily. (This was, of course, a time long before mobile phones, text messages, and social media.)

During the solid week I did not hear from her I am sure I tried to call her. When I finally reached her and asked what was going on, she said, "Oh, you know how it is. Sometimes you just don't want to be around people."

Okay. I got that.

Except she just told me she had stayed in town that week with her best friend. It was a while before it hit me like ice water dumped on my head: By *people* she meant a specific person—*me*.

When we spoke on the phone again, she was distant. I let her go. What else could I do? A while later I ran into her at a special meeting of the *Course* group where a film about the *Course* was being shown. She had with her friends from out of town. She introduced me to them as casually as one would a mere acquaintance. There was no indication of our romance, our love, our closeness. I knew we were over.

I was devastated and deeply embarrassed. My feelings for her clearly outstripped hers for me. I was still mortified by emotions, so I pretended to my friends that it was no big deal. No one had been certain how close we had gotten.

I was not to see her again for several years. But I did continue to write to her. I know at some point I laid out all my feelings and spiritual experiences with her. I do not know if it was during this time or later. And I do not remember any response from her during this time.

I thought then, and for many years after, that she *had* experienced the holy relationship and it scared her. I knew how threatened I was by it, so I assumed it had to be the same for her. I regretted not bringing it up at the time so we could support each other through it. The *Course* describes the beginning of a holy relationship as challenging and says that often it is broken off at that point. I was sure that referred to what happened to us.

I read many of the passages in the *Course* that were specific to Helen and Bill in a way that justified trusting Emily would be back. They were told by the Voice that they could trust each other as they worked together to bring the *Course* into the world. Later, I would discover these passages are often misread by students to indicate they are to trust everyone they meet. I used them to hold onto Emily for years.

I identified with everything I read in the *Course* about the holy relationship and those passages lit up my mind with Oneness. I clung to them. I could not understand how I could see Oneness with Emily and not be with her. I was torn between what I felt was the logical conclusion we were meant to be together and the fact that she was gone. And, worse, my intuition (Spirit) she was not coming back.

My job at the travel agency also came to an end. The company was going under and one of the owners, who had been my direct boss and somewhat of a friend (I never came out to her), asked me to go with her to a new company she was starting. But I sensed I was not going in that direction. I told everyone I thought this was a good opportunity to look for a job in line with hotel management, which had been my major in business college. But I was actually thinking about becoming a nun.

It came to me, I felt from Spirit, to clean homes as a

source of income while I decided what I wanted to do. I had some savings to fall back on as I built up a customer list.

Despite Emily being gone, I only had to think of her to experience Oneness and joy. But I did not want them without her. I wanted them only on my terms.

9

It was becoming clear that I was not going to follow a well-worn path in life. My spirituality led me away from my lesbian friends. And now I felt my spiritual experiences set me apart from my spiritual study group.

I felt, rightly or wrongly, that the group missed the point, which, for me, was the deeper, mystical reading of the *Course*. I felt they skimmed the surface and used it as an instruction manual for better relationships but did not seem to get that what it said about Truth and illusion was *true*. They tried to see Christ in the person of each other, rather than to invite the Vision of Christ. They did not seem to understand that spiritual Vision was an *entirely different way of seeing*, which is why it forgives. But I also was not comfortable bringing up my mystical experiences with them for the same reason I wasn't with Emily: If they were validated, it would increase my fear. If they were invalidated, I would wonder if I had lost my mind.

To understand my spiritual experiences, I read books written by contemplative nuns. They seemed to feel the Oneness with Jesus that I felt with Emily. I did not understand that I experienced Christ in me in those experiences, but I identified so much with what I read that I felt I was already living what they described. I became drawn to the idea of being a contemplative nun and spending my day in union with God.

Until I came out, I was never socially active. At any time, I had at most my family and one or two friends. (My parents did not have social lives. My father may have had his social needs met at work. My mother, and her father who had come to live with us, had a few acquaintances in the neighborhood, but did not have friends. My siblings had social lives.) I never just *hung out* with people. I did not join groups or organizations. I felt a good book was better than a party. I did not know what people socialized for, and only did it myself to find a mate with whom to build a home, so I could stay there and not have to socialize! So, the idea of living away from the world with like-minded women was not unappealing, and I started to consider it for myself.

The minister who led the study group was a very loving, gentle man. If there was anyone I thought of sharing my mystical experiences with, it was him. But I was never certain he would understand, as he was a mainstream Christian and the *Course* did not seem to challenge him. I felt if one had the mystical experiences I had, they would be as tossed up by them as I was.

However, I did tell him I was considering becoming a contemplative nun. He was appalled. He said he thought I simply felt a desire to devote my life to God. But he gave me the number for a contemplative who lived in a convent on the east side of the island. I called her and she shared how fulfilling she found her life of devotion to God. She seemed simple (minded? I wasn't certain.) and encouraged me to join a convent.

I went to the main library in Honolulu and borrowed books about nuns and had a fascinating experience: I so deeply identified with them, I felt I was already living the contemplative process. Later, I would recognize I already felt the union with God they sought.

My time in the house in Manoa came to an end at this time as well as several of my friends were moving out. I decided to go with two of them, a couple, to share a two-bedroom apartment in Kaimuki, a part of Honolulu east of Manoa.

So much came to an end at that time. Michele and I had been keeping in touch by letter. I had not revealed to her my involvement with Emily. I was waiting for that to solidify so I would know how to characterize it. And she never mentioned Emily saying anything to her. But I had gotten deeply honest about certain things in our relationship, and she had written back "thank you for sharing" and that she had a new girlfriend. I felt dismissed. Somehow in my move out of Manoa I lost the last as-yet-unopened letter from her. I never wrote to tell her. And she never wrote to me again, either.

In my enthusiasm over becoming a nun, I got rid of my music and books and other personal belongings. I had the sense of entering a new world. But first, I had to become Catholic. I discovered which parish I was in and found the appropriate church and spoke with what I can only describe as a disillusioned priest. He was clearly depressed and just going through the motions of his job. He was not encouraging but told me when catechism classes would begin.

I signed up and put it on my calendar and started going to church on Sundays. I sat in the back, feeling like a foreigner in a strange land, totally unmoved by the liturgy, unable to take communion because I was not yet a member. I thought it was an obnoxious waste of Sunday mornings.

I felt the whole Church idea distasteful in many ways. The way I looked at it, I would be *Catholic*, but not *Christian*. By this I meant I would accept the *culture*, but I could not identify with being a sinner or accept Jesus as my savior, which is how I understood Christians to define themselves. As a nun, I would have to take a vow of obedience to the Church, not to God, which I thought was silly. I did not intend to adhere to it. I also did not plan on being celibate. I knew about lesbian nuns. I had read a book about them. I could seek union with God and still have sex. Really, I was just looking for a place to be quiet and meditate a lot.

My interest in becoming a nun waned.

I went to services only two or three times. I decided I would wait until I was in the catechism classes to attend seriously. A few weeks passed, and the evening for the first class arrived. I went out to catch the bus that would take me to church. For some reason, that night it never arrived. I took it as a sign.

The contemplative nun phase was probably six or eight weeks long, but it ran its course and totally out of my system. I already had what I would have become a nun to seek. While there would be times when I would wish I could just go live a simple life on a desert island and not have to deal with people, and while I remained what I considered a loner (although I always lived with others) and spent much of my time in spiritual study and contemplation, I was never again drawn to a monastic type of life.

I eventually bought again the music and books I had given away.

10

Suddenly, in the middle of 1985, everything that had characterized the shifts of the past few years came to an end. Emily was gone, my job was over, I felt I was growing in a different direction from my friends as well as the *Course* study group, and my roommates were moving on.

The cost of living in Hawaii was so high that many young people lived with family or friends. I felt if I had to live with people, it might as well be people I knew well—my family. My parents, my grandfather, my sister, E, and her son, J, were still in the house in which I grew up. I thought my father might mind my moving back, but he did not. My nephew, who was now seven, had shared a room with my grandfather before I moved out and now had my old room. So, there was no bedroom for me. I slept on the bed that pulled out of the couch in the family room.

I was a little embarrassed about moving back home after only sixteen months on my own, but mostly I felt relief. I was hurting after Emily, confused but joyous about my spiritual experiences, and had spent my savings as cleaning jobs were few and far between. My mother charged my sister and me 30% of our gross earnings for room and board and we contributed around the house as well. Secure in my shelter, I could think about what I wanted to do for a living.

Whatever that would be, I felt the *Course* was my life's purpose. I finished the Workbook and felt I did such a poor job of it that, despite the introduction stating, "the training period is one year" and the lessons leaving me with Spirit in the end, I did it for another year. I did them no better the second time around.

Many students expect to be enlightened by the end of the Workbook. I do not know of anyone who ever was. It does not end as though it means for you to be. I did not expect it. My mystical experiences had revealed to me how far I was from Spirit-consciousness, although I still felt the glow and joy of It around. However, I had expected more to shift from the lessons and felt disappointed until I looked back over the first year and realized how much my thinking *had* changed. It was just not as much as I wanted.

I also finished the Text, the ending of which I found anti-climactic. I felt overall the Text was vague and indirect (this was me, not the book), and expected it would end with some sort of summary that would bring "the secrets of how to do inner peace" together in one place. Instead, it ends with "Choose Once Again", implying, like the Workbook, that I was setting off on a process with Spirit. I did not like that idea. But I started the Text again, as hungry for it as ever.

Despite wanting immediate relief from the pains and limits of ego-identification, I sensed I was in for a long haul. But I resisted this, adding to my discomfort.

Somehow, I learned that Emily left for Japan to join a spiritual community. It sounded, to me, like, or nearly like, a cult. She could receive letters but not write back. I wrote many letters to her, so it may have been at this point that I shared all I felt for her and my mystical experiences, including seeing our Self with her. But, of course, I did not hear back.

Later I would look at my coming out and marvel at how quickly that process went for me. I came to feel it was something that had to be put in order before I could embark on what my life was really about: Christ. I came to mark my return to my family home as the culmination of the Period of Undoing. I was certainly not aware of this then. It would not be until I entered the Period of Settling over twenty years later that I would recognize, in retrospect, when I had entered the three stages preceding it. It was difficult to discern because, like many students, I wanted to be further along than I was. Moreover, the descriptions for the stages are vague and each stage contains versions of the others. For example, they all begin in a kind of undoing and end in consolidation, like the last Period, Achievement. They also tend to overlap, making it hard to determine a stark line where one ends and the other begins.

Despite my desire to be further along, I was never able to fool myself into thinking I was more advanced than I was. My mystical experiences made me aware of the significant shift in consciousness that was possible, and I felt how far I was from it.

I often refer to Undoing as the *honeymoon period*. It was a golden time for me, despite fear and confusion. I experienced true joy and peace and knew they were real. The Light of God had come to my awareness and had not left, because I could simply recall It by thinking about Emily. Spirit-consciousness hovered around, even if I felt far from being able to sustain it.

I did not know if I would ever experience more than moments or episodes of Spirit-consciousness. I still wanted the Truth because it is the Truth, and I felt (mistakenly, I would discover years later) that if that shift happened it would be an effect of an awareness of Truth. This was the path ahead of me.

I would not experience again such an intense episode

of new spiritual experiences until decades later, in the fifth period, Unsettling, when I would find myself in another mystical holy relationship—and in Spirit-consciousness.

TWO: SORTING OUT

Next, the teacher of God must go through "a period of sorting out." This is always somewhat difficult because, having learned that the changes in his life are always helpful, he must now decide all things on the basis of whether they increase the helpfulness or hamper it. He will find that many, if not most of the things he valued before will merely hinder his ability to transfer what he has learned to new situations as they arise. Because he has valued what is really valueless, he will not generalize the lesson for fear of loss and sacrifice. It takes great learning to understand that all things, events, encounters and circumstances are helpful. It is only to the extent to which they are helpful that any degree of reality should be accorded them in this world of illusion. The word "value" can apply to nothing else. (M-4.I.A.4)

1

The Period of Sorting out was the longest and most difficult for me. The honeymoon was over, and I hit the wall that is ego. As a teacher and mentor for students of *A Course in Miracles*, I found this to be somewhat universal.

The first thing a *Course* student learns about is ego. Ego does not care if you love it or hate it, just so you believe in it. So, it thrives on examination. And, of course, our examination of it makes it loom larger in our awareness. It is not pretty, but it is necessary to see what ego is to let it go. So, it gets worse before it gets better.

It is not uncommon for a student to spend years looking at ego and lamenting it but feeling like they cannot get past it. They do not realize they are in a process and far more is occurring unconsciously than they are aware of.

Students often feel unmotivated at the start of Sorting Out. The *Course* tells us the world is not real. The first lessons in the Workbook lead one to see the material universe is meaningless. Ego goes into a big pout. And the student falls into apathy as they have nothing to replace their world and projections of meaning.

But the *Course* points out that the world is meaningless *in itself* to show the student that they choose the meaning it has for them. It empties the world of meaning *they have given it* so they can fill it with helpful meaning. But ego's resistance is such that even though this is stated clearly, they do not see it.

Of course, the meaninglessness of the world was more than theory for me. I had seen it, both in Revelation and in the miracle of the mystical holy relationship. And I was *angry*. I felt the world had been taken from me before I had time to become disillusioned with it on my own. I felt robbed of a normal life. I wanted a partner and a home. Maybe children. Possibly a career of some sort. I wanted to have the full experience of a *person*.

For seven years, I was *pissed off* about Emily and the holy relationship. First, I was angry with her for leaving. I was certain she fled the holy relationship. Then I was angry at God for showing me the real world and then taking it away. Of course, I still experienced it just thinking of Emily. But since when do facts matter when one wants to be angry?

And finally, I was angry with me for opening myself to the holy relationship in the first place. What a fool! What an idiot! I set myself up opening myself to God. Of course, God would take things away.

Of course, this was ego's point of view. My anger was not because Emily was gone, but because I experienced Seeing and Vision and knew ego was not real.

I did not deny that Visions of the holy relationship continued. In fact, I sought them by thinking about Emily so I could experience Love and joy. But then, perversely, I pushed them away because she did not come with them. If she was not returning, then I did not want to see my Self. I wanted joy *on my terms only.*

"I want it my way!" is the classic ego refrain. And if I could not have Love my way, well then, I didn't want It. I felt that to fully accept what I had seen in the holy relationship, which was that Love is here, within me, without an outside source, would cost too much—my identity; the whole world I knew.

Nowhere in the *Course* did it say I could not have what I wanted. In fact, quite the opposite. The *Course* is meant to be practiced within an ordinary life. It specifically says it is a short cut because you do not spend your life in meditation or fighting against the idea of sin (which *is* only an *idea*). You grow your awareness of Truth as you face your obstacles to Truth. The specific shortcut it offers is the holy relationship. And it reassuringly states:

I said before that the first change, before dreams disappear, is that your dreams of fear are changed to happy dreams. That is what the Holy Spirit does in the special relationship. He does not destroy it, nor snatch it away from you. But He does use it differently, as a help to make His purpose real to you. The special relationship will remain, not as a source of pain and guilt, but as a source of joy and freedom. (T-18.II.6)

But even if I could have what I wanted, the full experience of a person was impossible for me now. No matter I might acquire all the forms I wanted, I could never forget that I had seen my Self and could never wholly identify with a person and ego again.

Not that that was a wholly *bad* thing, either.

This was my split-mind, my conflict. Of course, I wanted to be my Self! Whole and complete and glorious; forever safe and loved. (And yet never labeled *Christ*, despite the *Course* making it clear this is what is seen in a mystical holy relationship.) But I also wanted ego and to be a person, which were lack and limitation and fear. *I wanted to be a person, but not to feel fear or lack or limitation.*

Mind naturally wants to be whole. Faced with this split, my first attempt was to integrate these two experiences, despite the *Course* making clear (and mystical experiences showing me) they are incompatible states, and one must choose between them. I got this intellectually, but my mind was not there yet. I unconsciously embarked on exactly the path most people do, whether spiritual or religious: Spiritualizing ego. I would struggle to make ego Spirit-like, attempting to keep both.

Spiritualizing ego is the way of many religions, which provide doctrine and dogma for this process. But I could not see I was making the same mistake. I set about repressing ego and perfecting the person to line myself up with what I thought God wanted or was God-like.

Like many *Course* students, I felt guilty for wanting a life partner—a special relationship. Anger over feeling robbed of a normal life and this guilt would characterize much of my twenties. Of course, they were related, because, as I saw it, I insisted on a special relationship with Emily to accept the Vision of the holy relationship, increasing my guilt. To a certain degree the holy relationship, through which I could have forgiven guilt, only highlighted my belief in guilt.

A new student is in a catch-22: You must trust the very thing (Spirit) that you fear to help you through the fear. The Period of Sorting Out is slow going because for a long while you take two steps back for every three steps toward trust.

Building trust in Spirit *is* the path of *A Course in Miracles*. This is laid out in the Manual for Teachers under the heading, "Development of Trust". But I was not yet aware that I was embarking on a path of building trust in Spirit. All I knew was I longed for what was revealed to me through my mystical experiences, even though they also scared me.

Sometimes I doubted the whole thing, even my mystical

experiences. I did not want to deceive myself. But eventually I realized during one of these doubting episodes that I had nothing to lose by opening myself to a possible…Something. If It did not exist, then I lost nothing because I had nothing yet. And if It did exist, then I would be better off in touch with It. It was a neutral-win situation.

I went through a few episodes of "testing" for Spirit and each time It came into my awareness in some way I recognized. Finally, I trusted that, yes, there really was Something there, even if I did not wholly trust It yet.

2

I may not have joined a convent, but I came to feel I was a kind of contemplative. (Really, *mystic* was always a better designation for me given my experiences.) My life's focus was God and my study of the *Course*. I lived with my family, but I did not pursue a social life, which was natural to my introverted personality. In fact, my only period of sociability was that brief time at twenty and twenty-one.

At some point I realized I liked being self-employed and decided to make house cleaning my full-time work. I did not mind the work; it was satisfying in its own way. I could look back at the end of a job and see what I had accomplished. It helped keep me fit. I was out and about and not tied to a desk all day. I did not have to worry about losing my job because I was gay. If it came up with a cleaning customer and they did not like it, I could move on. But mostly, what I enjoyed was my mind being free while the body was occupied. I had a lot of time to think about God and Truth and the *Course*.

The natural beginning for *Course* students is intellectual. It is full of many (usually) new concepts, blends psychology and spirituality, and is written rather densely, so it takes a lot of time, study, and thought. Of course, it is also "safer" to be immersed in concepts than in practice, which brings actual change. But this is a necessary beginning, and, if it is studied with Spirit as I did, it is a practice of its own kind as it is how trust is built.

The first thing a student needs to sort out is Spirit's still, quiet Voice (words, intuitions, unformed thoughts) from ego's cacophony of thoughts and feelings. As the student does this, ego will soften its voice and try to sound gentler. It will say what it expects Spirit to say, which is funny, because Spirit often says what one would *not* expect. It took me a long time to look to my *experience* to discern Spirit. When I heard Spirit, I felt liberated from whatever discomfort guilt and fear took in the moment. When I heard ego, my discomfort stayed the same or increased.

My awareness of Spirit, beyond feeling It as I studied (which I did not fully discern at the time), arose through seeking to understand the *Course* and any other spiritual ideas that crossed my path. While cleaning, I pondered concepts and chewed on questions. At some point, I noticed that sometimes my thoughts seemed to come from a deeper place, and I would receive clarity and answers. I understood this deeper place was Spirit. I began to consciously open to It as I worked. Eventually, I addressed It directly. I became more consistent with this as my trust grew.

I did not always receive answers the moment I asked a question, but I was always answered, usually within a day or two. Sometimes it came directly through Spirit in my mind. Sometimes I found the answer as I studied. Other times, it came through someone else, a fictional book I was reading, a song, a movie, a TV show, etc. Of course, those things did not directly address my question, so I realized Spirit was in my recognizing the answer.

After a few years of this, my trust was such that one day I wondered if I could bring more than just spiritual questions to Spirit. What if I brought It my practical concerns and decisions? Bit by bit, I offered It those things. I began to talk to

Spirit about what went on in me as well, using It like a Therapist as well as a Teacher and Guide.

To start, I simply lay things at Spirit's feet, so to speak. "Here's a problem. Take it." But nothing happened when I did this. At best I would feel, for a moment, that I had laid down a burden. But my upset or confusion was not resolved. I discovered "giving it to the Holy Spirit" did not mean passively laying problems at Its feet. It meant *looking at it with* Spirit. It meant bringing up all my thoughts and feelings about a situation, be it a relationship or a decision to be made. This is what I had hoped to avoid by giving things to Spirit! But my problems and decisions were symptoms, not the real concern. That was my sense of conflict, and Spirit could not help me if I wasn't looking at the real issue. So quite often I had to face uncomfortable thoughts and beliefs.

The result was a deep intimacy with myself because I had to be honest with myself to be honest with Spirit. This was the bare beginning of undoing my belief in guilt, because so often guilt was why I did not want to look at an issue in the first place. But the more I faced, the more I felt I *could* face, because I never did find the something in me that was supposed to be too horrible to see.

It was a while before I was consistent with this. Unconsciously, I held back areas of my life from Spirit. But when I realized this, I'd wonder what the heck I was doing. Spirit was always helpful, why wasn't I sharing *this* with It? I would feel foolish for having struggled so long when I did not have to!

Part of building trust in Spirit was accepting that there was Something in my life that was *wholly* trustworthy *always*. There is no model for this in the fallible world where I had to constantly measure just how far I could trust someone or something. But a large part of my piecemeal approach to trusting Spirit was simply fear of giving up control of my life. It was still "other" to me and I did not feel Its Will was mine yet. I let It in, but I was not *following* It. And It met me where I was and took me as I came.

Spirit was a great positive in my life, but I was still greatly conflicted. A couple of years into being a *Course* student I noticed a pattern. Whenever I had a significant insight, clear guidance from Spirit, or a mystical experience, afterward I had what I eventually called an *ego backlash*. Ego would get vicious, attacking my insecurities, Emily, the holy relationship, God, or anyone else. Or it would obsess angrily on something in the news, a social issue—you name it. This could go on for weeks after a single positive event, no matter how small.

It was not until I was teaching the *Course* that I learned how universal this is. It seems this pendulum swing between thought systems is characteristic of the split-mind. This pattern was there as long as ego was in my mind. But, over time, the duration of the backlash shortened considerably to hours rather than weeks or days. After a while I hardly noticed it.

Once I recognized this, I learned to anticipate it and ride it out. Being aware of what was occurring mitigated my discomfort somewhat.

In the early years, this swinging was what the path was for me. I was often angry. I often suspected I was grieving. I told myself I grieved over Emily, but really, I grieved the loss of ego and its world as I had believed in them. Sometimes I felt I could not possibly be aware of Truth and feel these things. Who was I, after all? How could I know these things? I wanted my experience of consciousness-as-illusion to be a concept, not something I had truly experienced. But I really did know that only God is real and everything else is illusion. I do not mean I thought about this or had it in my ongoing awareness. But if I did not know this, if it was only an idea in a book, I would not have been so angry.

Soon after starting the *Course* I read *Journey Without Distance*, Robert Skutch's story of how the *Course* came to be. He described Helen Schucman's resistance to the *Course*, both as and after she scribed it. In this early stage, I strongly identified with her. She, too, had profound mystical experiences that revealed Truth to her. I understood her conflict and found comfort in knowing I was not alone.

The *Course* makes it clear that a student will embark on a process of indeterminate length, but I did not want to accept this, increasing my conflict. My intuition was that I was not going to have any significant shift toward peace until my late thirties. But I found this idea intolerable, and I pushed it aside.

But one day, perhaps five years after I began the *Course*, when I was particularly conflicted and miserable, I reached out for help. One of my cleaning customers was a woman in her seventies who sometimes had a group of friends over to play Bridge. They would arrive just as I was leaving. They were the classic "ladies who lunch", white (again, so unusual in Hawaii), in their sixties, well off, and married to mostly retired professional men. They had spent their lives promoting their husband's careers, raising children, staying fit, working in charities, and traveling. One of these women lived in the same condominium as my customer and had a serenity that set her off from her friends. Somehow, she and I discovered we were both students of the *Course*. That day, I asked if I could stop by after work to speak with her privately and she said yes.

When I arrived, her husband went to another room and she and I sat in her living room. I poured out everything, including my mystical experiences and feelings for Emily. I am sure she asked questions along the way, but I do not remember our discussion. What I do remember is there came a point when she looked off into the distance and I knew she was tuning into Spirit. When she looked back at me, she said, "It's going to be a while." She meant until I had any shift toward peace.

On the surface, this did not seem like a conversation to bring relief. She did not say anything that lifted my sense of conflict. Instead, she confirmed my sense that I was going to be uncomfortable for a long while. But I *was* relieved, and it would be some time before I figured out why. She didn't say "never".

The result of this was I came to accept I was in a process and settled into it. From then on, whenever I sensed how long it would take before I shifted toward peace, I would brush it aside. If I was going to get there, I had to focus on the step in front of me, not agonize over the length of the journey.

While this did not make this stage any easier, it did mitigate my discomfort somewhat. I stopped adding resistance to being in a process to my already considerable conflict.

3

There is no zealot like a new convert, and I was proof of this. I itched to share what I was learning in *A Course in Miracles*. The *Course* teaches that we learn what we teach, and we inherently understand this. But I would not accept until many years later that my longing to have others *get it* was my own longing to *get it*.

The problem was, there was no one with whom to share it. The ideas were too radical to mention to someone who was not truly open to them. I found few people ask truly open questions anyway. Most people want their beliefs validated. Or they want simple yes or no answers to questions that, for a *Course* student, do not have simple answers.

For example: "Does the *Course* say I go to Heaven when I die?"

"Well...you haven't left Heaven. You are just unaware you are There. So, you don't have to put off Heaven until you die..."

This is not what most people want to hear! It is too complex. If I tried, I received blank stares and the topic of conversation was quickly changed. No one wanted to learn Heaven is available *now*. They might feel compelled to find out why they are not aware of It.

I very quickly learned that unless someone asked me directly what the *Course* teaches with a truly open mind, there was no way into a direct conversation about it. And I did not come across people who were like that.

I knew instinctively that no one in my family was interested. For one thing, the book was right there with me around the house, and no one asked about it or looked into it. My mother had become defensive about her spiritual beliefs. In fact, a few years later my sister, C, tried to engage her in a conversation about them and it led to an estrangement of many years. (I overheard the discussion—it became a loud argument—and could tell my sister simply wanted to talk, but my mother felt she was being attacked. Mom would die an agnostic, saying she could not believe there was a god who would make such a harsh world.)

C was the only person close to me I spoke a little about the *Course* to, but she thought along traditional religious lines and what I shared went right past her. (C searched for a religious home for years, always within Christianity. I told her I felt she was Catholic, which she had been raised for the first few years of her life by my father and his first wife. But she wasn't interested. However, in her fifties, she returned to Catholicism and finally felt home.)

But I was also aware that by *teaching* and *sharing*, the *Course* meant the extension of the awareness of Truth in *one's own* mind. It states three times that one's "sole responsibility" is to "accept the Atonement" for themselves.

I thought of starting a study group to share it, but I did not feel I knew the material well enough. But what truly overrode any idea of formally teaching was I did not feel moved by Spirit to do so. I knew my itch to share it had too much energy behind it to be Spirit's guidance. Spirit's promptings are quiet, not energetic or passionate. And if I taught from ego, I would only reinforce it in my mind.

Over time, however, I found I could share the ideas in the *Course* indirectly. Projection, for example, is well understood in psychology. The *Course* illuminates it because it is ego's primary defense. So, if a friend had an ongoing upset with someone else, I could suggest she was projecting. But I did not have to use the terms the *Course* uses. Instead of *Holy Spirit* I could suggest to someone in crisis that they get in touch with the *Quiet* at the center of their mind or the *wiser part* of themselves.

I learned to live with the ache to share. Sometimes I thought that maybe one day I would teach the *Course* in some formal way. But I did not necessarily expect to.

4

There was something else going on that dovetailed uncomfortably with my itch to share the *Course*. Without Spirit as Teacher, the *Course* can be a dangerous teaching for a codependent person, which I was in spades.

One's True Wholeness is their Identity in Christ, an Extension of God's Wholeness. Wholeness is what we seek in our relationships with others but can never find in them. Ego's substitute for True Wholeness is a false sense of union, or oneness, that comes from dropping identity boundaries with others. This shows up as taking responsibility for others or expecting them to take responsibility for you. This is codependency.

While ego is a false identification, and it is inherently neurotic, it does have healthy and unhealthy conditions. Ironically, a healthy ego is necessary to release ego. For example, a person with low self-esteem will not feel worthy of Spirit's Love and Guidance. One's self-esteem does not have to be perfect, but it must be healthy enough to let Spirit in.

Also, it is hard, if not impossible, to release an identity that is not clearly defined. You cannot let go of what you have given away to others. A codependent drops their identity boundaries to "love" others or to "feel loved" by others. They often do not know where they end and the other begins. The one who takes responsibility for others (often without others asking for this) takes on other people's problems. They feel responsible for solving another's issues, fixing them, or making them happy. They often spend a lot of time thinking about others' issues. This is stressful and leads to feelings of helplessness, sacrifice, and resentment. If the other is healthy and does *not* want to be dependent, they feel undermined, invaded, disrespected, and resentful. If they *do* want to be dependent (confusing this with being loved), they are enabled to remain immature and/or in addiction or illness.

Unfortunately, codependency is what most often passes for love in the world. It is one reason relationships are so conflicted!

My codependency came out of my family situation. While I never felt responsible for causing my mother's unhappiness, I did feel responsible for making her happy. Mom was also a model for codependency herself, taking it on herself to find solutions to others' problems, as was my father in the way he dealt with her unhappiness.

Mom seemed to carry guilt and shame, perhaps some of it the legacy of Catholicism in her family, even though her mother left the Church before she was born. During a crisis in her life (she never said what this was), Jesus came to her in a dream and told her everything would be okay. He told her to not tell anyone about the dream, but she told her mother. Later, she felt guilty for defying Jesus's instructions.

Twice she was pregnant out of wedlock, once with my sister, E, by a man she did not marry, and seven years later with me, by my father, who had recently been widowed. This was when abortion was illegal and being pregnant and unmarried was a source of shame. So, Mom told us that she was widowed by E's father. She said he—who, coincidentally, had the same last name as her family (it was common enough)—died in a car accident when my sister was an infant. We were told that she and my father married a year before their actual wedding to hide that she was four months pregnant with me at the time.

We children were suspicious. For one, there was the coincidence of the first husband's last name. And my sister, E, was old enough to remember Mom and Dad's wedding and the dates did not line up with her memories. But it was not until we were young adults that we came across information that confirmed our suspicions. Because of Mom's level of shame, we did not ask her about it, but respected her privacy. However, growing up with secrets, I came to value honesty and openness. I felt secrets created unnecessary tension, making what was hidden seem far worse than it turned out to be.

As well as carrying guilt and shame, Mom told how her mother made thoughtless comments that undermined her self-esteem. Mom was often insecure, anxious, depressed, and had chronic headaches.

A secretary at Westinghouse in San Francisco, where she met my dad, she became a housewife when she married him and went from being a mother of one to a mother of four overnight. A few months later, just after she turned thirty, I was born.

Dad and his first wife did not discipline their children. So, Mom took over three unruly children between four and ten years old who found her healthy boundaries and expectations of responsibility and respect harsh. Dad only became involved in discipline when she dragged him into it. It must have been very stressful for her.

Dad was the classic breadwinner, leaving care of the home and raising of the children to his wife. An engineer, when I was two years old he took a job as an executive with the electric company in Hawaii. So, Mom moved away from her family and the only home she knew in a city she adored when we moved to Oahu. Prone to anxiety and depression as she was, her chronic unhappiness was understandable.

Dad would usually do anything she wanted, but she had to ask, which she resented. She wanted him to anticipate her needs. (Another way we seek to feel one with another.) When I was born, Dad was forty-one. He was a genius, cerebral but affectionate even as he seemed distant. He seemed clueless about my mother's feelings. I remember him as often mildly depressed himself. When I was an older child, Mom told me Dad was experiencing mid-life depression.

Later in life I recognized that he probably had a condition I was diagnosed with, dysthymia, a chronic low-grade depression. There is also some speculation in my family that he was a functional alcoholic (an oxymoronic term). He was never sloppy, loud, or abusive. And he drank the same each weeknight and a little more on the weekends. But perhaps, given his depression and confusion about emotions, he numbed himself with alcohol.

For me, our family was stable, supportive, nurturing, and loving. I had a happy childhood. Apart from the secrets, which were flimsy anyway, any dysfunction in our family showed up for me later in life around the codependency I learned in it.

I felt Mom was the true head of the home. She was certainly its emotional center. And a great martyr. (I learned an attitude of self-pity and martyrdom from her, too.) She never articulated that my role was to make her happy. She was always the mother and did not lean on me. Yet I felt somehow that she had me to make her happy. I was her baby and she adored me, and I could feel her watching me as though her hopes and dreams were centered on the outcome of my life. And I watched my father mollify and cave to her, even to the point of agreeing to a decision about my eldest, mentally retarded sister, K, which he would regret to the end of his life. I learned that making Mom happy was what we were to do. And I extrapolated this to feel I was responsible for fixing everyone.

And mostly I did make Mom happy. Even as a teenager the worst I did was call her a bitch once within her hearing. She gave me a lot of freedom and allowed me my own self-expression growing up, so the message I received was I was okay with her—mostly. She had been a tomboy, so she accepted and supported my being one. But on the other hand, we struggled over her insisting I wear dresses occasionally, which was not in line with my masculine-female self-image and impractical for my physical lifestyle. This and my unsocial nature were the only areas where I felt she was not comfortable with me.

When I came out to her, she said—incongruently—that she knew I was different when I was a baby because I would sit and stare into space for long spans of time. I do not know what this had to do with me being a lesbian, but she had also seen other signs and was not surprised. She cried, but her concern was with how I would make my way in a world that was hostile to me. Down through the years, although always accepting and supportive, she would sometimes say things that indicated she still mourned an idea of a more conventional Elizabeth. (She never called me *Liz*, as I preferred, or any other of the dozens of nicknames for Elizabeth, until the last few years of her life, when she called me *Elspeth*.)

Though largely tolerant of differences—a happy model when growing up in the most racially and culturally diverse state in the union—she sometimes took it personally and felt rejected if I did not share her view on something. This became more pronounced as I grew older. On any occasion, I did not know if I would meet the tolerant or the insecure mom.

As a small child I felt loved, protected, and cherished by her. But when adolescence hit, I felt her attention was smothering and invasive. This persisted into adulthood, when I felt she was living vicariously through me and my siblings, rather than making a life of her own. She would *should* all over us, telling us what to do with and in our lives.

There were other issues, too, that fed my codependency. Because I came from a happy family that was comfortably middle class and I had above average intelligence, I thought I had more gifts than many others. I felt that meant I should take on more responsibility. In classic ego guilt, I felt as I did not *earn* my good fortune, I had to pay for it.

Codependency was so ingrained in my thoughts and feelings that I felt, unconsciously, that it was my God-given role to fix or take care of others. This was unrecognized, so undefined, but it was my relationship to the world. Whenever someone unhappy walked into my presence—whether I knew them or not—I felt a racing feeling in my stomach. I felt pressure to fix them. Of course, this was not about them, but about me. *I* was uncomfortable because they were unhappy, and I wanted to fix them to get rid of *my* discomfort. My problem was not their unhappiness, but feeling I was responsible for them.

It was a long time before I discovered the racing stomach around unhappy people and realized it signaled I was taking responsibility for them. And it was not until I worked out my belief in guilt that I was able to let go of the idea that I was letting God down if I did not fix them.

So, I was ripe to misread the *Course* to suggest, validate, and encourage codependency. The reason the *Course* takes such long and deep study with Spirit is it takes common words, phrases, and concepts and gives them new meaning to undo guilt. For example, the *Atonement* is not Jesus dying on the cross for you, but correction of your perception that you are separate from God. And while it uses phrases like "save the world" to describe your purpose, it does not mean, as a codependent might read that, that you are to take responsibility for others. In fact, it says explicitly that your only responsibility is to accept the Atonement (correction) for yourself. To understand *save the world*, you have to understand what it means by *the world*. It is not talking about the material world or others, but your *perceptions*. *Saving the world* means "saving" yourself from your sense of separation from God by correcting your perceptions. You "save your brother"—and therefore yourself—by seeing Christ in place of the person.

I *sensed* the *Course* did not mean what a superficial reading seemed to indicate, but for a long while I was not certain. I felt such guilt if I did not take care of others that I could not trust my own interpretations—or Spirit's, if it set me free. Codependency (I did not call it this yet) was what passed for love in the world and was in line with what most religions taught.

I was not sure if the *Course* was saying that I did not have to take responsibility for others or if it was saying I was supposed to take care of others but without a sense of sacrifice! So, I felt guilty as well for my sense of burden as I took responsibility for others.

This kind of confusion was common for me in my study of the *Course*. In many cases I could not tell if it was setting me free or if it was binding me and saying I should not feel bound. So, in this period, ego's resistance had a toe hold with me. With every new idea and lesson, I would find freedom, only to then fall into deep doubt.

During Sorting Out, I not only had to sort out myself and Spirit (same thing in the end) from ego in my mind, but also traditional religious values from what the *Course* taught. I sensed, but was far from seeing clearly, that the *Course* was comparing two different experiences of consciousness (ego and Spirit), not asking me to make ego and the person Christ-like.

Sometimes in the joy and sense of relief I felt reading the *Course* I wanted to express my Love in some form with the world. A few times I enthusiastically attempted to come up with a code of ethics derived from its principles. But each time, I lost my joy. It was a while before I understood why: I was doing what religions do, spiritualizing ego, thereby increasing guilt and blocking out Spirit in the process. The goal was to know Spirit, not perfect ego, the person, or the world, which are illusions.

5

In those years, I was only dimly aware of teachers of *A Course in Miracles*. Mostly I knew of teachers who contributed to a newsletter from a group out of southern California. One of the teachers they highlighted was Jerry Jampolsky, who had written *Love is Letting Go of Fear*, which had introduced me to the *Course*. But I felt about the articles in their newsletter as I felt about the study group I had attended: Disappointed that no one was sharing higher miracles (my term for experiences of Spirit-consciousness) or Revelation. They emphasized relationships and forgiveness in ways that seemed no different from how the world in general spoke about forgiveness. They seemed to aim at perfecting the person. No one shared experiences of Truth and how they revealed the world as illusion, which is what the *Course* teaches is true forgiveness. It was radical, yes, but isn't that what set the *Course* apart from other spiritual teachings?

What I did not know was whether they were not teaching this because they had not had experiences that showed them that only God is real, or if they had and felt it was too radical to share for one reason or another.

The only teacher I considered reading was Ken Wapnick. He was the third person involved with the *Course* and helped Dr. Schucman organize the manuscript for publishing. He set up the *Foundation for A Course in Miracles* and taught the *Course* extensively, from a very psychological and practical point of view. I saw his books on the shelves of a New Age/New Thought bookstore in Honolulu to which Emily had introduced me. But each time I considered buying one, I felt a gentle but firm *no*. And I would walk away without giving it another thought.

I learned over the years that when an idea came from Spirit, it would quietly persist. If it came from ego, it would come in strong, with a lot of thought and feeling, but eventually fall away. Sometimes, however, I was not certain if Spirit was there amidst ego's enthusiasm. Ego could piggyback on Spirit, with its own agenda for a situation (just as it did with my whole path). So, I learned to let go of a question or idea when I was confused about whether Spirit or ego was guiding me and wait to see if it quietly persisted or fell away.

Beyond Wapnick, any time I considered buying books about the *Course* or thought of somehow (this was pre-internet) finding someone who had experiences like mine with whom to speak, the idea fell away. So, as far as teachers went, it was to be Spirit for me.

Beyond the *Course*, the only teaching that resonated with me was the *Infinite Way* by Joel Goldsmith. Emily had introduced me to it, and I eventually bought many of Goldsmith's books. While what he taught did not wholly line up with the *Course*, somehow when I got bogged down in the *Course's* concepts, reading Goldsmith cleared my mind. This was largely because he brought me back to God. I would recenter on my awareness of God before diving back into the *Course*.

Goldsmith taught that if you were in touch with God, you would be supplied in form. Enough money, the right life partner, meaningful employment, etc. would all show up as manifestations of God's Abundance. Manifesting, not through action but through awareness, was certainly not a new concept, but was gaining traction in New Thought circles at the time. (This was long before *The Secret* and *The Law of Attraction* exploded this idea in popular culture in the early 2000s.) It was an idea that many students thought was in line with the *Course*. I was confused by it because while it sounded like it could be what the *Course* says, I sensed it was not.

Goldsmith was not suggesting you should manifest things to bring fulfillment. He was saying what appears at the material level is the result of your awareness of either lack (ego) or Abundance (Spirit). In fact, he cautioned students to not get so enthralled by what showed up that they lost sight of God, because then they would stop manifesting abundance. But it would be hard for someone to not then see the awareness of God as some sort of font of material goodness. This seemed more like magic than miracle.

The *Course* also teaches nothing outside of you can bring fulfillment. But unlike Goldsmith, who saw the material world as God's creation and therefore material abundance as everyone's correct state of consciousness, the *Course* teaches the material world is an illusion. The *real world* it speaks of is an awareness of Abundance, yes, but *just that.* Spirit-consciousness is an awareness of God's Reality that overlooks the appearance of the material world. (The *Course's happy dream* is happy because you see the material experience is an illusion and do not take it seriously.) Spirit's nonmaterial Seeing is precisely how it bridges ego-consciousness (interpretations and judgments on the material world) and Christ.

But some students seemed to think that the *Course* validated the idea of manifesting when it says you are responsible for what shows up in your life. However, the *Course* is always talking about your *experience* (conflict or peace), not the material world. I was confused about this at first, too, but the *Course* is very consistent in teaching that you are the source of your *experience*, regardless of what occurs in the material world.

It was just this type of incongruity that I brought to Spirit for clarification. I often encountered religious teachings or philosophies that did not seem to line up with the *Course*. Sometimes I even felt the *Course* contradicted itself. I would *feel* an incongruity, but it took me a while to home in on what it was.

It was confusing and often uncomfortable as my

thought system was challenged. And sometimes I discovered I misread the *Course*. More often, however, comparing the *Course* to other teachings was how it was clarified for me. And I saw just how different it was from other spiritual philosophies, theologies, and ontologies. I felt set free from erroneous ideas, whether I had ever taken them on as beliefs or not.

But when it came to the idea of manifesting, I ran into more than my confusion over what the *Course* taught about it. When I attempted to apply some practice for manifesting, I invariably felt I was "swimming upstream"—trying to make something happen that was not going to happen. Unfortunately, I took this to mean I was blocked. I dug around in my mind and feelings to find my obstacles to manifesting what I wanted. This was futile, self-defeating, and, sometimes, self-flagellating. Each time, however, I eventually let go of what I was trying to make happen because it was much easier to rest in what I felt was the "flow of the universe."

I did not know how to reconcile these *experiences* of flow with the *idea* of free will, which I sincerely felt I had. There is a popular passage in the *Course* about how *the script is written* (W-158.4). At that time, I took this to mean the outcome was inevitable—the Atonement (correction) would happen. I did not read this to be literal and to mean everything that happened was going to happen. There were other passages that implied predestination as well, but I took those to refer to which thought system I chose in any given moment. It would be a long time before I would have the issue of free will sorted out. But in the meantime, I was sure I had free will.

6

Because I was a sensitive child, I slowly laid down layers of armor over my heart, and by the time I entered my teens, I was threatening to become a hard person. But that changed when I was fourteen. E, my remaining sibling at home, had a son, J, just as she was turning twenty-two. She was not married, so they were to remain in the family home.

Late one night, when my nephew was a few days old, E put him in my arms while she went to change the sheets in his crib. Though I was thrilled by the fact of him in our home and had held him often before this, it was this night that I looked in his eyes and was a goner. I had bonded in what was to be my central love for the next sixteen years.

This relationship re-opened me to my softer side. To hell with hardness if it would keep me from loving this child! In fact, I credit this opening with preparing me for the one I would have a year or two later, when Spirit came into my awareness before I slammed my mind shut on It.

I had never had much of a social life. In high school I hung out with a small group of girls, ranging from three to five of us over the years. These were girls who, like me, did not fit into any discernable social group. My best friend among them was held back from having a social life by a controlling mother, but I rarely had anything to do with my other friends outside of school anyway.

In a class in high school, we did an exercise where we were asked how old we felt within. My classmates said anything from eight to twenty-five. I felt forty. I really had no idea how to be young. I had no interest in parties, drugs, or being popular. I wanted a boyfriend because I loved the idea of romantic love and it would raise my status. But when it happened (sweet guy; nice kisser), I felt, "What's wrong with this picture?" and broke it off.

I had always been happy in my family and by myself at home. I liked to do what I wanted to do with my free time, which was play with my nephew, read novels, watch old movies, and putz around the house and yard, doing chores and making my own projects. I could not understand why anyone would want to join after-school groups or activities or have friends who would cut into their free time with themselves.

So, the burst of sociability I had between nineteen and twenty-one was a new expression of me. And short lived. I thought at the time that I had been held back socially by being in the closet, and I expected after coming out I would be more social going forward. But my spiritual experiences seemed to change my life's direction. Of course, I did not have the hindsight yet to see that that social episode was part of settling my personal identity before the spiritual experiences that followed. There was no *change in direction*. My life was going as it was going to go, which was simply not what I expected.

Already not much interested in what others my age found important, I felt I could not talk with them about what was most important to me. Those on a similar path were not only not having my mystical experiences, they were also often much older. So, I had no social life through most of my twenties and found emotional fulfillment in my family, particularly with my nephew.

I did, however, continually fantasize about a partner. When I was twenty-four, I briefly returned to the lesbian support group that had been the source of my social crowd a few years earlier. The core of my group was gone, although one or two women I knew remained. But, except for a brief flirtation that I screwed up in an incredibly foolish way, I did not find any real connection or value there and soon stopped going.

I felt sorry for myself for not having a partner, despite being confused about whether a "good" student of the *Course* "should" want a "special relationship". Then one day on the further side of my mid-twenties, I got honest with myself and acknowledged that I was not doing anything to look for a partner. So, I could hardly act the victim. Although I sincerely wanted one, the reason I was not looking was that I enjoyed helping to raise my nephew, and I knew if I became involved with someone, I would pull away from him. I was wholly at choice. A partner would have to wait because there was someone more important to me in my life at the time.

As for sex, it had no meaning for me without an emotional connection. I could satisfy my own physical needs. I was only interested in being sexually involved with someone with whom I felt a mutual emotional connection and the potential to be seriously involved.

From then on, any time I felt powerless about something lacking in my life, I looked at the choices I was making. Always I found that, while sometimes it was a close thing, what I wanted more won out. I was always at choice.

I was growing up.

7

Throughout my twenties, I was often depressed. I certainly noticed the patterns of my moods with my menstrual cycle. But I seemed to be congenitally just below an even mood most of the time.

But my resistance to the *Course* and ego's backlashes to positive spiritual experiences caused the bulk of my general unhappiness. Sorting Out was a long, hard slog for me. And at least once, I consciously chose fear, and did it in the name of security.

I realized one day that I always felt secure, and I felt I would always be secure. This included, but was not limited to, financial and other forms of material security. And I wondered why. What was the justification? I concluded that, because I had a secure upbringing, I was projecting continuing security into the future. This did not feel quite correct, but I was concerned that blithely feeling secure was an illusion that one day would not stand against reality. So, I squelched the feeling of security whenever I discovered it, reminding myself I had no justification for it. I felt *this* secured me from future disillusionment.

But I *did* have justification for it. What I felt was, in fact, Spirit with me. If I was aware of this, I would have thought I was Eternally Secure in God, but I did not see how this would extend to being secure in my material life. I did not understand that what I felt was Spirit telling me I would have nothing to worry about in my material life as well. So, I rejected any sense of material security even as I grew my awareness of and trust in Spirit. Eventually, this became unconscious. I did such a good job that I did not feel materially secure for decades to come.

Sorting Out was incredibly difficult because of my physiology, my awareness of ego, ego's conflicts with my growing spiritual awareness, and not understanding how Spirit worked in my life, but in hindsight I see significant turning points in my spiritual life that culminated in an improved state of mind.

I still railed against losing Emily and the holy relationship. This sometimes showed up as grief. But it was still the case that all I had to do was think of her and I would be back in mystical Wholeness and Light and joy. One day, driving on the freeway, I had one of these experiences, and something struck me: If I had this experience when she was thousands of miles away, she could not be the source of it. The source had to be in me. And that had to be Spirit.

Suddenly, I realized I had not lost the holy relationship. It was with Spirit and Spirit was always with me. This was so obvious that I saw I had been resisting this awareness all along.

Of course, my attitude toward Emily shifted. I still looked at her as someone who had hurt me, and I held onto her in that regard. But I no longer felt she deprived me of the holy relationship. I also no longer had a basis to be angry with God or myself.

My mystical experiences of Wholeness when I thought of Emily faded away after this, but I hardly seemed to notice. They had a downside in that they did not last, so while joyful in the moment, they were also ultimately painful. My present and ongoing relationship with Spirit was far more valuable.

Another turning point came in my late twenties.

During the period of tremendous personal growth around the time I was twenty, I experienced panic attacks. The first was on the bus after work one day as it approached the freeway. I felt claustrophobic. I felt I would be trapped until it exited the freeway. I managed to ride it out, but every day I rode the bus my fear of being trapped increased until I was in panic. My heart rate shot up and I felt I was losing my mind. Rational thinking did nothing to diminish the fear. One day, I called a friend from a pay phone to take me home. After this, riding the bus was always a source of anxiety. But eventually, I stopped having panic attacks.

Until a few years later, in my late twenties. I do not remember a triggering event, but many years later I would discover that a mild allergic reaction, like subtle pressure in my bronchia from allergens in the air, would trigger subconscious thoughts about suffocating that would lead to panic. But at this time, I did not know what triggered them.

I ended up in a vicious cycle. Unchecked anxiety led to panic attacks, which only increased my ongoing anxiety, leading to more panic attacks. I saw that if left alone, this would lead to agoraphobia and I would be trapped at home, as my mother was in her forties when perimenopause triggered panic attacks for her until she went on hormone replacement therapy.

I did see a doctor, as ongoing anxiety led to myriad symptoms. Initially, she seemed to find something, which of course only increased my anxiety. But it turned out to be a false alarm. That's when I realized I had to get a grip on my mind. Despite turning to Spirit as my Guide and Teacher, I was very lax about my mind in general. But now Spirit inspired a regimen that reflected the practice in the Workbook: Meditation morning and night and taking moments several times a day to turn inward, quiet my mind, and open to Spirit.

Each day, when I reached a new home to clean, if no one was there, or as soon as I was alone, I sat for a mini meditation. And anytime I felt anxiety building, I stopped for a minute and turned to Spirit. This made workdays a little longer, but I did not care. It worked. I slowly came out of the anxiety and panic attacks.

Unfortunately, as soon as the crisis was over, I did not maintain this practice. But many years later, when I was *not* in crisis, I picked it up again and added to it, leading to my book *4 Habits for Inner Peace*.

<u>8</u>

In 1992, I overheard a man introduce himself to my sister, E, as he arrived to pick her up for a blind double date, and I knew he was the one for her.

G was from Las Vegas. They married, and my sister and nephew, now fourteen, moved away to live with him.

I expected to live my whole life in Hawaii. It is the most beautiful place on Earth, why would I go anywhere else? But E said I should come to Las Vegas. Hawaii's economy was going downhill, and Las Vegas's was taking off, and there was lots of opportunity there. Of course, the biggest pull was that my nephew was there, too.

And an odd thing happened: I felt *done* with Hawaii. This felt so complete that I was comfortable with the idea of leaving, even if very anxious about change.

My dad had retired the year before, and my parents were already thinking of moving to a better economy on the mainland. We all decided to move to Las Vegas to be near my sister and nephew.

I would turn twenty-nine just before I moved to a new city, sight unseen, that November. I felt if I did not like Las Vegas, at least I would be on the mainland and could drive to any one of the other forty-seven contiguous states. Because there was something I had to overcome to get there: I had a terrible fear of flying.

I did not like heights or speed. I did not even like being driven in a car at high speeds by anyone else. Something perceptual happened with my eyes and my inner ears and I felt like I was falling down a bottomless pit, a horrifying sensation. (As a child, I felt terrifyingly out of control on a merry-go-round.) Of course, with my experiences on the bus, I knew I did not like to be in enclosed spaces I could not leave at will. In a plane, I would be hurled through space in a sealed tube thousands of feet in the air at hundreds of miles per hour. This was worse than a bus on a freeway. I felt claustrophobic just thinking about it.

The only time I had flown since arriving in Hawaii when I was two years old was when Michele and I went to Maui. I made it by sheer will, forcing myself into the present, and using a lot of self-talk to remind myself I was at choice. It helped that it was only a half-hour flight in a prop plane that did not zip into the air but lifted gently off the ground.

So, besides being anxious about this huge life change, I was anxious about *getting to* the mainland. I was not sure I could do it. I went to a hypnotist to get over my fear of flying.

Before I left Hawaii, I called Emily's father to find out where in the world she was. I had long since stopped writing to her, but I wanted to see if I could find closure before I began a new life in a new place. It turned out she was back. In fact, she was in Pearl City, the town just west of Aiea. She was still with her cultish spiritual group, but I could call her, which I did. She told me she was not allowed to have visitors, and to come for an energy healing session with her so we could talk.

The organization had rooms in a small office building on Kaahumanu Street. Emily met me at the door, and we sat on mats on the floor in a room with others receiving healing. She sat behind me as she did whatever she was supposed to do. Energy healing was not yet in vogue in the US, and I did not know anything about it. I thought it was a bunch of hooey, but if that was the only way I could see her, so be it. Obviously, our conversation had to be quiet and was therefore restricted.

Emily told me she had received all my letters but was unable to respond due to the rules of the group. She thanked me for them. I felt long past whatever I wrote in them. I told her I was moving to Las Vegas, and she said something about having a friend there she might visit. I felt this could be a signal to me that she might want to visit me, too. This was typical of the vague way Emily communicated, leaving her words open to interpretation. I found it frustrating. I felt reading meaning into her words was how I hurt myself with her before. My lesson from that relationship was, when people are vague, it is best to assume they do *not* mean what I want. Better yet, seek clarity. But we were certainly not at that moment in a situation that was conducive to open, honest discussion.

I visited Emily one more time, and she was able to go up to the roof of the building to speak with me privately. I have a sense I pushed past my own discomfort and asked for some answers, but I do not remember what I asked or her answers. I know I felt uncertain if it mattered to me anymore.

I thought Emily looked wistful when I hugged her as I left, and I felt it would be the last time I saw her.

This time around, I did not have mystical experiences with Emily. My relationship with Spirit was integrated in my life, and spirituality had become everyday and practical. Mystical experiences were few and far between. But I felt if Emily was interested in a relationship with me, I would try again. However, I certainly did not need her, and I had no reason to think she was interested in me.

So, a few days later, I was surprised when Emily called me. The leader of her organization was coming to Hawaii, and Emily wondered if I would be interested in cleaning a couch she was to sit on. (Her group seemed to value cleanliness and purity.) I found this request odd. I did routine house cleaning; I did not have equipment for cleaning upholstery. Emily said I could just use one of those foam sprays you buy in a supermarket. Well, that was easy enough, so could they! I felt this might be her way of asking to see me again, but I was done with games. If she wanted to see me, she needed to say so. If she wanted me in her life, she needed to leave the group and come and get me!

I told her no, I was not interested in this job, but thank you for thinking of me. I did not hear from her again.

Inevitably, more than my fear of flying came up with the hypnotist. She told me that Emily and I had a *push-pull* relationship: If I got too close, she pushed me away. If I got too far away, she pulled me close. By telling Emily *no* I took back the power I had given to that relationship.

The hypnotism did not work. In our sessions, I felt I relaxed and was able to access things in my subconscious, but that was all. I did not feel I shifted into another state or was somehow freed from my fear of flying. I did not understand how it was to work. So, when the day of departure came, I got on the plane, took my seat, and went into total panic at the thought of the doors closing and not being able to get out as I hurled through space for hours.

I told my mother I could not do it. She rationalized with me over the safety of flying and when that did not work tried to motivate me with other ideas, like how terrible my nephew would feel if I did not show up. When that did not work, she tried to shame me, an old technique she used to motivate us to do the right thing when we were children. That just pissed me off.

A stewardess with a strong southern accent saw what I was going through and told me to call on Jesus. I snapped at her that I wasn't Christian. Her face closed and she backed away.

I couldn't do it. I got out of my seat and reached up into the overhead compartment to get my carry-on bag. My luggage was already loaded and would have to be sent back from Las Vegas. I tried to motivate myself to push through the fear with some of the same thoughts my mother used, especially thinking of J. Then I wondered where I would live if I stayed on Oahu. I would have to go live with my sister, C, and her family. They did not have room for me. I would be stuck in Hawaii forever if

I couldn't fly.

Nothing worked. But as I had my things in hand, I looked out a window at the tarmac and asked Spirit for help. And a thought went through my mind: *How would I feel about myself if I didn't go through with this?*

That did it. I would hate myself and I found that unacceptable.

I put my things back in the overhead, returned to my seat (having delayed the flight), the Dramamine I took for airsickness kicked in, helping me to relax, and I flew to the mainland without another hitch.

When I arrived in Las Vegas, my nephew flew into my arms, and I was especially grateful that I had made it.

9

Not long after arriving in Las Vegas, I had a dream unlike any I had before. There was no visual imagery to it, just the presence of what felt like an older, wiser, serene woman. I had the sense I was joining a spiritual community, of which she was a member. She asked me what I wanted my spiritual name to be. I told her I didn't speak her group's language. She said I didn't need to. I could learn it or not; it was my choice. She would translate my name into their language.

My first thought was *water*, which was my element, so that would naturally be part of it. And then I thought how wonderful it was in those golden years when I first found the *Course* and my life flowed. So that was my spiritual name: *Water Flowing*.

I felt this dream validated my move to Las Vegas, and signaled I was moving further into my spiritual process.

Anxious by nature and not one to like change, I determinedly threw myself into learning my way around my new city so I would feel settled as soon as possible. Las Vegas is in a valley, ringed by distinct mountains one can use as landmarks. Its major streets are laid out in a grid, north-south and east-west. It was easy to learn the way around.

In Hawaii, it took me three years to fill my schedule with cleaning jobs. In Las Vegas, it took me only three months. The city was booming, and everyone had a lot of money, especially those who worked in construction. My parents were building a home at the edge of the Peccole Ranch neighborhood, and I was to live with them initially. But I could foresee being out on my own in a way I would not have been able to afford in Hawaii.

I was shocked to find soon after I arrived that sodomy (which was defined as sex between two people of the same sex) was illegal. In *Nevada*? The only state where prostitution was legal? *Seriously*? I had not thought to research this!

But soon after, the law was changed. In any case, I went to a lesbian support group at the tiny gay community center on Sahara Avenue at Maryland Parkway. I found the gay community in Las Vegas to be about ten years behind Hawaii in both self-esteem and activism, which was dismaying. But here I was, and it was what I had.

I stopped pretending to myself that I did not want a life-partner. I did not care if this made me a "bad" *Course* student. It was what I wanted and there was no use denying it. I had learned to be radically honest with myself because if I wasn't, Spirit couldn't help and guide me.

Then one day while meditating I knew with absolute clarity I *would* have a life-partner. I told Spirit she would have to show up at the lesbian support group because that was as social as I was going to get. I never went to a gay bar or club in Las Vegas (and have not to this day), although I did visit other gay businesses in an area known as the *Fruit Loop* on Paradise Road.

But time passed and I did not meet anyone interesting. And I found I did not care. I cut back going to the support group to only every other week as on the alternate week I had a late job that made getting to the meeting a rush. I looked at my finances as I considered buying a condo and maybe getting a couple of dogs. And I thought maybe I would take myself on a road trip to think about letting go of the idea of a partner and spending my life alone. I was happy as I was, after all.

I had been in Las Vegas about a year and a half when I walked into the support group one week and saw someone I thought was "the cutest thing I'd seen there yet". I felt a knot I did not know I had in my solar plexus relax as the thought "you can stop looking now" went through my mind.

But then this woman—Jessie—spoke, and I thought she was the most arrogant and egotistical person I had ever heard. Moreover, she was surrounded by a bunch of angry friends, although she did not seem angry herself. The moment of recognition went out the window.

After that meeting, Jessie came up to me to apologize for something she had said that she thought offended me. I had not been offended and told her so. But there was something about the way she approached me, with child-like vulnerability, that I found appealing. She seemed like someone in need of rescue, which stirred my nurturing, codependent heart.

Jessie was there each of the next few weeks and our eyes met now and then. We sometimes addressed each other in the group conversation. I was fairly certain she was interested in me, as I was in her. One night, when the group went to dinner after the meeting, she maneuvered to sit next to me. We talked, my heart pounding, as she stole my French fries. I thought she smelled good. As we got up to leave, she said, "Why don't you call me? We can go out for coffee and some intellectual conversation." Her number was on the group's list.

I wondered if she was asking me to ask her out. And I thought about it, often, in the next couple of weeks. But it never felt right to call her.

Until suddenly one night it did. I was on the computer in the family room and shut it down. I did not hurry but made my way to my room in my own time and called her.

She answered, breathless, having just come through the door after a trip to the Grand Canyon, where she had had an important spiritual breakthrough. We spoke for hours.

And, again a few nights later, another marathon phone call. I was astounded by her. She shared everything; maybe too much. Everything dark that had ever happened to her, which was a great deal. And everything dark she did in the dysfunction that resulted from her early experiences. But it was all out on the table. I would realize later that I felt safe with her because nothing was hidden.

We shared the same values and the same ideas about relationships, like open honest communication. She was Christian and in a 12-step program. I told her about the *Course*.

Her asking me to ask her out had been vague, but I quickly found I could clarify things with her without risk of embarrassment. She could admit to her own vulnerability and could be direct. I did not have to interpret her. This was refreshing after Emily.

I was falling for her and I was a nervous wreck, afraid I would get hurt again.

The next lesbian support group meeting was coming up and I primped my car, washing it and cleaning the interior, having a vague idea Jessie and I might go out afterward. I made sure I had money to take her to dinner.

When I arrived at the GCC and saw her I said, "You want to get out of here?" We left before the meeting began. I drove to one of the many new housing developments and we walked through model homes. I took her to dinner, where she told me even more about her life. She had been abused in every possible way as a child, and had gone through, and was still in, therapy.

I talked about *A Course in Miracles*, but she asked me to stop, as the ideas I brought up made her feel "ice water in my veins." She felt as though she was falling through space.

Her life was messy, sure, but I had a more pressing problem. Despite my initial impression of her as "the cutest thing there", I did not find her physically attractive. I was falling for her, but I was not attracted to her. I didn't know what to do.

The next day my sister, E, who had heard about Jessie through my mother, called and said with a smile in her voice, "I heard you met someone."

"I don't know," I said. "She is such a mess."

Later, E would tell me that she knew from that statement that I was a goner.

I did not mention my lack of attraction to Jessie. How could I explain that? I was gaga for her. Yes, I thought she was a mess, and I was terrified of getting hurt. But what did that have to do with no physical attraction to her?

Two evenings later, I went to see Jessie at the apartment where she rented a room. She opened her door with her Cairn terrier in her arms and she looked adorable. How had I not found her attractive? This was a lesson in what fear could do. For a while it had totally blocked my physical attraction to her.

(Of course, for years I insisted it was the dog that won me over...)

That night, we acknowledged our interest in each other, and decided we were not going to pretend we didn't know where we were headed. A few days later, Jessie said to me that she was not in love with me yet, but she knew she was going to be. I told her I felt the same. It was wonderful to have the same level of interest returned. We were, unofficially, engaged to be married. Later we would joke it was almost like we had an arranged marriage, as we had an agreement to marry before we fell in love.

<u>10</u>

I lost a lot of weight. I couldn't concentrate. I couldn't

meditate. I ran late in my cleaning jobs because I would find myself daydreaming for minutes on end. I struggled to remember Spirit and just trusted It was with me.

Yes, I was falling in love.

Panic attacks had resumed for me not long before I met Jessie. I called on Spirit but was not sure if I could hear It through my fear. I decided to not suffer, which was, I now know, Spirit. After eight years with the *Course*, I still did not recognize all the ways Spirit reached me through my thoughts and feelings.

I found a therapist who specialized in panic and anxiety disorders, which she diagnosed in me. She was so tightly wound herself that I wondered if she was a good choice. When I told her about Jessie, she said we would never work out. Jessie had too many problems.

I stopped seeing the therapist. Besides a diagnosis, what I got from her was a model of what I did *not* want to become.

At some point, as we discussed our relationship, Jessie told me her sobriety came first for her. I told her that was okay since God came first with me. We realized we were saying the same thing, as her sobriety meant her 12-step program, which was the context of her relationship with God.

A while after this, referring to how I took responsibility for my feelings, she said, "It's like you have your own program." I told her that was the *Course*. It taught me that I, and no one else, was the source of my feelings. She said she had not met anyone outside of a 12-step program who was like me.

Jessie found the *Course* cold and cerebral. I was afraid that was how I presented it to her, but no matter how I tried, I did not seem able to convey the Love and joy of my mystical experiences.

Jessie had almost become a minister herself, in the Metropolitan Community Church, but had a falling out with board members and left when she was student clergy. She missed the "smells and bells" of religion but felt she could not go back. She realized there were other ways to fulfill her calling, particularly through 12-step sponsorship. She could not understand nonduality. She wanted a warm, loving, anthropomorphized God who had created her ego and body and the world, not an abstract Onlyness that transcends ego and the material world. In fact, she did not seem to understand there could be a shift in consciousness. Being "reborn in Christ" seemed to mean a transforming intellectual acceptance of Jesus as Christ to her (as to many Christians).

Jessie had a rough childhood and went through a lot of therapy, and our relationship was her first opportunity since to trust someone new. And she simply could not. Soon after we came to our understanding, we were in her apartment and I said or did something that triggered her, and she got up from the couch, went to her room, slammed the door, and played "Disarm" (*"the killer in me is the killer in you"*) by Smashing Pumpkins.

She was six months younger than me and acting like a teenager.

I sat on the couch and seriously considered leaving and breaking it off. This was not the first time she acted out, just the worst. I had other glimpses of what I thought was Jessie regressing to adolescence or younger. I did not like drama. I did not want this. But I also did not want to throw away what seemed, otherwise, to be the makings of a good relationship. Conflicted, I turned inward to Spirit.

And what came to me was to be still and unwavering so she could learn to trust me. I knew her whole story and no one ever offered her that. The image I got was of an anchor with the ship tossing on the waves above until the storm passed.

It was rough going. We moved in together and she left me often—for hours. She never actually left our apartment, but she would leave in words, and sometimes into another room. But I began to see a pattern. She would seem to really be going. I would be convinced of it. Then, suddenly, I would catch an opening; a glimmer of hope in something she said. I would stick a wedge in that, and the crack would widen, there would be a turnaround, and we would talk it out. I finally realized she was testing me, just as Spirit had indicated. She wanted to see how far she could push me before I would leave. I hated the drama, but I stood firm. And, sure enough, she acted out less as she trusted me more.

Eleven months after our first date, we married in my parents' living room. It was 1995, so not legally recognized, but called a Holy Union as it was performed by a minister for Jessie's sake. Our families and friends saw us as married, which was what the ceremony was for.

Three things had prepared me for the ins and outs of a long-term relationship. The first was my family, where I had noticed as a child that closeness in relationships shifted over time. For instance, I might be close with my mother for a while and then we would both move on and I would be close to someone else in the family. Neither I nor anyone else maintained the same level of closeness day after day, even if, over the course of time, we had members of the family we were closer to than others.

The second thing that prepared me was my high school psychology teacher who said, "Marriage is like this" and he brought his hands together and then parted them again and again in a weaving motion. He reinforced what I had already observed in my family.

The other reinforcement was the movie *The Four Seasons*. In the movie, Alan Alda's character tells a friend that over the course of his twenty-year marriage he and his wife went through phases where they could hardly stand to look at each other and other phases where they were like teenagers and could not keep their hands off each other. So, I went into marriage expecting that, over the long haul, Jessie and I would grow apart and together again and again. And this proved to be true.

Jessie said we worked because our "jagged edges" fit perfectly together. By this she meant our wounds. She recognized what the *Course* teaches, which is that we are drawn to others who (usually unconsciously) remind us of someone in the past. And we have the choice to either take revenge on the past in the new relationship or to heal. We chose to heal.

It was the perfect relationship for me to address my codependency. Jessie taught me that when she shared her problems with me, she was not asking me to fix them, but to just listen, empathize, support, and encourage. This was like an epiphany to me. What a novel idea—no one was asking me to fix them! They just wanted to be heard and understood.

With Jessie, I learned to recognize my codependent responses so I could address them. For a long while, though, I could only change my behavior, but not my emotional responses, which a therapist would point out was the source of my stress.

Jessie remained insecure, until one day when we had been together for a couple of years and she expressed concern that I would leave her over something I found to be a trivial difference between two people. I reassured her I would not leave, and said, incidentally, "Look—just don't abuse me and don't cheat on me. We can work out anything else." I inadvertently clarified the boundaries of our relationship for her, and she relaxed into us. If only I had known sooner that was all she needed!

But even these boundaries would turn out to be flexible. During a fierce argument one day Jessie warned me several times I was pushing past her stop sign and she might hit me. I kept pushing, and sure enough, she slapped me. I felt her pull back at the last minute, but that did not change the fact that she had struck me. Having been abused herself, in her family, and later by lovers, she was horrified. But I felt partly responsible. She gave ample warning and I kept pushing. Or was I doing what abused women do, taking responsibility for being hit? We talked and talked, that day and for days afterward. It was our agreement that if anything like this occurred, we would see our therapist together. But by the time we met with her, we had processed it out and were comfortable with ourselves and each other.

Our therapist could see we had worked it out. She asked how long we had been together, which was two years by then. She shrugged. "So, you hit each other every couple of years."

Jessie and I both understood that if it ever happened again, I would be gone. Jessie supported this, as she felt if it happened again, I *should* be gone. But we never came close.

Despite Jessie's insecurities, she never felt unworthy of my love. After Michele and Emily, it was wonderful to be with someone who wanted my love and absorbed it like a sponge. Of course, it was fantastic to have it returned as well. We wanted to be happy *together*. This laid a secure foundation for both of us to grow individually and as a couple.

But we had our differences. Some of them significant. I was used to effortless structure, organization, and order. It was how I was raised and just what life was to me. Jessie, it seemed to me, lived in chaos. Before we moved in together, I noticed she often had to dash to the store to buy something that anyone should just have on hand, like toilet paper or dog food. How did this happen? You make a list, you shop regularly…I could understand if she did not have the money, but she did. Good thing we lived in a 24-hour city where stores were open all night, because she often ran out of things at midnight.

Her idea of doing laundry was for everyone to throw dirty clothes in the washing machine until it was full, and then whoever topped off the load was to run it. But what if you ran out of, say, underwear before the machine was full? Well, then, you put on a dirty pair or did not wear any…*Who lived like this?* Just pick a day to do your laundry each week…like grocery shopping…

I was raised to put responsibility before pleasure. We had to do our homework and chores before we could go out to play. But after we moved in together, Jessie, when she wasn't working, would sleep or be involved with a hobby or friends as chores and shopping and other life-maintenance things all fell on me. I had always imagined a partner with whom I would shop and clean, etc. I could not live like she did without a great deal of stress. And she seemed constitutionally incapable of maintaining any kind of structure or prioritizing responsibilities over pleasure. Trying to do so caused *her* a great deal of stress.

This lifestyle difference was a deep source of conflict for me. I loved her and wanted to be with her, but I became resentful as I took care of everything around the home despite working all day, just as she did. My mind was often filled with angry, attacking thoughts about her laziness and irresponsibility. "Who the hell raised you?" I would ask.

I was wrangling with this conflict and folding towels for my cleaning business in our apartment complex's laundry room one day when Spirit gave me another way to look at it: We simply had different lifestyle values and *different did not mean wrong*. My problem was not our differences, but judging Jessie. I could not ask her to take on my values, but neither could she expect me to put aside my own.

I went back to the apartment and discussed this with Jessie. As I cared how our home was run, she gave me complete control of running the home. Jessie could go to work and come home and play, but she would have no say in the order or structure I imposed on the house and dogs. (We did make decisions together when it came to our finances or decorating our home, however). We were both set free.

I loved it! We could each live our lives as we wanted. I grieved a little not having the partner-as-constant-companion as I had envisioned. But I realized I had imagined a kind of twin, which was certainly unrealistic, a little ridiculous, and would probably have been stifling. This was better. I had both my freedom *and* someone with whom to spend my life.

Jessie did her best to not add to my work. The way she looked at it, if I lived alone I would cook and clean and do laundry anyway, so my doing it for two only added a little to what I would already be doing. She stayed out of my way and was largely oblivious to our home as she was absorbed with her own interests. Well into our marriage, she would tell her friends that she felt she lived in my home, and, essentially, she did. But she did not forget to be grateful, because she came to value the order even if she did not contribute to it. She often told me how much she appreciated all I did to make our home comfortable and her life easier.

We had different interests as well, but I found this kept us interested in each other over time. We came together over those interests we did share. For two codependents, this was important. It maintained the boundaries between us.

I learned it was more important to share character values, like personal responsibility, personal growth, spiritual development, social and political outlook, etc. in a long-term relationship than interests. While interests were about time spent together, values were about respecting each other. Two people can always find something to do together. But without respect, there is no desire to spend time together.

I did not forget the holy relationship. I invited Spirit into my relationship with Jessie and then we did this together. But it was a practical, not a mystical, holy relationship, and I felt my relationship with Jessie was "Plan B". I felt I was supposed to be with Emily, but that she had not wanted it, so I was given another path.

However, I felt that I had with Jessie what I had wanted with Emily. We were open and honest with each other, we communicated as deeply as we could, we loved and supported each other, and hauled together in every practical area as partners in life. All that was missing with Jessie was the mystical awareness of Oneness. But just as I could not make Emily want the material relationship I did, I could not make mystical experiences with Jessie. I would just have to wait and see if they came again.

11

When I came out to myself, I questioned if I really wanted a life partner or if I had just taken on that value from the dominant culture. This was no small inquiry, because I had spent so much of my time fantasizing about marriage that wanting it seemed part of my identity. But it seemed that, as the rest of my personal identity was up in the air, it was a good time to look at this value, too.

I was fascinated by the idea of two strangers choosing to spend the rest of their lives with each other. I wanted to know what it was like to love and grow with someone I chose through ups and downs, trials and triumphs, and every phase of life. I wanted to discover the depth and breadth such a connection could reach. So, yes, wanting a partner for life was my own value.

And finally, at thirty, I had met that someone and was embarking on that lifelong journey with her.

I loved Jessie and valued our relationship more than I could say. But my theme song in our early days together was Suzy Bogguss's "Hey, Cinderella". I was old enough to know there was no happily ever after, but marrying meant facing that illusion for the final time. I mourned it a little.

I knew Jessie could not fulfill me. I knew when I felt lack what I lacked was an awareness of my Wholeness in God. But sometimes when I felt empty or needy, I still turned to her. Of course, affection, sex, or time together did not fill the emptiness. I was never upset with her for not making me whole, as I knew she could not. But I just could not seem to stop reaching outward for wholeness. Then one day, feeling needy, I decided instead to turn to Spirit. And it worked! My feeling of lack subsided as I rested in Spirit.

This signaled another significant shift in my spiritual growth. I had told Jessie my relationship with God came first. I discovered the holy relationship was with Spirit. Now I decided to make Spirit *my primary relationship*. It would come first and all other relationships, even my marriage, would follow.

In practice, this meant I turned to Spirit first in every circumstance, whether it was to deal with a sense of lack, a personal problem, a decision, etc. Spirit was my Partner and I found fulfillment in this.

I never told Jessie, but she felt it as I took even more responsibility for myself. She felt free without knowing why.

Practically applying my spirituality was the only way I could share my spirituality with her (really, with anyone). She was occasionally threatened by it because she did not understand it. And sometimes she feared it could somehow lead me away from her. I reassured her I could not see how that would ever happen.

We found we did not need to share the same path. It was enough to encourage and support the other on her path. This did mean, however, that I did not share with her my deepest, most meaningful experiences. I did not share them with anyone else, either. But I did not need to. I had Spirit.

I felt I had an inner life apart from Jessie, although in practice I felt Spirit was *between* us. But Jessie shared her spiritual process with me as I could listen to her without judging her path or being threatened by it.

However, I did share the psychological aspects of my process with her. I just did not put them in the context of my spirituality. And I did the same with a therapist when I decided to deal with my depression.

Jessie had a fantastic therapist, and she became mine as well. The overriding issue of my thirties was my conflicted relationship with my mother. I told the therapist that I did not know where my mother ended and I began—classic sign of co-dependency. She told me I had to take steps to sort myself out from my mother.

Discussing my depression, she drew a line on a piece of paper and said that was an even mood. She asked where I would place myself in relation to it most of the time? I pointed just below the line. She said that's dysthymia, a chronic low-grade depression. She told me there was no treatment for it. The anti-depressants at the time did not work for it.

I left her office crying. But then I knew there was only one thing to do. I had to apply the mind-training the *Course* offered, which I had been avoiding. I had no choice; it was my only way out.

I finally began to pay attention to my own thoughts and watched how they contributed to my depression and worked to change them. And I stopped seeing the therapist.

12

When I was young, I expected to be a mother one day. I discovered that it was while loving that I felt love, so I enjoyed nurturing. But helping to raise my nephew took a lot of the shine off the idea of motherhood. I found out how much work even one child could be. And I discovered my need to nurture was met in my relationships with Jessie and our dogs.

Jessie and I did discuss having children. We considered artificial insemination, but neither of us had a burning need to carry a child, so we felt adopting was the moral choice in that case. There were obstacles to same-sex couples adopting children in Nevada back then, but it was not impossible.

But, over time, we came to discover that Jessie had various physical and mental health issues including—no surprise—Attention Deficit and Hyperactivity Disorder. The bulk of raising children would fall on me, and in that case, I would want to be a stay-at-home mom. This was not realistic on Jessie's income alone. It was also possible that one day Jessie would go on disability.

These are the reasons I gave others for not having children. But within myself, the real reason was I felt children would tie me to the world more than I wanted to be. My goal was inner peace, which I understood could come only from an awareness of Truth. And I did not want anything to distract me from that.

But my study of the *Course* continued to be almost completely intellectual. I was often bogged down in theory and concepts. I understood this bit and that bit, but I could not see how it all fit together. I felt guilty and was often tormented by it. Once, reading it in bed, it hit a nerve and I hurled it at the wall across the room. "Didn't like what it said, huh?" Jessie asked drily beside me.

I brought up some of my torment to my therapist once and she said, "It's just a book!" I felt she just could not understand.

Jessie got fed up with me one day and said, "I've never known anyone who *thinks* about God so much!" This was like a slap upside the head. I *was* too much in my mind with it. I eased off the theory for a while and started to put it in practice more. And I was happier. I read theory through guilt; I practiced from Love.

Torment and confusion characterized the Period of Sorting Out for me. So did putting intellectual understanding over practice. I had rare mystical experiences. And they hardly seemed worth it, as the swing back to ego afterward was extreme. My trust in Spirit grew slowly, even after it became my primary relationship. The thing about trust is, you can't fake it.

I would come to think of that period as though I had seen a Bright City on a ridge in the distance during the Period of Undoing and then, to reach it, I had to descend into a dense, dark valley for the Period of Sorting Out. I could put my hand on Spirit's back to guide me through the forest, but more often than not I felt out of touch with It.

In 1997, Jessie and I bought a house. And it was not long after this that my interest in the *Course* and all things spiritual tapered off.

I read the *Course* with diminishing frequency, until the blue books just sat on my end table gathering dust. Months went by without me opening them at all. Finally, I acknowledged I felt done with them. As I put the books up on a bookshelf, I was baffled by this complete dropping away of interest. My spirituality had defined my life until then. But I could not pretend an interest no longer there.

For the next couple of years, the only thing I felt moved to do that could seem even remotely spiritual (which it was not for me) was read the Bible front to back. I used one of Jessie's modern-English versions. It was dry and boring and struck me as irrelevant. It took me a year. The only things in it that resonated with me were Paul's experiences of Christ.

I could not dismiss my own experiences of Christ, but they seemed remote. I also could not dismiss Spirit. It had always been there for me, but now I was not sure what It was. So, I was not quite an agnostic as I acknowledged that there was *Something* that I had clearly experienced. But I also was not sure how to characterize It anymore. Moreover, I was not motivated to do so.

THREE: RELINQUISHMENT

The third stage through which the teacher of God must go can be called "a period of relinquishment." If this is interpreted as giving up the desirable, it will engender enormous conflict. Few teachers of God escape this distress entirely. There is, however, no point in sorting out the valuable from the valueless unless the next obvious step is taken. Therefore, the period of overlap is apt to be one in which the teacher of God feels called upon to sacrifice his own best interests on behalf of truth. He has not realized as yet how wholly impossible such a demand would be. He can learn this only as he actually does give up the valueless. Through this, he learns that where he anticipated grief, he finds a happy lightheartedness instead; where he thought something was asked of him, he finds a gift bestowed on him. (M-4.I.A.5)

1

Not just *A Course in Miracles*, but my spirituality had fallen away. I felt no connection to a Presence within. I wasn't even looking for It anymore. I couldn't fathom what that had been about. Jessie was uncomfortable with me not having a spiritual awareness and practice. A large part of her sense of security— her highest value—with me had been my foundation in Spirit.

But I was not unhappy. In some ways, I was personally happier without struggles with the *Course's* concepts and my belief in guilt in my face all the time. I was just living a normal life in the world.

I did not mind cleaning houses, but I reached a point in 1999 when I wanted to do something more meaningful; something that used my mind. This was a little awkward, because it was the kind of thing I would have shared with Spirit and that had faded for me. Yet, something of that posture remained. As I folded work towels one day, I put this desire "out to the universe". And a week later I read about life coaching in a magazine and recognized my answer.

I entered the life coach training program at Coach U. Classes were internet and phone based, as that was how life coaching was done. I squeezed this into my life, which was already filled with my house cleaning business, my marriage, taking care of our four dogs, and maintaining our home and yard. I was excited as I was taking my life in a new direction. I told everyone, and Jessie okayed our getting into debt for this as potentially I would make more money as a life coach.

At Coach U, we were strongly encouraged to get a life or business coach ourselves and build a coaching practice as we took the two-year course. Since we were our business, our natural markets were the communities we already had. I could think of only two I had in the past: The gay community and the *A Course in Miracles* community. So, I picked up the *Course* again to attend a study group and market myself.

And then my life did what felt like a one-hundred-and-eighty-degree turn. Although I had not felt lost or as though I was missing anything, reading the *Course* again I felt I was home. My spirituality was front and center once more, and I knew I was never going to leave again.

Try as I might to bring the new direction of my material life to the center of my attention, I could not. This was my first conscious experience of feeling something of greater significance occurring within than what appeared to be happening in my material life. It *was* going in a new direction, but I felt an unexpected shift in my mind that seemed to be the real change. The material change was secondary.

I had "heard" Spirit before, of course, as ideas and intuitions and, rarely, in words. But this time I felt something fundamental changing in me that I had seen but not been in touch with before. And it was real. I knew this was not the shift to Spirit-consciousness, but I felt I had a taste of what was necessary for that to occur in this feeling of fundamental change. And it would be HUGE. I was already a little afraid of *this* shift. Frankly, I was grateful it was not THE shift.

In those couple of years away from the *Course*, I had forgotten its central principles. At one point, I had a coach who was also a student of the *Course*, and when I discussed my fears around putting myself out there as a coach she said, "You know what the *Course* says about fear." I could not for the life of me remember.

She reminded me: "It's not real."

Oh, yeah.

But I did not find it helpful to be reminded of this when fear was currently very real to me. This approach to the *Course* was what I had found frustrating in the study group I had attended and in articles about the *Course* that I had read. It was not enough to merely *think* "it's not real." I had to *see* and *feel* it was not real. I wanted help to get to *that* point, not empty phrases. In the meantime, I needed help dealing with fear.

For my coaching practice, I built a website called *LovePeaceJoy*. I also wrote a blog by the same name to stay in front of potential clients. I tried to focus on traditional life coaching ideas, but spiritual concepts kept coming through. So much so, that I would later learn that my mother told my sister, E, that she felt that maybe I should be a minister. (I learned this after my mother died, and while clearing out her things, we discovered she printed out all of my articles and kept them in a folder.)

My articles reflected the growing conflict in me. With my spirituality my undeniable focus again, I felt pulled away from traditional life coaching, which is generally about helping people reach material goals for fulfillment. When I brought this up to my coach, she shrugged and said people had to make their way in the world whether it was real or not. It was what they experienced as real. That was true, but that did not mean

I had to teach what I knew to be false. I did not want to teach what I did not want to learn and reinforce ego in my mind. It didn't feel authentic. I felt pulled in a different direction—away from the world and into my Identity in God. But this sensation was new to me and I could not articulate it, even to myself.

While in conflict about a coaching practice, something amazing slowly emerged: *Complete willingness* to follow Spirit. If during the previous periods I was in the driver's seat and asked Spirit for directions, now I had moved over to the passenger's seat and was going along for the ride.

This deep willingness signaled my entry into the Period of Relinquishment. This was the significant shift toward peace I had sensed ten years before, when the-lady-who-lunched told me "it would be a while". From here on, it only got easier. My peace only grew. The long, hard slog of Sorting Out was over.

Relinquishment was uncomfortable to start, but only because I compulsively attempted to take the wheel back from Spirit until that habit wound down. To build a coaching practice, I had to decide what kind of coach I would be, and therefore who my market would be. I knew I would be a life coach as opposed to a business coach. But there were so many ways to approach that, and I was to try them all on: Relationship coach, woman's life coach, gay and lesbian life coach, ACIM coach, spiritual coach, etc. I would get excited and passionate about an approach and get it going…only to feel each time I was running down a dead end. It was not the way to go.

Even after I concluded I could only authentically be a spiritual coach, none of my attempts worked. I briefly considered focusing on coaching students of the *Course*, but that seemed limited, and I could not see making any money at that.

Complete willingness to follow Spirit felt like a gift. It was refreshing. It felt natural. And each time I hit a dead end and let go, I felt relief because I sensed I was trying to force something that was not going to happen. After several months of this, I finally figured out what these dead ends meant: I was not going to build a coaching practice. And I did not want to accept that.

It was awkward to be in the classes and not building a practice. The only others not doing so were retirees taking the classes for the fun of learning new skills. Once again, I was doing something outside of the norm. A familiar position, but was I *ever* going to run with a herd? I had known all my life the answer was *no*. This cow always had and always would follow her own star.

I was not just embarrassed in the classes. I had enthusiastically told family, friends, and some customers that I was taking my life in a new direction. And I had to tell Jessie that I did not know what I was taking the classes for. She was supportive, because she loved me, and she wanted me to be happy. But she was disappointed, too, as I had gotten us into debt, and I would not be making more money.

It was a relief when I finally accepted that I was not to build a practice at that time. It felt like I put down a burden, despite my desire and enthusiasm. I did wonder if I had made a mistake enrolling in the classes in the first place or if I was meant to quit. But I felt I was to continue and get my certificate. My embarrassment faded as I rested in my willingness to follow Spirit.

2

To reacquaint myself with the principles of the *Course*, and because I felt I did such a poor job those first two years, I began the Workbook again. I did do better, but about two months in I had to concede I found the lessons rudimentary. I sensed that, although reading the Workbook as I did the Text was helpful, applying the lessons again was holding me back. I was past them.

After I put the lessons aside, I found I was given a thought to use each day by Spirit. This was usually in the form of a succinct phrase that encapsulated what I was learning at the time. Sometimes, it was a line or lesson from the *Course*. Usually, it was in words I honed with Spirit. I realized that where the lessons in the Workbook were introductory and for everyone, this was a curriculum tailored to my mind. I would use a thought for two or three days and then be given a new one. This went on for several months.

For over a decade of study before my two-year hiatus from all things spiritual, I held my mystical experiences at bay when I read the *Course*. They did inform how I read it. I intellectually embraced what I felt was the *Course's* radical message: *Only God is real*. It was, for me, a path to awaken to Truth rather than simply a guide for better relationships or a Spirit-centered life. But I did not let this message *in*.

So, the shift in willingness continued as I realized I could *only* understand the *Course* through my mystical experiences. I *had to* let them in. This seemed so obvious. What value could study have without the experiences that illuminated the words? How could I ever have kept them apart? Well, fear, of course.

It was like something cracked open in me that I did not know had been a hard block of resistance. I accepted Truth as I had never done before. I accepted my *experience* of It. And I began to accept that Reality was other than the world I was used to. I knew this changed everything, and my life would never be the same. And it wasn't. This was my first real shift toward Spirit-consciousness. I was not entering it, but Spirit was real *in my experience* and I willingly followed It.

In a way, this shift seemed more significant than my early profound mystical experiences. Those seemed to come out of nowhere and to simply happen to me. And although I was not aware of choosing this great willingness to follow Spirit, it still felt like *my* willingness. I was involved in my growing awareness of Spirit as I had not been before. It was finally real to me.

Another aspect of this shift was an amazing understanding of the *Course*. When I read it before The Spiritual Hiatus, I understood *this* concept here and *that* concept there, but I never formed a complete picture. But now, I saw how every part fit with every other part. A whole picture formed. And where I anticipated bumps in my understanding, they were gone before or soon after I reached them. It was as though the Text was a wrinkled cloth being smoothed before me. This was so exciting that I read the Text faster than I had ever done. And to test my new understanding, I quickly read it again—and it held.

It would be many, many years before I came to understand what The Spiritual Hiatus had been for. It seemed I had gotten off the path, but clearly, I had not. I returned to it too easily and naturally for that to be the case. And I more than picked up where I had left off. I had advanced into a new period. I did not realize this at the time, but I was certainly aware I was experiencing willingness like nothing I had felt before.

Two things went on during that time. One was settling into my life with Jessie in our new home. By 2000, we had been together for six years, married for five, and in our new home for three. In fact, for a long time I thought that was all The Hiatus had been about. But that explanation never felt complete.

The other was something I saw much later. For thirteen years or so after starting the *Course*, I read it pretty much the same way. My reading was intellectual and conceptual, with little application. But, more than that, I read it through a filter of guilt. I often felt it was harsh. I felt it condemned me for my ego-identification. Oh, there were many loving passages as well. But while it said that sin, and therefore guilt, was not real, I was never certain if that was only true if I was Spirit-identified. Was I not guilty at all or was I guilty when I identified with ego? (It was saying I was never guilty, but I would *feel* guilty as long as I identified with ego.)

The Hiatus was to get me away from the fixed way I read the *Course*, so I could come back to it with an open mind and fresh eyes. Where I used to read condemnation, I now read fact: This is how ego works; this is how Spirit works. It was not condemning me, but simply showing me how my mind worked. The judgment I had read in it was my own.

3

When I began life coaching classes, I attended a *Course* study group to become grounded again in its principles, and to market my life coaching practice. To share with them, I picked up their language and labelled things I simply never had to label on my own. For example, I started to refer to my Inner Teacher as *the Holy Spirit*.

This was also the only time I tried to use Jesus. I felt from the beginning the *Course* was written by the universal Christ Mind, despite the "I" statements attributed to Jesus. I knew there had been a man named Jesus who was crucified for teaching radical things two thousand years ago, as the Romans had written about him at the time. And I accepted the *Course's* idea that he was a brother who had a unique role to play in the Atonement and walked the path before me. But I just could not get with calling on a dead man.

This episode may have been the influence of the study group, as *Jesus* and *Holy Spirit* are often used interchangeably in the *Course* community. Some find *Holy Spirit* too abstract, as it supplies no image. Others find *Jesus* too concrete, as it conjures an image of a man. (I have known students who use both, depending on circumstances.) Abstract worked for me because Spirit *is* Abstract.

In any case, I decided to try giving Jesus a go. And this did indeed conjure up a very concrete image for me—a man of European descent (even though he was from western Asia), with long blond hair, a white robe, and Birkenstocks.

The only notable experience during this episode was one

morning when I was meditating with our cairn terrier curled up in my lap, her usual place in the colder months. I strongly felt the presence of Jesus, and the dog sat up in my lap and stared upward at the ceiling for several minutes.

My Jesus experiment did not last long. Jesus was, for me, too much of a personification for What I felt was nonmaterial.

Eventually, the study group served its purpose and I left it behind. But still thinking in terms of marketing a life coaching practice, I started a study group in my other community, at the Gay and Lesbian Community Center.

Only women came, and in diminishing numbers as the weeks went by. Few of them were familiar with the *Course* at all and those that were, were hardly so. Basically, they were all new and needed to be taught from the ground up. This was quite different from the two study groups I had attended fifteen years apart, which were made up of students with varying degrees of experience with the material. I was truly the expert in the room and felt pressure to not only do the *Course* justice, but to be truly helpful to the attendees.

Not long after I started the group, New York, Pennsylvania, and Washington, D.C. were attacked by terrorists on September 11, 2001. It was a Tuesday, the day the study group met. I cancelled it as many of us had to cross the Strip to reach the meeting, and it had been shut down due to the attack.

But we met the next week and, of course, everyone was still reacting. To me, the terrorist attacks were simply another expression of what the world is. It just happened on US soil, which we were not used to. But most in the group were upset, some personally, even when they had not been directly affected. This was my first lesson in meeting others where they are rather than teaching what I know. I realized I could not go right into discussing Truth and illusion and how this fell under illusion. That would not be helpful to people for whom this was very real. In fact, it would put them on the defensive, increasing their fear, as they would feel they had to defend their reality.

After a moment of wondering how to be helpful, I was inspired by Spirit. I taught something else the *Course* teaches: Ask for another way to look at it.

The next week only one woman reported she was given another way. She realized she could focus on the fear or the love. She spoke of how the attacks brought out the best in some people and brought people together. This made her feel better.

This began my awareness of how the *Course* would be read at different levels as one advanced. After all, Spirit always met me where I was. When I came out, It assured me I was okay with God. But later, when Spirit was an ongoing Presence in my life, but the Religious Right was loud, I had doubts. I asked Spirit directly about my sexuality. I was willing to give it up if it was an obstacle to Truth. And I received an answer that I could understand then but certainly would not have understood before: Heterosexuality is no more real than homosexuality. There is no hierarchy of illusions.

Asking for a different way was helpful when I was in conflict. While I felt I needed meaning, meaning was given, and it was something that pointed, no matter how dimly, toward God. But over time, an awareness slowly sunk in as I was given a different way to look at things: If I could give things a different meaning, they had no meaning in themselves. Without my being aware of it, the world was slowly emptied of meaning for me. But unlike when I read that as a new student and went into an ego pout, the actual experience of it was liberating. The world did not determine how I felt; I did.

4

After a meeting of the study group I led, an attendee mentioned to me that the moment she wanted something, it manifested in her life. She implied her desire caused things to show up in her material life. This is how I had always understood manifesting. But I was still confused about it. I did not live in isolation. Anything that came to me affected more than me. How could I know what I needed or was good for me, or how it would affect those around me?

But for the first time, I saw I had it backwards. I saw that the desire she felt for an object or situation was the flow of the universe through her just before the manifested object or situation showed up. She did not *cause* anything with her desire. The *desire itself* was a manifestation of what was unfolding. They were the same thing.

Of course, not every desire I felt was me tuning into how things would unfold. A lot of it was ego suggesting how to fill a sense of lack. But there were certain long-standing quietly persisting desires that, in retrospect, I could see represented an awareness of how things would unfold.

For example, my desire for a life-partner, a home of my own, to work from home—each of these persisted quietly long after I was aware they would not bring fulfillment. It felt like I *wanted* them, and perhaps I did, but not *personally*. I was in touch with the whole unfolding.

And sometimes a desire would show up suddenly. This exchange with the student occurred at a time when I was extraordinarily busy. One day around this time, Jessie and my sister, C, and I went up to Deer Creek at Mt. Charleston, a forty-five-minute drive from where we lived in the middle of the city. Sitting by a trickling stream, I relaxed and felt a deep, deep peace and felt, "*This; this* is what I want." Much later, I would remember this, and see how from that time on, my material life progressively simplified as my peace grew. The desire for that deep peace did not *cause* but *signaled* what was to unfold.

The experience with the student caused a fissure in my understanding of free will, but I just could not accept predestination. For one thing, I *felt* I had free will. For another, if everything was predetermined, that meant I could do something terrible, and it was supposed to happen. I did not see the release from guilt in this, only that it meant I had no control, even over me. This was central to a sense of personal autonomy, so it was unacceptable to me.

I found if I tried to apply the idea that everything that happened was going to happen, I became confused. How could I make a decision if it was not up to me? I never read or heard anyone explain *how* predestination would work. I did not understand that what felt to me like my individual will and desires and choices was a story (the Atonement) unfolding through me. In other words, I could go on as I had done, just knowing my actions, and what felt like my desires and motivations, were a part of something larger. Another way to put it was that my will was something other than I thought—it was that larger will. But not yet seeing this, I continued in confusion and lost that moment of clarity when I understood desire was a signal, not a cause.

More than a decade later, my understanding of predestination would unfold as I released the personal identity. It would come to me not through concepts, but insights and experience. And it made perfect sense.

Study group attendance diminished progressively, and I brought it to an end. After all, I was not building a life coaching practice.

5

What attracted me to life coaching was a desire for purpose. Of course, I felt more complete following Spirit, but I still wanted something I could look to as my purpose. Then one day while meditating the turn I was in was made complete. I felt God and knew, "*This* is my purpose."

Of course! My purpose was not what I did in the world.

How could it be when my Reality (Christ) was in God? My "purpose" would be my Oneness with God, and in consciousness that is expressed as communing with God. This felt obvious and natural.

My self-concept had transformed to a Spirit-centered person. I was still purpose-driven, but that purpose was not to fulfill my personal identity in various ways. It was to commune with God. How simple was that?

I had had an experience in the Period of Sorting Out when while meditating I simply opened my mind to God with no agenda but to be open to God. I considered this to be truly *communing* with God. I do not remember the details, but this brought an amazing shift in my mind. Despite this positive experience, however, I practiced it only for a few days and it faded away. Over the next years I revisited this very rarely, even though each time it had a remarkable effect on me.

I never was a great meditator. During Sorting Out, I was inconsistent about meditating and when I did meditate, I was often just going through the motions. I sat *as if* I was meditating while my mind wandered, and I made no attempt to bring it back to Center or to connect to Spirit. The only thing I got out of this was some processing and relaxation.

In Relinquishment, however, I became disciplined about a daily meditation practice. But I still got lost in a busy mind. My discipline was more an expression of willingness than an effective practice of quieting my mind.

However, during this period, I realized at some point that often I worked on myself in a certain direction—for example, I thought there was someone I needed to forgive or some character flaw in myself I needed to "fix"—only to find a shift occurred in a different, unrelated place in my mind. This made me aware that I had no idea what I needed to advance spiritually.

Remembering the effects of communing with God, I developed a meditation practice where, after processing or bringing something to Spirit to look at with It, I simply opened myself to God with no desire but for God to come into my awareness. My posture was, "I have no idea what I need. I am willing for You to come into my mind and do what needs to be done." I did not aim for a perfectly quiet mind. I was more concerned with being truly open. My mind would dip back and forth between chatter and Quiet as I sat for a few minutes in this attitude.

Communing with God daily did not necessarily bring effects in the moment. But I found I had answers and insights I needed or experiences of true peace throughout the day. I felt that while communing, I opened my mind to God and God walked in when needed. And, as I looked back over the day, it seemed to me a river of peace had flowed beneath it.

Relinquishment was, for me, *I will step back and let Him lead the way.* (W-155). Although my Self (Christ) still felt *other*, my trust in It had reached a tipping point. I willingly followed Spirit, accepted my mystical experiences, and found purpose in communion with God.

It was around this time that I wondered casually one day during meditation what it would be like to die. And Spirit said, "Here, let me show you." And then…nothing happened. Except… I was not aware of the boundaries of the body. I was still fully here. I existed, but without limitations. And then I was back in them.

<u>6</u>

When life coach training classes were over, I left them completely behind. I continued to clean houses, and sometimes I wondered in bafflement what I had taken the classes for. I was tempted to attack myself for wasting money and embarrassing myself by announcing to everyone a new direction

I did not take. But always I came back to feeling I was meant to do it. It was not a waste of time or money or effort. In light of this feeling, I could only go forward and see what happened.

With my new understanding of the *Course*, I felt moved to teach, and this time it was not for marketing purposes. So, I began another *Course* study group at the Gay Community Center (which had moved into a larger building across the street). This was simply the space I used for the group; it was open to everyone.

Las Vegas is notorious for transient residents, and historically it was difficult to keep groups of any kind going. For the two and a half years that I led this group, only one woman was certain to come each week. And quite often she was the only one who came at all.

While I was long used to hearing Spirit for myself, I now learned to hear It with others. This was an exercise in following Spirit on the spot. Sometimes I had to answer difficult questions that I could barely answer for myself. As others were waiting, I didn't have the leisure to work them out. So I had to listen for Spirit rather than think. I heard words in my mind and then said what I heard. Often, I was learning as I spoke.

I was frustrated with the material. Putting aside the concepts, which are already challenging enough for new students; ego's resistance to its message, which is powerful; and the guilt in the mind of the reader, which leads them to read it through a filter of fear; the style of the *Course* adds another layer of difficulty for students. The *Course* is written in dense, sometimes flowery, and often figurative language. Its language and symbols are Christian, and its pronouns masculine, turning some students off immediately. It is in the context of Helen Schucman's mind and her relationship with Bill Thetford, so it is often personal and conversational and without helpful elaboration. Dr. Schucman loved iambic pentameter, the meter of Shakespeare, and the Voice dictated most of the *Course* to her in that meter, perhaps to make her more amenable to taking it down. But this resulted in often stilted language and double negatives that seemed to be there simply to satisfy the meter.

It takes years of study to sort out what is literal and what is figurative in the *Course*, the new definitions for loaded Christian symbols, what is personal to Dr. Schucman, what in her relationship to Dr. Thetford is specific to them and what the rest of us can generalize, to untangle double negatives, and to piece together a whole picture so that seeming inconsistencies and contradictions can be undone in the context of the *Course's* entire message.

Reading the *Course* for myself, I had encountered these issues, but they were secondary to the message and I mostly disregarded the style. My chief obstacles were guilt and fear. But now, teaching it, the style was a distinct nuisance. I spent so much time clarifying the language of the *Course* for students that I spent far less time on its message than I wanted. This frustration would be turned to something significant later.

In sports, an athlete must put in a certain number of hours before they are considered proficient. Somewhere around my fifteenth-year cleaning houses, perhaps I reached the hours necessary, because it suddenly flowed and became easier. I felt I had reached a level of mastery with it and it was second nature.

But it was twenty years before I felt this way about the *Course*. I never felt I mastered the *material* of the *Course*. I cannot cite it chapter and verse. But I felt I hit my stride, perhaps in trusting Spirit. What else would spiritual *mastery* be but letting the Master lead the way?

What came with this was personal maturity and equanimity. Wisdom and confidence seemed to arrive unexpectedly, rather than through time and experience. I no longer wallowed in the "bad", but I didn't cling to the "good" either. The more I was aware of the Eternal in Spirit, the more I accepted all in the world as passing.

But while spiritually Relinquishment represented a positive turning point for me, my personal life entered a very rough patch. I was fortunate that they coincided.

As much as a loved one's terminal illness (or advanced age) brings the discomfort of an imminent, but indefinite, end, at least you can prepare for the looming loss. I always felt *suddenly* was the worst way to lose someone, and I was to face this dreaded experience more than once.

My brother-in-law, G, died unexpectedly in his late forties at the start of 2001, when I was still in life coach training. He had had surgery and seemed to be recovering but was felled by an infection. The family was still adjusting to this loss when my mother literally dropped dead at only sixty-nine in the middle of 2003. Only that morning I was driving on the freeway considering my parents getting older and someday losing them, when the Voice in my mind said quietly that I should prepare myself. I did not think It meant for that night.

When my sister, E, called to tell me our mother had died, it was so unexpected I turned instantly to Spirit and asked if it was true. I heard *yes* and felt acceptance. Because of this, I seemed to bypass shock and numbness, which I considered the worst stage of grief because you know you have received a blow, but all the pain, processing, and healing are yet to come.

We often do not know how we are progressing on a spiritual path until something out of the ordinary occurs and we discover our actual state of mind. My usual experience when I was younger was to think I was further along than I was because nothing occurred to "test" my peace. This experience was the opposite. It was a worst-case scenario, and my trust in Spirit and my own peace—these were always in direct proportion to each other—did not waver. I got through it much better than I would have predicted. It revealed that I had advanced in my spiritual awareness without knowing it.

This made me aware how much spiritual development occurs unconsciously. I had seen this after The Hiatus, as obviously Something had worked in me, tipping me into trust in Spirit and great willingness to follow It. And when I returned to my path, my peace continued to grow with my trust, mostly out of my awareness. Ego dominated my conscious mind, but Spirit was always here in my unconscious, and so was my trust in It.

True to form, my dad was baffled by his grief and depression. He could not understand why he missed so much the woman he had been married to for over forty years, as they had spent so much time in their own spaces in the house.

Dad was almost twelve years older than mom, so we knew it would probably not be too long before he was gone, too. Mixed in with my grief for Mom was anticipation of losing him soon as well.

Two years later, in the winter of 2005, we had to put down our beloved cairn terrier. My sister, C, was diagnosed with breast cancer and my dad with lung cancer. C had a mastectomy and recovered. Dad was gone in the spring—the day before the second anniversary of mom's death.

Jessie's mother died that autumn. And the following year, Jessie was diagnosed with a mental illness. In the long run, this would be a good thing, as she would be properly medicated. But it came after years of losses as well as other physical and mental health diagnoses, and she was emotionally shattered. She had a breakdown, falling into a depression unlike anything I had dealt with before. She could only lie in bed and stare at the wall. I asked our therapist at what point I would have her hospitalized, and she said when Jessie would no longer get out of bed for even fifteen minutes, if only to sit in a chair. We never reached that point, and eventually Jessie rose out of the depression.

But she had reached her limit with her emotional and physical disorders, which included fibromyalgia and herniated discs in her lower back. It was time for her to go on disability. We had prepared for this, buying the maximum disability insurance through her work. So at least we were spared a financial crisis as we could not live on my income.

These six years of major loss after major loss would once have sent me spiraling into anxiety and depression and probably panic. I got through them by staying present, returning to my awareness of God, and trusting Spirit to guide me through anything that came up, in myself or in the world.

7

Between my parents' passing, I turned forty. Finally, I was the age I had felt inside all my life. Yet it took me three years to overcome my shock. It was like I woke up one day and found I was middle aged. How did it happen? One day at a time, obviously, but I felt that, somehow, I had missed the passing of time.

The summer after my father passed, I went to our therapist. I told her I did not know if what I was going through was grief or mid-life issues. She said, "Yes."

This was the therapist who had told me that I had to build boundaries with my mother to sort out my identity from her. I spent my thirties doing this within myself. But it was only just before Mom passed that I finally figured out how to do this in our relationship.

A few years earlier, while I was in life coach training, I tried to tell Mom that her relationship with her children would probably be better if she wasn't always judging us and telling us how to live our lives. She said she was just being a mother, but I pointed out that we were no longer young children in need of guidance. We were adults now and our relationships with her should reflect this. She became defensive and suggested that the life coaching I was into must be some kind of cult. I dropped it.

Another angle my sister, E, and I took to reduce the tension in our relationships with Mom was to encourage her to take up interests outside the family. But Mom didn't want to do anything without Dad, and he was not interested.

Then one day, not long before she died, I was inspired. I

simply stopped talking to Mom about my life. I kept our conversations to the family, weather, news, and other interests, like old movies, that we shared, but I steered clear of my own life. This was so obvious and easy to do I could not believe I hadn't seen it before. For me, this dropped the tension in our relationship. I enjoyed speaking with her, without dreading her judgments and nagging. Because, aside from her judgments, I did enjoy my mother. She was intelligent and generous and funny. Apparently, she noticed my change in approach to her. She asked my sister, E, "Does Elizabeth talk to you about her life? She doesn't with me anymore."

So, when she was gone, I had no baggage from our relationship. I grieved her and my role as her daughter as well. And when my father was gone, I grieved him and my role as anyone's daughter. But I felt set free, too. I felt I had the space to come into my own.

Over the years, when I had less to figure out and to ask Spirit, I amused myself while cleaning houses by working on plots for novels. I started writing fiction when I was ten and did so on and off until I was thirty, but I no longer had interest in writing. I was simply entertaining myself as I worked. But after my dad passed, my mind was filled with stories. So much so, I sometimes had to write down the plots to get them off my mind. But I still did not feel moved to write.

When I told my therapist about this that summer, she got a faraway look in her eyes that I recognized was thinking with Spirit—whether she knew this or not. She turned to me and asked, "What are you not doing that you need to be doing?" She asked what I wanted the rest of my life to be about. We discussed my "mission", and she had me think about it as a homework assignment.

At first, I thought she was asking what I needed to be doing about writing, since that's what I had brought up. But I truly did not have a desire to write. However, a couple of days later I realized she had asked an open question and was not necessarily pointing to writing.

When I saw her after my mother died two years before, she had me begin a journal that she wanted me to handwrite. She felt that writing by hand I would get more in touch with my feelings. I had continued this on and off.

But in August, I began a new journal, which I typed on the computer. I called it *Dialogues* because it was conversations with Spirit. (This is my journal to this day.) In my second entry, I reference the handwritten journal. In it, I had written that after this discussion with my therapist, I felt weary and wanted to get on with whatever I was here to do.

In the middle of that month, I wrote:

"All my life I've wanted to express something. From the time I was a kid and started to write. However, I often felt the pointlessness of what I was trying to express. I remember writing as a kid and getting frustrated and telling Mom what I was writing wasn't saying anything. She couldn't understand. Why did it have to have a message, have to 'say something'?... I stopped writing. It wasn't as though I really wanted to be a writer. I've wanted to express something vague and inchoate."

And on that same day, I continued, referencing a story that had been on my mind:

"When I wrote on August 2nd it was a burst of creativity like I've never experienced. It flowed and could not be stopped. And then it was followed by the installment called the Dialogue, which meant far more to me than the notes I wrote for a story. It was much closer to what I want to express."

I wondered if that burst of creativity was Spirit trying to come through:

"When I was a teenager, didn't I begin my relationship with you like this: Writing, asking questions, and getting answers? Writing has been a part of me and a part of my relationship with

you all along."

I felt it was pointless to write for others if it wasn't inspired by Spirit.

I was sure it could not be a coincidence that just before this began, I bought a laptop I had wanted for a long while. A laptop gave me greater flexibility, as I would not be tied to a computer at a desk. I could write anywhere.

"There's something simple, succinct, crisp and clean I want to express, but how do I access it, let it through? It is first and foremost for me a crystallization of all I have learned but not been able to bring into focus. Because I have not been able to bring it into focus, I have not been able to walk it, embody it fully."

Clearly, I felt it was time to consolidate all I had learned, something I realized later I did through writing.

Between August and November, I finally knew what I was going to do with the life coach training. In November, I wrote in Dialogues:

"I feel it's time for me to do whatever it is I've felt about me and the Course *all these years. The mentor thing came to me out of the blue, after, a while before, I had said I felt ready and I would leave my mind open."*

I felt strongly I was to be a "teacher of teachers"—students of the *Course* who are all, in *Course* terminology, "teachers of God". I did not know if I could make any money at it and was concerned about that when I was in doubt. But overall, that did not matter. Everything now was secondary to following the movement through me. I trusted I would be taken care of.

As I knew a few of my fellow trainees in life coaching had been students of the *Course*, I was certain there were others out there doing this already. But when I looked online, I didn't find anyone. It seemed I would be the first. It was a niche market, too, so that would make marketing easier.

Each day I got up and knew what to do. "Today, get a business license", "Today, put up a website", "Today, start a blog", etc.

I struggled for a while with what to call myself. I didn't want to use *life coach*, as I felt that was not all I was to do. I really liked *teacher*, but all *Course* students are called that. I eventually settled on *mentor*, as a mentor is a teacher who has more experience in a given area, and that seemed to nail on the head what I felt I was to do. *ACIM Mentor* was born.

(I would discover that for others, *mentor* invoked an adult who worked with teenagers. So, in conversation, I would say I was a spiritual *teacher* or *life coach*.)

Jessie was supportive because she wanted me to do what made me happy. I was to continue cleaning houses as well, but I knew that would eventually come to an end. In fact, I felt Spirit was guiding me to let that go, but I wasn't ready. A total commitment to mentoring made me nervous.

Instead, I dropped some, but not all, of my cleaning customers. But I found this split in my time was obnoxious. I was pulled more and more toward simplicity, and one business would certainly be simpler.

Ever afterward, Jessie harbored a wish I would become the next Marianne Williamson (*A Return to Love*), a best-selling author, speaker, and teacher of the *Course*, for the money she thought I could make. But I pointed out that not only did I not have the charisma that would inspire that kind of following (which she well knew), but my message would never be popular.

Once I started writing my blog, I knew I could not hold back what I knew to be true: *Only God is real*. I felt this message was *why* I was teaching. And it brought me joy! But I knew it would be viewed as radical, even among *Course* students. Everyone wants freedom from the belief in sin and guilt, but most do not want to pay the "cost": The awareness that what they thought was real is not real. I felt this was why many *Course* teachers taught forgiveness as the world teaches it, rather than as the *Course* does. Either they themselves did not understand what the *Course* teaches, or they did understand but were not comfortable teaching it. (I was eventually to hear of a teacher who was popular in the *Course* community, as well as in the general population. who was asked once why he did not teach that the world is not real, and he said, "Because then I would lose my following.")

As well as teaching what I felt was the *Course's* central, radical message, it was important to me that my teaching be practical rather than theoretical, and my writing reflected this. I wanted to provide what I felt had been missing for me as a new student: Someone to speak with who understood the message of the *Course*, but also knew how to apply it in their day-to-day lives. In my writing in particular, I focused on clarity.

As much as *only God is real* burned in me as Truth and gave me joy, I was not without conflict teaching it. I knew it could sound nuts, and in my lower moments questioned my sanity. Mentoring was the first real threat to ego since the holy relationship, and it went on the attack.

Sometimes I also felt trapped. I had to commit to my process as never before, because I would have to continue to work on myself to stay ahead of my clients. Moreover, Spirit would *have to* be my Partner for my work to be of any worth to them (and me).

Reading my journal entries from that time, I am struck by the conflict I felt. It was short lived, and I did not remember it, because it felt good—refreshing and cleansing, actually—to teach the pure message of the *Course*, in writing, in a telephone study group, and mentoring. *Only God is real* must have been the "something simple, succinct, crisp and clean" I wanted to express. Over time, I forgot how radical the idea was for others.

Looking back, I see that in the time between life coach training and building a life coaching practice, two things occurred: I learned to hear Spirit when I was with others. This prepared me for mentoring. And room was made in my life for its new direction by the loss of my parents. I was not particularly busy with them before they died, but those relationships took up space and energy in my mind and life. In retrospect, I understood why everything unfolded the way it did.

As I had sensed the shift to peace that would come in my mid-thirties, I sensed another shift way up ahead. I felt it would come in my mid- to late-fifties. But as my peace was growing and I was happy in my personal life, I rarely thought about this. Anyway, all I could imagine was my work or my teaching would change, or I would write a significant book or something.

FOUR: SETTLING

Now comes "a period of settling down." This is a quiet time, in which the teacher of God rests a while in reasonable peace. Now he consolidates his learning. Now he begins to see the transfer value of what he has learned. Its potential is literally staggering, and the teacher of God is now at the point in his progress at which he sees in it his whole way out. "Give up what you do not want, and keep what you do." How simple is the obvious! And how easy to do! The teacher of God needs this period of respite. He has not yet come as far as he thinks. Yet when he is ready to go on, he goes with mighty companions beside him. Now he rests a while, and gathers them before going on. He will not go on from here alone. (M-4.I.A.6)

<u>1</u>

Together, the Periods of Relinquishment and Settling Down were the most productive and most Spirit-centered of this mind's experience of ego-consciousness. They blended so well that I would not know when Relinquishment ended and Settling began if it were not for a Revelation I had in August of 2007.

Between my first and this my last (so far) Revelation, I had two or three others. I was never again as shattered as I was the first time, and each time I was less shocky afterward. As I came out of one of them, I was surprised to find not only *no words*, but *no thoughts*. I did not know that was possible! Another, I felt approaching in the days before it happened, which had never occurred before.

As I came out of Revelation this time, I vividly experienced the split in my mind. I found myself beside what seemed like an Ocean of Joy. I felt if I had one more drop of Joy, I would *be* the Joy. I then swung, as though on a pendulum, all the way to the extreme of ego's fear of nonexistence. It was terrible.

It was always the case after a higher miracle, as well as any strong insight, that what followed was a period in which I seemed to learn the lesson of the higher miracle or insight from all angles. It was like I walked in a circle around the lesson, seeing it from the 1 o'clock position, then the 2 o'clock position, then the 3 o'clock position, etc. until I completed the circle and thoroughly learned the lesson. This usually took several months. After this higher miracle, however, it seemed I spent the following *years* seeing the split in my mind with ever growing clarity.

A few days later, I awoke early one morning and lay in bed still feeling the remnants of shock from the Revelation. And the Voice said clearly, "You have entered the Period of Unsettling." This is not a typo. I had no doubt I heard *Un*settling, the period that follows Settling. But somehow, I did mishear.

Even though I was not thinking about the periods of the Development of Trust, it is possible I simply heard what I wanted. In an entry in Dialogues in 2006, I reference feeling I must be in the Period of *Un*settling because I was so uncomfortable. (I had no idea yet how uncomfortable it could get!) Always wanting to be more advanced than I was, I decided that I must be in Unsettled.

But for the next few years, I was often doubtful about that *un*. There certainly were times when I felt unsettled, as I had episodes when I was pretty stirred up within for one reason or another. But they came and went, and besides, I could not place Settling in my previous experience. I was also fairly certain, given that Unsettling comes before Achievement, that it would be pretty recognizable.

I was aware ego had not been undone. I had experienced no shift in consciousness. In fact, I came to realize that all that had gone before, as well as what was going on for me at the time, was only *preparation* for undoing ego. The description of Settling says the student "has not yet come as far as he thinks". I felt this awareness was how that showed up for me. That line also made me wary of thinking I must be in Unsettling.

Although it took a while for me to be clear about what period I was in at the time, it was in this period that I was able to look back and see when I passed through the other periods. Before, I could not see them.

For a period called *Settled*, I accomplished a lot. However, this work was "consolidating my learning", as the description says. I discovered I wrote books as I integrated their topics and moved past them.

It was not long after I entered this period that one day, I realized peace had come to stay. I was used to peace coming and going, but I realized that it had come and had not left for quite a while. And I knew it would not go but continue to increase. This is the same as saying I felt I always had the Answer to any question, conflict, or situation, in Spirit. My trust in Spirit and my peace were in direct proportion.

In fact, this "reasonable" peace is what I look back upon as the sign I was in Settling. This was not perfect peace. I was still in ego-consciousness and knew it. But I had access to peace any time I needed it. I was advancing as a Spirit-centered person.

At one point, I wondered why I still saw the material world if peace had come to stay. And the answer was, "What difference does it make if you have peace?" I realized I was focused on the wrong thing. It was peace, not the continued appearance of the material world, that was significant.

This was not a snooty ego question meant to tear down my peace. Nor did I have the illusion I was in Spirit-consciousness. I was wondering at the process, especially as peace was at hand. I still had the idea that a shift to Spirit-consciousness would lead directly to God taking "the last step". The *Course* says this occurs after you see the *real world*, which is consciousness that purely reflects God's Love (Spirit-consciousness). It says this is seen only briefly before all consciousness disappears and only God (Knowledge) remains.

But I was to learn that some are in this consciousness for years, even decades, before putting the body aside. So, it is possible that those passages were specifically for Bill Thetford, who joyously told a friend after taking a walk one day "I'm *There*" and died hours later. (It could also have been Helen Schucman's experience, but she died alone, so we do not know.)

Also, some passages indicate that consciousness ends when Sight of the real world is *perfected*—when you see nothing else. For some—perhaps in Bill's case—that may happen in an instant. For the rest of us, it is a process.

2

In great conflict, but feeling the rightness of it, I quit housecleaning at the end of 2007. I loved the idea of a simplified life, but I was nervous about what I felt was deepening commitment to my spiritual path. However, I wrote in Dialogues that taking this step away from housecleaning and into mentoring I felt I was "walking into a Big Light."

When I was in life coach training, after I met with a client I played over and over what we said and wondered if I could have said more, or maybe less. I wondered if I should have said *this* instead of *that*. I worried that maybe I wasn't helpful. In other words, I had baggage after a call. And that baggage was my co-dependency. I took responsibility for the client.

But from the moment I began ACIM Mentor in 2006, I had a different experience of life coaching. I showed up for the call and when it was over, I carried nothing away. I felt I sat between Spirit and the client, and that what happened was between them. This was very liberating! It was not like work at all.

Through coaching, I became aware that there is a missing step in the *Course*. It has a built-in assumption that the student is aware of Spirit in their minds. In fact, many of the lessons in the Workbook imply this. That is because it was for Drs. Schucman and Thetford. Obviously, Helen was aware of Spirit, personified for her as Jesus, as this was the Voice that dictated the *Course* to her. But many, if not most, new students are *not* aware of Spirit. At best, new students are confused by the *Course's* assumption; at worst, they feel they are failing even before they begin.

So, often I had to teach students to discern Spirit before they could take the steps the *Course* asked of them. And many clients *were* aware of Spirit, just not *as* Spirit. They had, at times, received answers or guidance, or experiences of peace or comfort, but attributed it to something else in themselves or someone else. Or, like me, they felt Spirit when they read the *Course*, but they did not identify it as Spirit.

But there were some who had nothing to point to that indicated Spirit, and I asked them to open to Spirit. Some would have an experience they could point to as Spirit. Others did not, and fell away as clients.

I found that students who came from a Christian background were easier to work with than those who were New Age. Christians or former Christians came to the *Course* because they did not find what they were looking for in traditional Christianity. Their minds were open. But New Agers often mistakenly thought the *Course* validated what they already believed. Their minds were closed, and they missed the *Course's* new message. Often, they didn't seem to want it anyway. They wanted to continue in the way they were used to and were not looking to have their minds blown open in a new direction.

Clients often asked what I did to stay at peace throughout the day. I had to think about this because, outside of meditating every day, I was not aware of any other efforts I made. But I discovered that, indeed, I had unconsciously developed four practices to remain centered in Truth. They had become habits, so I did not think about them.

Certainly, Spirit had become my Constant Companion and turning to It as my Teacher, Guide, and Therapist had long been built into my life. It was my first consistent spiritual practice. In fact, for me it was not a *practice*, but an ongoing *relationship*.

And, by this time, I had incorporated communing daily with God into my life as well. In fact, I felt that if I did nothing else, communing daily with God would be enough to shift me to peace.

When I had that bout of anxiety and panic in my early twenties, I turned inward to Spirit several times a day. This was a practice I took from the Workbook, which leads the student to remember an idea throughout the day. I recalled this one day in Relinquishment, and I thought, *why wait for a crisis*? If that helped pull me out of an anxiety and panic cycle, certainly its benefits would be greater if I made it a regular practice, no matter what was going on in my life. So, turning inward to Truth several times a day became another practice I unconsciously put into practice.

There were certain practices that the *Course* encouraged that I felt I failed at. One was forgiveness. I found I could not forgive as the *Course* teaches, which is recognizing that only God is real. The other was "seeing Christ in your brother". Despite my experience of Vision in the holy relationship, I could not *make* myself see Christ "in" others. I only saw ego in people.

One day I decided to throw out everything but the two practices I knew at that point worked for me: Communing with God daily and calling on Spirit. And, lo and behold! In time I found forgiveness simply happened as God became more real to me than what was appearing.

As I consistently put into practice turning to Spirit with

others, I found I was aware of Spirit *instead of* others. I had been looking for Christ *in* others rather than looking *at* Christ, which made how others showed up irrelevant. This encouraged me to begin a practice of looking inward to Truth, or Christ, when I encountered something upsetting, to remind me of my True Self.

Communing with God daily, Spirit as my Constant Companion, turning inward to Spirit throughout the day, and looking on Love (Christ) to remind myself that I am Love became what I called *4 Habits for Inner Peace*. They were the practice of forgiveness the *Course* teaches.

3

Before Christmas, 2008, Jessie and I got a cairn terrier we named Ginny. We had gotten a golden retriever, Mulder, when he was five months old, but Ginny was our first true puppy.

From the start, I had a special relationship with Ginny. My actual attachment was not so much to her as to the role of mother I played with her. We had had five dogs before her, and Paavo, who was ten years old, remained. In a year we were to have another. Yet none were to me what Ginny was.

I realized I had a special relationship with the role I played with her, but I let it go. I had learned there was no point in resisting the ways of ego; that only strengthened it. There was no point in judging myself for it, either, as that could only be ego, too. If this relationship was an obstacle to peace, Spirit would let me know and we would work it out.

This would be my last special relationship, which of course I did not know at the time. But early in it, I had a preview of things to come.

(Dialogue 20090402) *"Yesterday Ginny got spayed and*

beforehand fear like I'd experienced when we took Mulder to be euthanized. I knew I was just seeing the past in the present—the last time I took a dog to a vet for a procedure, etc. I kept reminding myself that she was getting spayed, not <u>euthanized</u>, but the fear kept coming. I knew it was the fear of death that had gotten me so good the night we took Mulder in. Then I had so much grief on top of the fear that I couldn't work through it and reach You. This time I welcomed the opportunity to look at this fear with You. I knew I'd asked to have it again because I want to really see it and know what I am telling myself underneath it all.

The terror came in huge waves and I used affirmations, 'I will never die. I am One with God and Eternal', etc. Then I suddenly realized what I was feeling <u>was</u> death. 'Death' is a phantom, an illusion. It doesn't exist. But the fear I was experiencing was as close as I could come to death: It was the absence of God. Death was right then upon me—and yet I wasn't dead. I will never die. The body will fall away but I won't die.

So the fear of death goes out with a whimper instead of a bang. It just dissipated like fog before the sun. The more I tried to grasp it the more elusive it became—not because I was unwilling to face it but because nothing was really there. I think something important happened here but because it was so anti-climax the ego is saying it wasn't particularly significant. It's also saying it can still get me. I wasn't really faced with 'death', only a symbol of it, but wait until I am really faced with death.

I doubt there will be anything real to grasp then, either."

This was largely an intellectual insight about death, but it was a start. It is fascinating to see how my relationship with Ginny began and ended with the idea of death.

<u>**4**</u>

Because I found the style of the *Course* made it difficult

to teach, I sometimes played with the idea of translating it into plain, everyday language, but not seriously. For one thing, they were sacred books to many, and I felt they would find it offensive. For another, there were now many teachers clarifying the *Course* for students.

I also felt that for all the obstacles the style of the *Course* presented, they could be useful. For example, they pushed me to study with Spirit, for which I was grateful. After all, the value of the *Course* is not in the words on the page, but in that it leads a student to Spirit within. It *is* what my therapist had said, "just a book!" Without Spirit, it is frankly meaningless.

However, I was aware that many did not trust they could discern Spirit, got so bogged down in its style that they never reached for Spirit, or were not given to the kind of analytical thinking required to get past the style to the deeper message. So, the idea of a translation arose when I was frustrated, but fell away the more I thought about it.

Until one day. I was again thinking about my frustrations with the *Course's* style when I heard in my mind, "Why don't you try it?" Meaning, translating part of the *Course* into plain language.

Seriously?

I opened the *Course*, skipped over the Introduction and 50 Principles of Miracles, went for the first paragraph, and rewrote it in plain language. It was easy and natural and satisfying.

(Dialogue 20071111) (Spirit in bold.):
"*YOU HAVE FUCKING GOTTA BE KIDDING ME? You have me re-writing the* Course*! Are you insane??????*

I knew I was given this insight into the Course *for a reason, but not this. This is just so wrong.*

What is more important: The books or the message?
I'll be vilified.
Yes. But is that really a problem for you?
You know I enjoy the process itself. It isn't that it flows; it's

less effort than that. It is like _being_. But I don't think You are editing enough.

You already know what it says. And I am right in there with you, as with all the other writing. I will correct any mistakes, you know that.

But can this be real? This is ridiculous. Who could be so arrogant.

Me, I guess. Ha, ha, ha.

Funny.

What is more important: The form or the message?

I will be despised.

You know the truth. You are indulging ego. You know exactly what the Course says. You know it says the same thing over and over. You know there are people who can't get through the language of the Course as it is. It's the message that is important, not the form it comes in. The Course is not sacred, but its message is. The goal is to save time. You know all this.

I can't believe this.

You knew from the beginning that your work would be about the Course.

Not this! I vaguely knew it would be about teaching or something.

And you've sensed that mentoring is not the central work.

Jesus, Mary and Joseph. Fuck. This is huge. You want me to take a sacred work and put it into plain language.

It's different than it was for Helen because she didn't know what was coming, it was new to her as it came out. But I know the whole message and can see how each part fits into the whole.

Remind yourself of these things as you go along to cope with your sense of being overwhelmed. Really, you are making too big a deal of it. You are indulging the ego. I need this to be done and you have been prepared for this.

You have liked writing since you were a kid.

You knew from the beginning the Course was your life's work.

You learned to listen to me as you studied the Course.

You accepted the gift of understanding the **Course** *more deeply.*

You have willingly been a teacher. You have willingly done all I have asked. You are ready. It is time.

Maybe nothing will come of this. Maybe this is something that is just for me. Maybe there's something I will learn in the process that this is preparing me for.

And if that were so you'd freak about whatever it was preparing you for. Liz, you have a choice. Follow me or the ego. How are you benefiting from this fear?

Can't I just be shocked for a while? Jeez.

How about gratitude? You think this mild freak you are having is not significant, but as you have it are you listening to the voice you really want to hear? Isn't it painful?

Somehow a pain I still seem to want. It's back to the ego's question: What's in it for me? I see, yes. This is what's in it for the ego. This mild freak indulges it, plays to it.

Okay. Gratitude that I get to spend time with You, immersed in Your Word, so to speak. Gratitude that I get to share this gift I have been given but have been unable to adequately share in my blogs and booklets. Of course, I feel a complete confidence in this and in the rightness of this. In fact it's so natural it's beyond natural, it's just <u>being</u>."

I expected to be attacked by others for translating the *Course* into plain language, because I experienced every possible attack in my mind as I wrote it. I rode out overwhelm, doubts about the value of the translation, doubts about the rightness of it, doubts about myself, intense feelings of unworthiness, ego's grief and fear of death, and distracting fantasies, sexual and otherwise. I learned to step away for a while when the attacks or fantasies became too strong. They would pass, and I would resume a few hours later.

Sometimes, resistance took the form of ego pumping me up rather than tearing me down. But I saw through that to the heart of what I was learning.

(Dialogue 20071115) (Spirit in bold.): *"I wonder if my seeing this as 'huge' is my wanting it to be huge? Yes, that's it. That is all ego. 'Look at how great I am doing this big job with the Holy Spirit'. I resist the idea that it is the connection, not the product from the connection that is important. But that's like the principle of miracles that says it's the Source not the form of the miracle that is important. Of course! This reverses the way it is in the world. What you do is supposed to glorify where you are coming from (ego). And what I am learning here is that what you do is nothing; where you are coming from is everything. The form that shows up in the world is nothing. Oooooo, I feel resistance to this!*

So: I connect with You. The product of this connection is a PL Course, which is insignificant?

It attests to the connection.

But in itself?

In itself its value is whatever one wants to give it. It will be useful for some; not so for others.

So it would be no different than if I was baking pies with You. I'm being deceived by the seeming spiritual nature of what I do..."

As far as how to approach it, a shift occurred when Spirit told me to write it through the lens of my mystical experiences and—the classic advice for writers always—for myself. If I was not writing the translation through the lens of my experiences, what were the experiences for?

(Dialogue 20071126) *"The argument in my head goes like this: It starts with me thinking about the PL Text. Then I start to argue that it is pointless to re-write something that is already complete. So I move on to the argument that perhaps I should just write a book about the* Course, *illuminating its concepts. This leads to an argument that points out that many people have written books about the* Course. *And I know some of them have helped students. So why do we need one more? And then I'm back to students strug-*

gling to grasp the Course *as the* Course. *There's a difference between reading a book about the ideas in the* Course *and reading an interpretation of the* Course.

So, I just sat down and reread and cleaned up my summary of the Principles and You told me to delete the other parts I have already written. I did so. Again, I begin to dimly sense the value of my writing this as clearly as I can as I understand it, discomfort with interpretation and elaboration be damned. It is what it is. I have to write it as purely as it comes to me."

Of course, arguments about the value of the translation could go either way, so clearly it was not for me about landing on which of those were correct. I was doing the translation because I was doing the translation. My own judgments on the matter were irrelevant.

It bothered me that I was not doing a straightforward translation of the *Course*. Of course, it was bound to be interpreted through the filter of my mind, but I realized my translation was more advanced than the original. For example, for *the world* I wrote *the world that you perceive* or *your perceptions* or *your entire mind*, going right to the heart of the message that you do not live in the material world, but rather in your perceptions of it.

I was uncomfortable as I realized I stripped from the *Course* much that ego could use as obstacles, stripping ego from me in the process. I was more uncomfortable cutting out many of the references to *others*, emphasizing that I saw either my own projections or extensions.

I debated whether to focus on simplifying the language or on getting to the message. But I got bogged down when my focus was on the language and writing flowed when it was on the message. That answered that.

There were many ways to convey the message, so I sought to be as clear as possible. I felt, as I did writing my articles, that *clarity, clarity, clarity* was my purpose. And since the average adult in the US reads at the eight-grade level (alas),

I made sure to keep it there to make it accessible to more readers.

I had many practical decisions to make. Which figurative language should I change, and which should I keep? Should I keep the original chapter titles and subheadings, or should I make new ones to reflect the plain language? (I kept the originals.) And then there were those mixed metaphors —keep them mixed or fix them? (I used footnotes to clarify them.)

As I was doing a paragraph-by-paragraph translation, there were things I could not "fix" or "clean up" as I would in a wholesale rewrite. For example, I discovered at the beginning of the Text, where it is more conversational, that subsections, and even paragraphs, sometimes veered off topic. I needed to make this clear, while sorting out the topics from each other. Jessie suggested I use footnotes or brackets to distinguish one topic from another, which I did.

There were passages that I knew from my experience leading a study group screamed for elaboration or an example, as well as passages that seemed to contradict something said earlier. I used footnotes to clarify these as well.

We learn through repetition, which ego knows well, replaying the same false and negative ideas over and over. So, the *Course* presents ideas to consciously counter ego by being repetitious itself. If a student does not grasp a concept in an early chapter or lesson, it does not matter as the *Course* will revisit it again and again. But often it uses different words for the same concept, confusing students. For example, *forgiveness, true perception*, and the *Holy Spirit's perception* are the same thing. I decided to use *True Perception* as the singular term for all of these to prevent confusion. This made the translation more noticeably repetitious than the original—I felt annoyingly so. My translation was often an awkward read.

5

As I learned that I write a book when I am consolidating my learning on, and moving past, the topic of the book, I speculated in my journal that I would no longer study the *Course* for myself when I was done translating it. This turned out to be true. I read it in study groups and used it for my writing, but I no longer felt moved to study it—or anything else. When I tried to read spiritual material, I felt pulled inward, so I would put the book aside and commune with God. This was, after all, what I was really looking for.

Consolidating my learning meant I occasionally ran into a gap in my understanding. When this occurred, I hashed out the concept with Spirit until I was clear. But there was one area that was tricky for me because, concerning it, Spirit had led me in a different direction from the *Course*. This had to do with physical healing.

There is a lot that the *Course* says about illnesses and disorders in the body that is misunderstood and misrepresented. For example, it does not suggest, as some think, that you use the mind to heal the body. In fact, it says the body is an idea in the mind and that it is a misuse of mind to put it in the service of the body. But any misunderstandings have to do with the minds of students, not with what the books say. In fact, I found as I translated passages about illness that by far what the *Course* said and what I got from Spirit were in line.

But there were two crucial points where Spirit led me in different directions. I wrote about these in detail in articles that are contained in *The ACIM Mentor Articles* Volumes 2 (#76) and 3 (#22, #23), so I am only going to touch on them briefly here. (It was interesting that, despite my detailed explanation, some readers could see no difference between what the *Course* said and what I had been taught by Spirit. They read in the *Course* what I had been taught, although Spirit did not give me a different *interpretation* of the *Course*. It taught me something altogether different.)

The *Course* says that since the body (and therefore illness) is a thought in the mind, taking medicine to alter the body is "magical thinking". (It also says you should take medicine as long as you believe it will work, a point often missed by new students.) But what Spirit taught me was *magical thinking* was the idea that treatments for the body or even a healed body—or anything else in form—will make you whole. It also taught me that there *is* cause and effect at the level of form and that medications and other treatments *do* affect the body—but, again, they never determine your *consciousness* (ego or Spirit).

The *Course* says that the cause of illness in the body is one's identification with it. If you did not identify with the body, it would manifest perfect health. But what Spirit taught me was that, as the opposite of God, the personal experience is never perfect, and that experiencing illness and disorders is part of that experience. These are not wrong or bad, but meaningless, as a healthy body is no more real than an unhealthy body. Your identification with the body does not cause illness in the body, but your experience of the body is the cause of your *experience* of illness, whether you identify with the body or not.

In the end, I found so little discrepancy between the *Course* and what Spirit taught me that I had little conflict translating it. Where there was a difference, I translated the *Course* directly and did not mention how I had been taught differently.

There were, as well, passages that dealt with Dr. Schucman's use of illness to make others feel guilty. Obviously, not everyone does this. In fact, Dr. Schucman's psychology is all over the *Course*, and this became clear to me as I did the translation. I began to see just how much of the *Course* was personal to her and Dr. Thetford. I was already aware that the holy relationship described in the *Course* was theirs, but I discovered that much was *specific* to their relationship. For example, there are several passages referring to their relationship touching thousands, obviously referring to them bringing the *Course* into the world. The *Course* was their relationship's "special function".

Eventually, I wrote about discerning how much of the *Course* was specific to Drs. Schucman and Thetford—something that has become clearer to me over time. I thought this was important because I saw how those passages were misunderstood or used for guilt. But this turned out to be more controversial than the translation. In the years since my translation was published, I received at most a half-dozen objections to it. (There seems to have been far more resistance in me to the translation than in the *Course* community at large!) But students are dubious when I say they need to understand the *Course* was specific to Helen and Bill, and the rest of us must learn to generalize it for ourselves. It is as though I take something away from them when I point this out.

It was my experience that each time I read the *Course*, new ideas or concepts stood out. Sometimes, in previous readings I simply had not paid much attention to them as I was learning other things. But with some ideas it was as though I had never read them before. Of course, the book didn't change, I did. As certain ideas sunk in, others emerged for me. And while translating the *Course*, there was one overarching idea that was hammered home to me again and again: *The whole spiritual process was between me and me*. It was not between me and a world outside of me. It was not between me and a god outside of me. It *only* went inward. This was a pivotal insight that would continue to unfold and deepen, to this day.

I was not cleaning houses anymore, and my mentoring practice was slow to start up, so I was able to devote many hours to the translation. Once past the intense resistance of ego, I thoroughly enjoyed everything about the process: the structure of writing days, the work itself, collaborating with Spirit. It was deeply satisfying.

It took me ten months to translate the Text. When it was complete, I wondered if I would be promoting the book as authors do, going to bookstores and study groups around the country. What I heard in my mind was, "You won't be going that route." And I felt that to be true.

In fact, what I heard was, "It's time to come within now."

6

When I was done with the Text, I was still frustrated by what I felt were the limitations of the *Course*. I wanted to write something concise and direct, and I considered a book based on the four habits I had discovered were my natural practice. But I felt either it was not the way I was to go, or it was not the right time.

Two other things came up for me: A strong urge to spend a lot of time in contemplation. And I found I was looking a great deal at guilt with Spirit.

The *Course* takes a psychological approach to spiritual awakening and teaches that guilt—and the fear it induces—are one's chief obstacles to being aware of God. Guilt is built into the ego thought system and is its primary defense against Truth. If ego is real, you must believe you have succeeded in defying (sinned against) God. And, as ego makes God in its own image, it teaches God will punish you for this. There is no ego without guilt and there is no guilt without ego.

To keep you from looking inward, and so possibly looking past it to Truth, ego says you are so sinful that you will be destroyed if you look inward and see it. This feeling that they are, deep down, wrong or bad, keeps many from seeking out even psychotherapy when they need it. They may not *think* they believe they are sinful, but they *feel* they are, and this stops them.

For years I could not grasp what the *Course* says about

guilt. Certainly, I felt guilty when I did something I judged as wrong. I also knew my guilt was often disproportionate to the occasion. But I did not see how the circumstantial guilt I felt represented inherent sin for "separating from God".

Finally, I grasped the concept of inherent guilt in ego when I returned to the *Course* after The Hiatus, but I still could not find that guilt in me. However, I eventually recognized my *feelings* showed I did believe this. I found, when I was able to sit with disproportionate guilt over some ordinary social transgression, that deep down I expected punishment. And what would punish me but God?

After I discovered this, I learned to pay more attention to my feelings than my thoughts. Thoughts can contradict beliefs, but feelings reveal what you really believe.

For a couple of years, I had nightmares once or twice a week. In these dreams, either I had killed someone, or I was helping someone to cover-up a murder. I would awaken feeling terrible guilt. So much so that I searched my mind for repressed memories of some major wrongdoing in my past. I never found a thing. I finally realized these dreams represented inherent guilt rising to conscious awareness.

In time, I reached a point of willingness to look at this idea of inherent sin with Spirit. I wanted to know what it was ego said was so bad about me. I knew it was just an idea and was not real, but even so I knew I would not have been able to attempt this before my trust in Spirit had reached a point where my belief in It was greater than in anything ego said.

So, I girded my loins and set to it. In meditation, I saw myself lowering into a dark pit in my mind and felt Spirit above, holding the rope tied around my waist. I felt trepidation about what I would see but trusted Spirit would pull me out if I saw something I was not ready to face.

I found nothing. I took this journey a few times, with the same result. I checked in with my willingness—it was intact. I truly felt ready to face inherent guilt. So, what was going on?

I asked Spirit and what I got was laughter: "I told you, *there is no guilt.*"

Of course! I had fallen for ego's ruse. I expected ego to present some deep-seated ugly idea of me that justified feelings of guilt. But there was nothing, nada, zilch. There is no sin, so all it could offer was *belief* in and *feelings* of guilt.

From then on, when guilt came up in any form, I sat with it and remembered my experiences of Truth—direct Revelation, miracles, Spirit. They undermined ego's whole premise for guilt, that I was separate from God. This sunk in over several years and my belief in guilt was undone.

As the belief in guilt was what the *Course* said was the chief obstacle to God, when it was gone, I wondered, what could possibly come next?

7

For *The Message of* A Course in Miracles: *A translation of the Text in Plain Language* I went with a publisher in the UK. It took sixteen months to come out, which was frustrating, but they were faster than most publishers. In the meantime, I heard from clients and readers who wondered if I would also be translating the Workbook. I was, again, reluctant, especially as I felt I would also need to do the Manual for Teachers. It would not make sense to leave it out. (The three books of the *Course* are in the public domain, but there are copyrights on the supplements.) I decided that if I was going to translate these books, I would include mentoring notes to address questions and obstacles I knew students to have.

It seems odd that I was resistant, as I enjoyed translating the Text. In fact, part of my resistance was that I enjoyed it so much I did not want it to end! I preferred anticipating the work, as starting meant the beginning of the end.

Both the Workbook and MFT were easier to translate, as they were already more practical and direct than the Text. As I was also in the rhythm of translating by then, I finished both in less time than it took me to do the Text alone. They were published together in one volume in 2011. (*Practicing* A Course in Miracles/*The Way of* A Course in Miracles).

While I was waiting for them to be published, I gathered my newsletter/blog articles into a book (*The ACIM Mentor Articles*). Readers had been asking for this, and I did not want to wait another sixteen months for a publisher to put them out, so I self-published it. This, and following collections of articles, would be my most popular books, as students like a practical approach to the *Course* that they can use in their everyday lives.

The *Course* says we will go through many shifts in self-concept until self-concepts fall away. This was my experience. And as I worked on these books, I went through one that was uncomfortable. The self-concept I had for myself as a teacher of God in the Atonement fell away. I no longer felt it defined me, and I was not sure if I was going to continue teaching. I often felt "done with the world." The ontology I had been given (shared at the end of this book) still made logical sense but seemed like a story that had nothing to do with me. But as I recognized it was a useful tool to use with students who still needed a purpose for their life in the world, I continued to use it in my work.

An awareness that followed this shift was that there is no such thing as *personal enlightenment*. I realized I had envisioned becoming a *peaceful person*. Without conscious thought, I expected ego would eventually *transform* to Spirit. But now I became aware, beyond theory, that *the* Enlightened Mind (Christ) was already whole and complete in me, and that ego would fall away, not transform.

The analogy I came up with for this realization was if you have a splinter (ego) in a thumb (mind), you heal the thumb by *removing* the splinter, not *fixing* the splinter.

I remembered this insight, but I did not realize it signaled a major shift until I read through my journal for this memoir. In fact, I was floored to find I did not know how much I changed after this. I came to feel part of me was *There* (Christ) while a part of me continued in a process to get *There*. I was no longer just seeing the split in my mind—I experienced how *I* was split. I did grasp the significance of feeling partly *There*, but I continued to identify with the part in a process as it occupied my day-to-day mind.

Around this time, I had a quiet thought: "Never ever, under any circumstances *ever*, do I have to listen to ego." I had never thought this before. It came in subtly, but I saw and felt the truth of it. My relationship to ego was never the same.

One day, to motivate myself to release ego, I looked at how painful it was, and Spirit said: "I don't want you to let it go because it is painful. I want you to let it go because it is not real." Of course! That is true release, true forgiveness. This was one of those thoughts that reoriented me as it reminded *only God is real*. But I felt it was a tall order, to see this, much less accept it.

Reading my journal, I see how much I was given to hyperbole. I often thought my shifts in self-concept were more significant than they were. Or, perhaps, I *wanted* them to be, even though I knew they were not shifts in consciousness but shifts in place. But this shift in self-concept was an important step toward dropping any self-concept, as I went from seeing myself as a spiritual *person* to a Spirit-centered *mind* (individual consciousness).

I did not come to understand I was a mind and not a person by thinking "I am mind." This awareness had grown over years of looking at my mind and how it made my "world" through its perceptions.

I had begun to know myself as a Son of God. I called it a *split-mind*. But I was caught up intellectually in the insights that came with this and did not fully realize they signaled my identity had shifted.

Besides feeling "done with the world" I also felt "this is all over"—a feeling that persisted for years. And with it, cause and effect began to be corrected through insights that came to me slowly over the next years.

My experience of insights from Spirit had evolved. To start, they felt like they came from Something Else or from deep within me. They seemed to come from out of the realm of my ordinary thinking. Especially when writing, and often when speaking with clients, I became used to ideas and clarity surprising me; "I didn't know I knew that!"

In the Period of Settling, however, the boundary between Spirit and me began to blur. When clarity and insights came, it was as though they were in the ether around me, or I was in their essence. Instead of ideas coming to me singly, I seemed to be aware of the Greater Reality from Which the insights flowed to me. It was like I could almost see the Bigger Picture and was aware I was connected to It.

This shift in my experience of insights progressed subtly over time and I only recognize it in hindsight, as that Greater Reality has become my ongoing Context. In Settling, I would say I felt the boundary between me and Spirit blurring, but I would not have been able to express how I knew this. This is another example of how the boundary blurred. I knew things without being able to point to any "proof." What proof could there be, as by definition Spirit is nonmaterial? Spirit reveals Itself in a mind. It does not show up in the material world.

This was the beginning of spiritual Seeing and it began with the slow correction of cause and effect.

For years, I thought I often stepped off the path and had to choose Truth again and again. Eventually, when enough time had passed and I could look back, I realized I had never stepped off the path. What seemed like stepping away had been part of the process. And at this time, I felt I saw I made the choice for Truth as a teenager when I let Spirit into my mind, and I did not have to make that choice again. I felt everything that followed was merely that choice unfolding.

This meant I had not been, as I thought, on a path of *attainment*, but on a path of *acceptance* of the Truth I had allowed into my experience back then. This reoriented the whole way I looked at myself and my life. But I could sense this was not yet the full picture. In fact, it would turn out I was not seeing accurately, but it was a turn toward seeing correctly.

I still thought very much in terms of choice and free will. I felt I had *allowed* Truth into my awareness, or It could not have come into it otherwise. I thought that every step along the way had come at my independent decision, conscious or not. I felt that I overcame obstacles to peace in my own time. I saw the split in my mind more clearly all the time, but I thought the split was perpetuated by my choice. I felt I was an autonomous being and I was right to take responsibility for making a choice. I did not see the contradiction between this view and my willingness to follow Spirit, which would imply I was not—or at least was *no longer*—autonomous.

In January of 2012 I saw, probably for the first time, "*...the personal unfolding is not toward a purpose but is an expression of my awareness of Truth. Both are in my mind. The personal unfolding is not for a reason, but is simply an effect...*" I would have realizations like this contradicting what I felt about choice and free will for several years before my confusion was unraveled by experiences that showed I had no will autonomous from the whole unfolding.

It was at this time that I became fairly certain I was not in the Period of Unsettling after all. Despite feeling unsettled quite often, I felt a pull to contemplation, meditation, quiet, and simplicity. I also felt intense resistance to this. I felt it would be a kind of death to withdraw from the world that way, just as would dropping ego. This feeling would show up in my journal repeatedly.

8

With the translations of the three books of the *Course* and my book of articles behind me, I started thinking about writing *4 Habits for Inner Peace*. I was itching to write something that said what the *Course* says, but was clear, concise, and did not use the loaded Christian symbols of the *Course*. At first, I was not sure it would come off, as it didn't flow. But I collected and organized my thoughts, and eventually I found the rhythm of it.

I never confused *Christ* with Jesus, but many readers did, and I had long dropped the term in my writing. But I did work a long while to get past, for myself, the connotation of the word *God* as a symbol for a father-figure sitting in judgment on me, but I could not. So, I shifted to using *Truth* for myself and in writing. I called Spirit *the Teacher* (later, *Awareness*) *of Truth in my mind*—although *Holy Spirit* was a term I fell easily into using again. Ostensibly, I threw those terms out because I wanted symbols that were not loaded with heavy connotations and which I felt got to the point. God *is* Truth, after all. But, in retrospect, I see something more was going on.

Having dropped the term *Christ*, I simply lumped anything applicable to Christ with Spirit. This reflected my understanding at the time, which I now know was incomplete. And that continued until I shifted consciousness.

There are thousands of different forms of spiritual practice, as the *Course* points out. But I have found that nonduality paths take one of two (there may be more) approaches to Truth. One I call *state-spirituality*, which is expressed as those who seek a *state of consciousness*—what I call Spirit-consciousness. Often, they have had a taste of it and seek to return to it.

The other approach I call *identity-spirituality*, which is

expressed as those who seek God, or Truth, because they want to know what (they may think in terms of *who* to start, as I did) existence is and how they fit into it.

These are not necessarily exclusive, of course, as one could say to be in Spirit-consciousness is to be the Self God created. And both approaches emphasize quieting the mind, observing thoughts, and releasing ego. However, those who use the state-spirituality approach seek a perfected state of mind, some believing Spirit-consciousness *is* God. And those who take an identity-spirituality approach look past consciousness to God.

The *Course* is a form of identity-spirituality:

"Except ye become as little children" means that unless you fully recognize your complete dependence on God, you cannot know the real power of the Son in his true relationship with the Father. (T-1.V.3)

(For clarity, for *Son* read *Part* and for *Father* read *Whole*).

Your *True Identity* (Being, Existence) is God's Extension in your mind, Christ. However, this Identity is different from identity as a person. Christ is *What* you are, not *who* you are. Christ is given, so It is a passive Identity. But the person, as an identity, is constantly being made while you identify with it. (The person remains after the shift, but not as your *identity*. It is no longer *what* or even *who* you are but is merely an experience you have.) So, when your identity shifts from person to Christ, it is a different experience of *identity*. For one thing, you no longer have a *self-concept*, as Christ simply *is*. There is nothing to conceptualize about Christ.

When I recognized my *Self* in Emily in our holy relationship, I characterized It that way and did not label It *Christ* until I began this memoir, but Christ is the Self I saw. (To recognize my Self *as* my Self I had to be that Self.) But over two decades later, when I recognized that Enlightenment does not happen to a *person* but is already here, incongruently I moved away from identity-spirituality. I so equated *ego* with *identity* that as I moved away from ego, I moved away from concepts like *identity* and *self* as they always brought me back to ego. And, completely unaware, I threw the baby (Christ Self) out with the bathwater (ego identity).

Ego did not fall away in one fell swoop. It dribbled away, beginning in this period, as I started to think of myself as *mind* rather than *person*. But Christ was gone for me, too, as I rejected any idea of *identity* or *self*. I began to lose a sense of anything as *me*. It seems I had so entangled *identity* and *self* with ego that the only way to "purify" those concepts was to throw them out for a while.

9

I became aware I was not learning anything new. Old lessens deepened and I saw them from new angles. But that was all.

After the Revelation of '07, all lessons seemed to be variations on the theme of seeing the divide in my mind between Truth and ego more clearly. I was coming to accept that ego could not be transformed but would have to be released. I also accepted that there was no such thing as *personal peace*. It was a relief to let go of pursuing it! After all, I had True Peace instead.

More and more I was aware of a part of me *There*—in peace—and a part of me still seeming on a journey to peace. I was divided between Stillness and a process meant to attain Stillness. From Stillness I watched the process. And in the process, I reached for Stillness.

As time went on, Stillness grew in my awareness and it became less significant that a part of me was still in a process. I could access memories, but I could no longer conjure up how it felt to be consumed with the world and its dramas. The more at peace I grew, the fewer people there were to whom I could relate.

During this time, my one friend went through a crisis in her marriage. I tried to step into her shoes, but I found I could not do that anymore. It resulted in intense disorientation—like I had slipped "down the rabbit hole". She and her husband were both intensely fearful and projecting, but when I tried to get her to see this, she could not understand. And what she saw as her problem made no sense to me. I found I could not help her.

One day, very confused, I asked her what she would say to a friend in her situation. She said she would tell her that she would be okay no matter what happened in her marriage. This seemed like pablum to me. Didn't she want to resolve the problem? I had slipped back into my codependent habit of trying to fix her situation—in this case, her perceptions— rather than just be there for her. I adjusted and began to support her as she wished.

Besides letting go of my codependent responses again, what I took from this episode was the awareness that I was no longer able to relate to the way most of the world thought. It simply made no sense to me anymore—to the point that it seemed insane.

I started to understand that there is a difference between living *as* a person and living *through* a person. No matter my level of awareness, ego-consciousness or Spirit-consciousness, I would experience a body and personality—a person. But only in ego-consciousness would I reach through the person for wholeness through various forms of personal fulfillment.

My trust in Spirit had grown so deep that answers came faster, and guilt and fear resolved quickly. I would hear much later that Ken Wapnick said that the gauge of a *Course* student's advancement was not that they never came from ego, but how quickly they could let it go.

I saw clearly now how I made my "world" with my thoughts. I do not mean the physical world, which is just the material of consciousness and is neutral. My "world" was beliefs and judgments about, projections on, and subjective experiences of the physical world. I had understood this for years. In my translation, I used "your perception of the world" for "the world." But I was indeed "consolidating my learning" and moving past concepts to true understanding through experience.

As I responded to my perceptions, rather than to the physical world, I developed a practice when upset of sorting out the *facts* of what was occurring from the *story* I told myself about them. For example, if someone was angry and yelling at me, the facts were this person was manifesting anger through their gestures, expressions, level of voice, choice of words, etc. But any story I had about this ("this is unfair"; "this is just like when I was attacked as a child" etc.) and any judgment ("they're wrong"; "they're bad") was my perception and the source of my discomfort. With these sorted out, I could look at what *really* bothered me—not the other or their behavior, but my own beliefs, thoughts, past, filters, judgments, etc. I no longer felt out of control of my "world", as I dealt with my problem where it was, in me.

Eventually, I realized that just like me, everyone was projecting, and I stopped taking their responses personally. Everyone truly does live in their own little world.

The more I looked at guilt, the more I became aware of it everywhere. I discovered that guilt did indeed underpin ego and the whole world it perceived. I had self-published *4 Habits for Inner Peace* in 2011 and I would go on to write a supplement to it, *Releasing Guilt for Inner Peace*, which I self-published in 2013.

As I wrote the latter, I could imagine readers asking, "Can you give an example?" so I peppered it with a lot of everyday examples. To release guilt, I offered my practice of sitting with guilt and contrasting it with experiences of Truth, which undermines the premise for guilt. I considered it a supplement to *4 Habits*, because the four habits were what I suggested for building one's awareness of Truth.

I continued to write articles, but as far as books went, I felt done. Everything I had learned and needed to consolidate for myself was out there. I knew eventually I would gather up the articles I had written since my first collection for another, but that was all I expected.

My personal life was settled, and I was happy in it. Peace had come to stay and continued to grow. I anticipated a shift in my mid-fifties, but all I could imagine it would concern was my work. Perhaps it would go in a new direction. Sometimes I thought I might write a significant book. I sort of always expected that one day I would write an autobiography or memoir as a student of the *Course*.

10

Single clients often asked about my marriage. They were curious because Jessie and I were on different paths. They could not imagine being involved with someone who was not also a student of *A Course in Miracles*. They could not imagine *not* sharing their path with a life partner.

I explained that my primary relationship was with Spirit. No person or relationship could provide the wholeness I found in Spirit. As far as my spiritual path and practice went, all I wanted from Jessie was the space and support to follow my own path, and this I got from her.

She certainly was aware of, and grateful for, its effects on me. She would sometimes tell people living with me was like living with Gandhi. When I explained to her that he was more a political than a spiritual leader, she changed it to Buddha.

Personal and spiritual growth was a shared value of ours, which also served our happiness together. Ours was a long-term relationship, so we each had our personal ups and downs over time and rode it out together. Jessie was uncomfortable when I seemed to be off my path during The Hiatus. And she went through a long period of disillusionment with her own spirituality, which meant she was quite dark before she found her way again. But we never stopped growing, individually and together.

We also weaved in and out of emotional closeness over the long haul, just as I expected. We both understood that is what marriage is. It always seemed that when one of us became uncomfortable with how far we had drifted from each other and mentioned it, the other was ready to come back in as well. We fell in love with each other again and again over the years.

When we had been together for maybe five years, I realized one day that I felt single. By this I meant I did not feel, as many seem to, that marriage deprived me of the freedom to be me. I felt I was the same person married that I would be single. This never changed.

To protect each other, our relationship, and our assets, we set up wills, a trust, and powers of attorney. Even though it would not be recognized in Nevada, we went across the border to legally marry in California in the summer of 2008 in the brief window before marriage rights were whipped away there. In 2009, we formed a domestic partnership in Nevada, which was marriage in all but name. And in 2015, the Supreme Court recognized same-sex marriage and our legal marriage was finally recognized by all states and the federal government. But these were all simply legal formalities as we considered ourselves married since 1995.

It is difficult to adequately express how much I valued my wife and marriage. They were the very heart of that life. Of course, it wasn't *perfect*. Jessie did not meet my every need, blah, blah, blah. But what I had with Jessie far outweighed anything I felt was missing. We were awesome partners, communicating openly and honestly. It is true that I did almost everything around the house and took total care of the dogs. But I enjoyed having complete control of our home and finances. Jessie provided the greater income and never took me for granted, always certain to express her gratitude and appreciation for a better quality of life than she would have on her own. I felt it balanced out.

Sometimes, we did repair or assembly projects about the house together. In those cases, I stepped back and let her take the lead, as she usually had the greater knowledge and experience—or, at least, *opinions* on how things should be done. This helped keep the peace and we worked very well together.

As Jessie's disabilities developed and intensified over time, we checked in on our codependency regularly. My concern was that I enabled her to remain dependent on me. I did not want to stunt her growth. But she pointed out that while I took care of her in many practical ways, she did continue to grow as a person through her relationships and 12-step program, and in her spirituality. This was true. I also did not feel burdened or resentful. So, we agreed to a certain level of codependency.

Although we were home together all day after she went on disability and I began to work from home, we spent our weekdays in our offices across the house. Jessie played her virtual reality games with her online community and wrote in-depth scenarios for live role-playing games that she ran on weekends. I had no interest in any of this whatsoever, but I was interested in her. I told her early on that while she blathered on about her (intensely boring to me) games, my attention would probably drift in and out. She understood and was okay with this. I usually tuned in enough to follow and ask appropriate questions.

Jessie never read my books, and some of my clients could not understand why this did not bother me. But I understood. She did not understand my path and it scared her. She had come to be afraid, not just of what the *Course* said, but that my spirituality would pull me away from her. I assured her I could not see how that could ever happen. We were great partners, supported each other's spirituality, and were happy together. Our marriage was not an obstacle to my spiritual awareness.

We found that having our own lives, we remained interested in each other. We came together over what interests we did share, such as certain TV programs.

We had a very nice standard of living, but always wanted something, of course. More money to fix up the house. More money to take a vacation each year. But these were petty dissatisfactions.

I spent my weekdays meeting with clients, writing, working out, taking care of the house and dogs, and, more and more as time went on, taking Jessie to doctor's appointments. I cleaned the house once a week. On weekends, I shopped for food and did yard work. I saw my family when we all got together for holidays. Now and then I saw a family member for some other purpose. On rare occasion, I spoke or met with my one friend outside the family.

Of course, I meditated each day. I no longer needed structure and let it flow into the day as it would. I read books (I had stopped reading spiritual material a while before) and watched baseball and other things on TV. I did all of this with Spirit as my Constant Companion, the source of my sense of fulfillment.

That was my life as a Spirit-centered person. And it was a damned good one.

11

As I shared about my early life, romantic love was important to me. As a teenager and young adult, I shared an interest in Harlequin Romances with my mother. I tried my hand at writing romances as well. I loved love stories and the love stories within other stories.

Like many other *Course* students, I equated *romantic love* with *special love*, which the *Course* teaches is an obstacle to peace. To refresh, a *special relationship* is one in which you see another, or a particular form of relationship, as the source of wholeness. Of course, this does not have to be a *romantic* relationship. People make idols of children or parents or siblings or friends. I made an idol of playing mother to our dog, Ginny. In fact, you can have a special relationship with money or status or something else you hold up as the source of what you need to feel whole.

Suddenly, in my forties, I lost all interest in romantic love. I still loved Jessie in a romantic way, but that was all. Romantic love as I saw it—special love—struck me as absurd. I could not think of anything more ridiculous. I could not watch or read romances, and I slogged through the romantic parts of other books, movies, and TV shows.

I wasn't certain at first what this was. For one thing, my libido had diminished greatly (and temporarily, it would turn out). My parents had died, and I was in perimenopause. Was it grief and/or lack of hormones? This did not explain my total lack of interest in the other aspects of romantic love, though. I felt, in fact, that this was the result of coming to a certain spiritual awareness. Special relationships made no sense to me.

And then, sometime around the time I turned fifty, I realized one day that I was enjoying romantic storylines again. This shift had crept in quietly and subtly. And I noticed I was viewing them in a different way. I saw romantic love now as just one way that Love is expressed. It was no longer special. All love is Love and the form of expression is irrelevant. In fact, no form is inherently special. It is focusing on the form that makes it special.

It was as though romantic love had been "purified" of specialness the way I would come to see, much later, that the concepts of *self* and *identity* were purified of ego when they fell away from me for a while.

In early 2014, Jessie and I celebrated 20 years together and looked forward to our 20th wedding anniversary the following year. We experienced an intense rekindling of our relationship that year. I was used to our feelings weaving in and out over the years, but we were gaga for each other as we had not been since we got together.

While our relationship was rejuvenated for a while, it now seems like that was, for me, a flame out. Subtly and quietly my feelings for Jessie, and my family as well, were purified of any leftover specialness. No longer did I feel a unique love for each depending on the form of our relationship. I felt the same detached Love for all.

These experiences put greater distance between me and ego as the contrast between Spirit and ego grew starker. As I understood the only way to liberation was to release ego, my journal was peppered with ego equating this with death. I felt its grief.

By 2012, I moved from feeling "this is already over" and "then this means it (life in the world) is over" to dimly feel that I was "someplace else." I would put it this way: I began life in the world feeling I was in a room in the midst of a party. I embarked on a spiritual path, and in time I felt I was still at the party, but standing on the sidelines, along the wall of the room, watching more than participating. And in this period, I felt I had left the room and I observed the party from outside.

As I wrote *Releasing Guilt for Inner Peace* in 2013, I felt I was in the labyrinthine depths of the mind, getting to the root of the ego thought system and how it worked. As always when I wrote, I was consolidating my learning. I wondered what would be left of ego after my belief in guilt was gone, as guilt was what held up ego in my mind.

(Dialogue 20130403) "...I've felt since my last Revelation in 2007 that I've only been seeing the next step in this stage, not taking it yet. I think I may be moving into the next step now. What-

ever that is! I would think it was to really start to release the ego. And I feel a joyful anticipation of that! But, I do not really know. I will let it unfold."

The material world had become devoid of meaning and value for me. I often described feeling I was on a stage with scenery and props but no story to give them context. This was a neutral, not negative, emptiness. I recognized the world was not my source. Any meaning I experienced was within me.

In both my personal life and in my work, I found I now tended to see people as more advanced both psychologically and spiritually than they were. Even if my intellect and common sense told me where they must be, I could not seem to *see* it. It was as though there was a limit to how far back I could recall my own experience, so I could not see past that limit with others. Often, when taken aback by something that revealed how unconscious they were, it would strike me, "Ohhh, they just don't *know*."

To meet others where they were, I had to put aside my own discernment of them as more than they thought themselves to be and listen hard for where they thought they were. But in time, I stopped seeing others as more advanced than they were. Instead, I found almost everyone immature or underdeveloped as I was aware of their potential.

I did not know that these experiences of detachment signaled life as I knew it was ending. Oh, I knew a long, slow shift had been occurring for a while. This was manifestly apparent. My awareness of Truth grew as ego diminished in value to me. Insights were revealing a new way of understanding existence and myself in it. But, despite feeling "someplace else", I did not grasp the larger implications of these things.

At the end of April 2013, I wrote:

"I told (Jessie) last night that I don't live in the world anymore. She reminded me that she has been telling me this for a long while."

And:

"I don't think I really understand where I am now. It is so recent. I wonder if I am seeing what ACIM *calls the real world. It's the world stripped of guilt. If so, I've only just begun… I feel an even greater distance from the world. It's a sense of, okay, I'm done here. I just do not belong here anymore."*

LIFE II: ONE MIND (CHRIST CONSCIOUSNESS)

FIVE: UNSETTLING

The next stage is indeed "a period of unsettling." Now must the teacher of God understand that he did not really know what was valuable and what was valueless. All that he really learned so far was that he did not want the valueless, and that he did want the valuable. Yet his own sorting out was meaningless in teaching him the difference. The idea of sacrifice, so central to his own thought system, had made it impossible for him to judge. He thought he learned willingness, but now he sees that he does not know what the willingness is for. And now he must attain a state that may remain impossible to reach for a long, long time. He must learn to lay all judgment aside, and ask only what he really wants in every circumstance. Were not each step in this direction so heavily reinforced, it would be hard indeed! (M-4.I.A.7)

INTRODUCTION

(Dialogue 20130611) "...There have been many other times I felt 'unsettled', but they passed. And they did not have the depth of this. Now I have no doubt I am in the period of unsettling."

(Dialogue 20130624) "...my self-concept seems scrambled. This has happened before, of course, but this time I feel no need to unscramble it..."

A Buddhist parable:

A monk set off on a long pilgrimage to find the Buddha. He devoted many years to his search until he finally reached the land where the Buddha was said to live. While crossing the river to this country, the monk looked around as the boatman rowed. He noticed something floating towards them. As it got closer, he realized that it was the corpse of a person. When it drifted so close that he could almost touch it, he suddenly recognized the dead body—it was his own! He lost all control and wailed at the sight of himself, still and lifeless, drifting along the river's currents. That moment was the beginning of his liberation.

One reason Buddhism scared me when I was young was that it seemed I always came upon descriptions of ego death that I vividly recognized and never, ever wanted to experience. Oh, the joy! And oh, the terror! Well, it did not matter. Buddhism or *A Course in Miracles*, it was where I was headed. I was to go through what can only be described as classic ego death. And it was just as awful as I thought it would be.

I want to make it clear that it was only difficult because I was in a false state and for me to be free and happy and in my True State, I had to break free of it. It was not done to me, I was not tested by God, God did not ask it of me, nor was a difficult passage laid out by God as a requirement to reach God. It was simply the process of correcting a massive misidentification. My discomfort was all due to my false identification with ego and had nothing to do with Spirit.

It is not always clear when one period described in the Development of Trust ends and another begins. The shift that began in 2010 when I fully realized ego could not be changed and would have to be released, was the beginning of the end of ego-consciousness for me. I was soon hearing and feeling impending ego death, as I shared at the end of the last part. But that was more an anticipation of ego death than the real death. I was aware that so far, I had only shifted in place; the real undoing was up ahead.

And that began in August of 2014, when it came to me that I was done with pain, so I consider that the beginning of the Period of Unsettling.

As I write this, I am still in Unsettling. So far, I identify six stages of ego winding down as I gradually emerge into consciousness of myself as Christ. I share them here.

A. END GAME

1

Your starting point is truth, and you must return to your Beginning. Much has been seen since then, but nothing has really happened. Your Self is still in peace, even though your mind is in conflict. You have not yet gone back far enough, and that is why you become so fearful. As you approach the Beginning, you feel the fear of the destruction of your thought system upon you as if it were the fear of death. There is no death, but there is a belief in death. (T-3.VII.5)

(In email to client, 20140424) "...But I find often I am reluctant to detach from the ego. If I ask myself why, the answer is 'end game'. This is it. This is all there is left to do. And that's what scares me."

I was ill in August of 2013 and was diagnosed with Irritable Bowel Syndrome. On and off for the next year, I looked at issues of power and choice around the body and illness and money and self-worth. None of this left an impression on me. I did not remember any of it until I read my journal for this memoir. But in hindsight, I find it interesting that I looked so much at *power* just as I headed into a stage of weakness preceding claiming my True Power.

In July of 2014, we put down Paavo, our fourteen-year-old dog. He had been sick for a while and required a lot of care. He was a noisy, demanding dog and had been with us for twelve years, so I really felt his absence. But I was surprised by a sense that a huge chunk of my material life was falling away. It seemed like more than missing a beloved dog, no matter how much attention he had taken up.

A month later, our little cairn terrier, Ginny, was ill, and the week between her vomiting and fatigue manifesting a destroyed liver and finding her (not wholly unexpectedly) dead under our bed one morning, was one of the hardest in my life. I could not understand these responses.

(Dialogue 20140811) *"...it seems like something more. Some fear of a loss of something much larger than the absence of a loved one... Because as much as I would miss her specialness and our unique bond it's not something I cannot live without."*

Of course, it was an awful experience to see a dog I felt was my baby so sick and possibly dying in such a horrible way. I felt responsible in the sense that I did not do my job and protect her. (From herself, most likely, as she was never hesitant about eating anything on the ground.) But this cut into me so keenly, I could only take it a day at a time and just *breathe* my way through that week and the weeks of grief that followed her death.

What I did not know at the time was the depth and sharpness of my pain was a signal that a significant shift had begun in me. Four years later I would have similar experiences of intensified feelings and come to understand why I felt as I did when Ginny died.

It did not help that I was in perimenopause, symptoms of which had begun for me when I was thirty-six and only increased in number and strength through my forties. Now I was fifty, and I still had an unknown number of years of annoying physical symptoms and wild mood swings ahead of me. So, for the time being, I put my experience of unusually cutting emotions at Ginny's death down to perimenopause. But I was never satisfied that was the explanation.

I was aware even as Ginny was sick that my attachment to her was really to a role of *mother-nurturer*. It was a self-concept. (The last one, it would turn out.) I was also aware that I did not need it to feel whole. So, when she was gone, I found I *was* relieved to be free of my attachment to the role I played with her, and I felt no need for another of any kind. I wanted this to be the "last useless journey". But I wondered if I was ready for the freedom that would come with dropping roles that were not necessary for peace.

I was disappointed that I felt so much pain, as though that was a failure. But:

(Dialogue 20140814) *"...One nice thing that I have discovered through this is that I feel like myself when I am in a place of detachment observing rather than in the emotions. The emotions now seem like the alien experience. Familiar, yes, but not like me. This is a turnaround from past experiences where the detached observation felt like a nice relief but it was also frighteningly different."*

Before these deaths, my journal was filled with tedious ego blather about perimenopause mood swings, my slow life coaching practice, my low earning, and wondering why ego was still in my awareness. I was still looking at guilt, although I felt that by the time I wrote *Releasing Guilt for Inner Peace*, the premise for it was gone. Spirit told me that it was only that "you believe that you still believe" in guilt.

About a week after Paavo died, I was looking at a belief that was recurring: That there was some darkness in me that I believed in and had to be honest about and face. This was different from my experience of looking for ego's story for guilt for me with Spirit and not finding it. I *felt* this darkness. Of course, I knew this was a manifestation of guilt and fear. I understood it could only be a *belief*.

And I realized fear was no more real than guilt. I figured that just as it took a while to undo my belief in guilt, it would take a while to undo my belief in fear. Obviously, I could not undo the belief in fear *in ego*. For fear to be gone, ego would have to be gone. What I did not yet understand was that seeing fear was not real was seeing ego was not real.

This awareness had been showing up for a while in other

ways as well. The awareness that I used to shift me out of guilt and fear was *only God is real* and *God is untouched by anything that seems to happen in consciousness*. Having used this awareness for quite some time, I started to feel that what I experienced in my conscious awareness was not relevant for two reasons: Clearly, I did not have to be *always* conscious of Spirit for It to work in me and through me. It rose to conscious awareness as needed. And, ego dominated my conscious awareness, and it wasn't real.

I also became aware that my ongoing practice for inner peace was often merely managing moods and I judged my sense of success or failure on the path by how well I did this. This was dismaying because I realized I was not working at anything real. An even or good mood was not inner peace. But, as I came to see what happened in my conscious awareness was not significant, I realized a bad mood was not failure as Spirit was *here*. I was growing less concerned with the limited experience of this individual consciousness and, dimly at this point, more aware of this mind as part of something larger. Truly, what I experienced minute by minute was irrelevant.

But even as I began to see the unreality of ego, I resisted peace because I experienced it as *no-feeling*. Having no feelings felt the same as losing loved ones. In fact, when Ginny became ill, ego told me that my desire for detachment and peace was the same as wanting to lose loved ones. It told me my desire for detachment was the same as my own desire to die. I recognized these thoughts were ego. I understood that detachment from the world really meant detachment from ego, because it teaches that the world is the source of wholeness. But its resistance now was intense.

After Ginny died, I went through a significant episode I call *The Mansion/shack Insights*. Something was different within me. I found I was thinking with greater clarity and immediacy about ego and Spirit.

(Dialogue 20140821) *"Last night I was thinking about this*

reluctance to let go of not-Truth this way: I needed shelter so I built a shack (not-Truth). It's shoddy and ugly but it's mine. I actually have always had a Mansion (Truth) but I have been unaware of It. At first I felt unworthy, etc. of the Mansion because of guilt but I've worked through that. I now see the Mansion is not bestowed out of worth but has simply always belonged to me. However, I still have this shack I'm reluctant to release because I've believed I need it for shelter. I also value it because I made it. I'm afraid of who I will be without it even though this perfect Mansion that offers me complete safety and every comfort and has always been mine is available to me. I feel that to live in the Mansion full time will 'cost' me the shack."

My journal does not reflect this, but I spent quite some time with this metaphor. I felt something significant occurring around the realization that the value of the shack (ego) to me was one simple thing: *It was mine.* I was frustrated because I wanted to let it go and could not seem to. I felt this meant I must value it more than I could see. I eventually accepted this and stopped trying to release it. But I was disappointed in myself. And to my dismay, I dimly sensed it would be several years before I released ego. I could not understand how I was not yet ready. But as I could not force release of ego, I could only accept this and go on.

My sense that I was in a long-term process was correct, however that process *was* releasing ego. And I had been in it for a while.

Some have famously dropped ego in a moment. Some go right to joy when ego drops. It is understandable that much is made of their experiences. But it did not happen like that for this mind. And I suspect it does not for most, making the actual process obscure.

I actually envisioned how it *could* be when ego falls away. But although I have since heard and read of experiences like this, it was not to be for me.

(Dialogue 20141024) *"...The conscious and unconscious in my mind would go silent and there'd be a vast spaciousness that I recognized was everywhere, always. But the body/personality of the self would still go on, an empty (without meaning) shell merely observed with the rest of the universe of form.*

At first I would probably find this silent vastness of mind disconcerting. I'd also find it liberating and therefore joyful. I'd have easy 'access' to Boundless Truth. I'd be amazingly present in my interactions with the world. Boundless Truth would always be in the background when It wasn't in the forefront. I would be so here, yet nowhere specific. As I acclimated I'd settle into a deep, abiding contentment. And eventually all consciousness would fall away and only Boundless Truth would remain.

This is what I've imagined anyway. Very gentle. Startling at first. Somewhat uncomfortable because unfamiliar. But nothing dramatic; nothing dark. I've left darkness behind with guilt."

Sometimes, I *did* catch on to how it was unfolding for me.

(Dialogue 20141028) *"I'm not so sure this would be as dramatic as I think it would be. I think I have been prepared... Mine has been a gentle, slowly unfolding preparation. I feel, in fact, that a lot of it has already happened...I just have not...dropped the ego 'all the way'. I also think that it is possible that for me there will not be a moment but a continuation of gentle undoing. I suppose there will have to be a moment of recognition that it has occurred. But I think it will be so natural that it won't be dramatic."*

I would turn out to be correct about a continuation of a slow undoing, but wrong about the drama.

It has always been the case for this mind that it embarks on a process of integration when an event occurs, whether that event is triggered within itself, as with an internal shift or something dropping away; or by something in its life in the world, like a loss or change. Another way to put it is an event happens and it takes a while for this entire mind to catch up with itself. (Perhaps this mind reflects its path. The *Course* describes an instant of Atonement unfolding as the story of time —a process. Or perhaps this mind reads its own workings into the *Course*.)

Only in retrospect do I see that ego died to me around Ginny's death. Certainly, something felt different after The Mansion/shack Insights. Before Paavo and Ginny died, my journal was filled with whining about not being able to release ego. Afterward, it was a record of new experiences and insights that I am the dreamer of the dream (*the* Son of God) rather than a figure in the dream (*a* Son of God). I was rising in consciousness and did not know it. Ego no longer tethered me, although it would take years for my entire mind to catch up with this fact.

2

There were many signs my mind was shifting consciousness. The premise for guilt— that I was separate from God—was undone. I was aware, in my experience, not just my intellect, that God was untouched by ego. And that meant God in me (Christ) was unchanged by ego. I was aware that ego in my conscious awareness in no way prevented Spirit from working in me or through me, although I still granted ego's continued presence in my mind too much significance. And I was beginning to sense it did not matter. I was not yet manifesting Spirit-consciousness, but the line between me and Spirit had been blurring for a while.

I had for a long time felt I was done with the world, culminating with feeling with Paavo's death that a big part of me was gone. My last special relationship was my role of "mother" with Ginny.

I spent a great deal of 2013 looking at the issue of my power. And in April of 2014, Spirit said to me about ego "...you will stop empowering it at all because you will fully recognize that it *is* you who empower it. And then it will cease to be for you." During The Mansion/shack Insights, I got in touch with my responsibility (not to be confused with *blame*) for ego.

My sense that I valued ego *only* because I made it was not *personal*. It was the Son of God. But I did not know this at the time, because these experiences did not come all at once. They came over a long span of time, and they were not ongoing, but rose to conscious awareness now and then. I knew I was in some sort of shift, but I did not know what it was. Sometimes I did sense that I was more advanced than I was ready to accept. But my continuing mistake was thinking that ego in my awareness was significant and that I had to do something to release it.

At the end of September 2014, I wrote:

"The thing is this: I know I'm in a process, a large shift, that is happening 'for me'. By this I mean I do not have to make it happen. All that I've been writing about in here lately is really just me scrambling around trying to get comfortable on a day-to-day basis. Because I am lost right now. I do not know how to look at myself. I do not know where to stand within myself. I do not have a practice that seems to work to make me more comfortable. But none of that has anything to do with the process. It will not make it happen. And it will not impede its happening. The shift will occur. It is occurring. 'I' am irrelevant to it."

Spiritually themed books were often mentioned or suggested to me, but for years I had not felt moved to read spiritual material. But after mentioning to a client that I felt without a self-concept, he suggested I read Bernadette Roberts. I felt moved to look her up and was drawn to *The Experience of No-Self*. As it turned out, I could not understand much of this book and suspected that she meant something other than *ego* by *self*. (This was correct. Though in this first book on the self she was a bit murky, in her later books she makes it clear that by *self* she meant *consciousness*.) But what I did take away from her book was how idiosyncratic is each spiritual awakening.

This was reassuring, but I realized it also meant I was on my own. There was no template to refer to for understanding a process I felt occurring whether I wanted it to or not. And less and less did I have a sense of Spirit *with* me, to turn to for guidance, understanding, and comfort, as I shifted to identifying with It. I could only watch and ride what unfolded for me. I was increasingly uncomfortable.

At the end of September, I saw and felt something I had not before. I had been having more experiences of detaching from ego and feeling I was "not here". However, my mind skittered away from these experiences before I could understand them. But this time, I experienced this long enough to feel that *not here* meant *not in the body*. And I realized I would not *cease to exist* without ego; I would *exist differently*. I did not experience this as a higher miracle Vision of a future state. I felt I could make the shift right then. I felt it was waiting for me to accept it.

In October, I took our Maltese-Shi-tzu mix, Joey, to the vet for a routine check-up. I was grateful to have him. It would have been terrible to be completely dog-less so unexpectedly. He had adored Ginny, so he was a bit dazed and uncertain too, but we had each other for comfort.

Dr. G gave me Ginny's autopsy results, and they were what we already expected: She had no underlying liver disease. She had been healthy and died of acute liver poisoning. But I was not responding to this the way I once would have.

(Dialogue 20141010) *"This is where the interpretation of 'numbness' comes in. It's that I'm not feeling what and/or how much the ego wants me to feel. It tells me that I must be in denial and uses the threat of some future emotional breakdown. But this time I saw that I am not in denial and I do not have repressed emotions about this to erupt in the future. I am beginning to 'exist differently'. I am, and have been, transitioning to that. It's just not showing up the way that I expected, but that's how it's been all along. Expectations have often confused me and made me wonder if I'm not getting it. But of course I have no model for what goes on internally in this process."*

This is not unfolding as I thought it would was a recurring theme with me, and often showed up in my ACIM Mentor articles. But frankly, I had not given a lot of thought to what the shift in consciousness would be like. I certainly knew it would be a *qualitative* (wholly different) shift rather than like the *quantitative* (a different degree of what I was used to) shifts I had been having all along, because I had glimpsed it in higher miracles. Also, the *Course* mentions a (false) sense of sacrifice or cost comes with it, so I knew it was not just more of the same.

That I was surprised, even as the shift began, by how different it was turning out to be from what I expected is indicative of how much ego-consciousness was still at play in my mind. Ego was slipping away as my identity, but I was about to take a long journey through ego-consciousness as I awakened from it.

These new, surprising experiences occurred as material life went on. I knew Jessie and I would get another dog eventually. I liked having two, so they would not be alone when we were not home. And I loved watching dogs interact, as it highlighted their distinct personalities.

Jessie had always wanted a West Highland Terrier and she saw her opportunity. I did not care which breed of dog we got, but I wanted a young rescue. I found the thought of a puppy excruciating. They are a joy, yes, but also a lot of work. Ginny was supposed to be our only puppy experience because of the months of vigilance and training required. And now, grieving her, I simply felt I did not have it in me to raise one.

But Jessie wanted a puppy and was pretty insistent. She promised it would be our last and that she would help more than she had with Ginny, as she wanted this puppy to bond more with her. Of course, something more than grief for Ginny was dragging at me, but I couldn't explain this to Jessie as I didn't understand it myself. In time, in the way it works with couples, Jessie's need for a puppy outweighed my reluctance. We chose a dog that we would not pick up for a few weeks, giving us more time to process our grief.

Rory was born in November, and we picked him up from a breeder in Utah at the New Year. I liked terriers for their feistiness, which gives them a lot of personality. We had had two Cairn terriers, and they are a notoriously independent breed. But as Rory was a Westie, he had the terrier feistiness, but was devoted to me. I felt that balance made him the perfect dog for me.

And yet...it didn't matter. Something in me was gone. I loved Rory, but I couldn't form an attachment. This was a relief, certainly, but also somewhat disconcerting. It was as if around him I was feeling for a missing limb with which to connect with my perfect dog.

(Dialogue 20150428) *"...all along I've had the feeling that I'm raising Rory for someone else. At first this showed up as it feeling as though there was something temporary about him...But in time I realized that the temporary referred to me, not him. I've temporarily come back into the world to raise him. This feeling has morphed into a strong feeling that I'm raising him for someone else. And beyond this feeling is the sense that 'I've already left.'"*

I sensed shifting, of being done with the world, and had new experiences of existence, but none of this was my ongoing experience. I did not know what this was; I did not define it. I seemed to see and feel just enough to be moved to write these experiences in my journal. Yet, while clearly only feeling the outer edges of this, I also recorded feeling that I was "acclimating to a new state."

3

For the first periods of my spiritual path, I thought I was taking steps toward a goal. Each step built on what had gone before. I felt wholly autonomous and at choice. I felt that I could step off the path, but that I had seen too much and would not want to.

This changed in the Period of Settling in a slow shift as the boundary between me and Spirit blurred. I sensed something I could not see fully, which was that what I thought of as me was part of something larger. I still held onto the idea of free will, but in limited form. I felt that the only choice I had had to make was for Truth, which I did when I let Spirit into my awareness as a teenager, and that after that my path was out of my hands. But in early 2015 I began to see the whole picture:

(Dialogue 20150113) "So I seem to have this vision now where I see that there is no goal; this is all an effect. Every choice I've ever made as a self has not been the free and independent choice that I thought it was. Everything has all been a part of a larger story, a great tapestry. My seemingly-independent choices as a self are influenced by the tapestry and they play into the tapestry… This seems to be a higher vision…This is why the 'law of attraction' never worked for me, too. The feeling of swimming upstream trying to make something happen in my life always led me away from those gimmicks. I always looked for the stream—the feeling of flow. Sometimes I could feel something was not going to happen for me. Sometimes I felt it was maybe one day but 'not now'. But it never felt right trying to make something happen…"

While the *Course* says "the script is written" and that we are living a moment that was over as soon as it was thought, as long as I felt autonomous and guilt was very real to me—while I was ego-identified—I could only interpret this to mean the outcome was inevitable. So, my seeing and feeling through spiritual Sight that I had never been autonomous was another signal that Spirit had come to take the place of ego.

But my experience of ego was not over. Along with these new experiences indicating I was moving into a new State, I entered an episode I call *The Barrenness*, an indication that I was experiencing ego-consciousness as I had never done before.

Somewhere, somehow, and I suspect slowly and subtly, I had slipped into a deep forgetting, and I had no clue that this occurred. Truths I had long relied on were gone, but as I had forgotten them, I did not realize this.

It was not that I had not truly learned them or that my learning was incomplete. They were the basis for my true peace. But it was like, to make myself whole in my awareness, the part of me still buried under darkness (ego) had to emerge *through* the darkness, seeming to get lost in it for a while, to join the Light (Spirit) that was already here. Of course, I did not know this at the time. I did not know what was going on.

To start, my discomfort was only a small part of my overall experience. In moments, I had the sense of dark beliefs to undo, and that was how I sometimes explained my discomfort to myself. But I expected those to be individual beliefs, and I did not realize I was to take a journey through ego-consciousness.

For a long while, I used *split-mind* to describe the state of the Son of God as well as of each of us as seemingly-individual Sons of God. I found it useful as a way to remember that I always had a choice of where to come from in my mind, ego or Spirit. It was a helpful self-concept for a long while, until during The Forgetting it became a way of denying that I was usually in ego-consciousness. It was not that I thought I was usually in Spirit, but I seemed to think I could find some neutral ground when I could only ever be in one thought system or the other.

One of the first signs of The Forgetting was, as I described in Settling, dropping any idea that there was a true experience of *identity*, *self*, or *I* in consciousness, and It was of God. I so associated these concepts with ego that as I began to detach from ego, I came to feel that there was no experience of *identity*, *self*, or *I* in consciousness that reflected Truth. I had intermittently felt this before, but always came back to identity-spirituality. Not this time, however.

I seemed to totally forget the experience of my Self in the holy relationship. Instead, I came to feel that the concept of a *True Identity* was rudimentary spirituality and dismissed any spiritual approach or practice that included any sense of identity. I embarked on attempts to practice state-consciousness by focusing on my state of mind, unwittingly losing God in the process, yet feeling I was stepping into a more mature spirituality. But it never caught on, and I was left without any meaningful spiritual practice.

This had been the case for a while when I saw something that threw me, although it was something I had learned before. While I never consciously chased a perfected state of mind, early on my path I considered what I experienced in what I called *higher miracles*—love, joy, a sense of expansion, oneness, etc.—to be the experience of Truth. However, as time went on, I heard of people having these experiences while taking certain drugs and even sometimes during a stroke. At first, I assumed they felt only *high*, which is not the same as *joy*. But as I heard more details, I realized that many felt what sounded *just like* a higher miracle experience. I could only conclude that these experiences, no matter their source, were only a physiological *effect*.

Of course, source is important. A sunlamp may produce light with the same properties as the sun, but that does not make it sunlight. But that these effects could be caused by things other than an awareness of Truth diminished their significance to me. This was an important adjustment, and reinforced for me how important it was to remain focused on Truth rather than to pursue a state of mind. But it rattled me for a while.

Eventually, however, I realized that there was no loss. I would still have those experiences in consciousness as an effect of an awareness of Truth; I would just not be taking them beyond. And that did not matter as I knew from Revelation that God's Glory was far beyond those effects. In the end, I felt relieved of an illusion.

So, I was surprised when this came up again with a client and I felt hurled sideways by it, as though I had never realized those experiences were only effects. I felt as though I had still been in denial in some part of my mind, and it was stripped away, and I was not on the path I thought—just as I had felt when I learned this years before. What was going on?

I could not find any new angle or belief about it that I had not seen before. I was not only feeling the confusion that is the state of feeling thrown off, but I was also confused by feeling thrown off! I was very disturbed; the whole thing felt foreign. I knew my mind well, but I felt in wholly new territory. I could only conclude that I would understand whatever this was in time. It was a powerful experience, yet an isolated occurrence.

On top of forgetting that the split-mind is never neutral and denying my Self and God as I dismissed identity-spirituality, realizing, again, that oneness and peace and joy are only effects reminded me that God is completely different from consciousness. As consciousness is existence, God is Nonexistence in the truest sense. I shifted into desolation.

This was a familiar experience as ego's response just after Revelation. But after Revelation, I always remembered the Glory of God and knew that the desolation I felt was *ego's interpretation* of God. Now these facts simply did not come to mind. I totally forgot them.

In fact, I felt that I was being strong and facing facts: There is no God-inspired identity in consciousness, God is Nonexistence, and God is desolation. I expected that I would acclimate to these dismal facts and somehow come to feel that they were not dismal. I felt that if I could not do so yet, the fault was with me.

It baffles me now that I never saw through these various forms of denial of Truth. I never even questioned them. But this, of course, is how forgetting works.

So, I found myself with an inner landscape that was dry, desolate, and barren. This was not my entire interior; just a place in it. But eventually I would not be able to find my usual routes to Spirit and peace, although I trusted that Spirit and peace were there.

Contemplatives write of a *Dark Night of the Soul* at ego death, which they describe as feeling they lost God. I felt that I lost me. Bernadette Roberts wrote that she felt she lost God with ego because she had connected to God through ego. She eventually found God again when she realized God was the Void left when ego was gone. I never felt I lost God, although I was unconsciously pushing God away. I knew God was here, whether I felt It or not. What else could be carrying me through my sense that I lost all that was familiar within?

I knew Spirit (God within) would be left at the end of whatever process I was in. I just did not know if anything that I felt was me would be there.

4

In my journal and articles, I suddenly found it confusing and awkward to use *I* and started using *this mind*. In essence, I felt less ownership of this mind. It did not feel like my mind alone. I did not know it, but *I* was becoming de-personalized as

I sorted it out from ego. My mind was becoming de-individualized (*a* Son of God) and preparing to expand (to *the* Son of God).

Using *this mind* exclusively did not last long, which indicates to me that this must have been a shift manifesting rather than beginning. Soon I was able to feel that *I* and *this mind* were the same. I would eventually return to *I* but would use *this mind* whenever it felt appropriate.

It was also increasingly difficult to express my experiences in words, since everything I wrote sounded like things I had written before. I had new experiences, but I didn't have new words to express them. I was entering an experience that really could not be captured in words. So, I just had to accept the limitations of expressing the inexpressible and the misunderstandings with my readers to which that would lead.

It would come to me at times that I was *"still thinking like a person."* I felt it was time for this to change, but I could not turn this into a practice, because I could not force myself to think like Spirit (whatever that would be). However, I intuitively sensed the correct approach:

(Dialogue 20150607) *"I sense identifying as a self is a habit of many layers. It's (undoing) going to happen seemingly-automatically. So it's a matter of catching it and letting it go.*

Without an identity what is there to think about? Nothing, really. Just observational and informational thoughts."

Personal stories that I was guilty *for*, afraid *of*, grieving *for* persisted, but, really, those stories were gone. When I experienced those things, it simply meant that I had slipped back into ego-consciousness. This was the source of my feelings of guilt, not anything occurring.

I sometimes had the itch to write a book that would encapsulate all I had learned in plain, ordinary language and with a lot of examples. This came around at this time, but:

(Dialogue 20150707) *"Perhaps what this mind is feeling is*

not something to be written but to be experienced. Especially given that it is in an active learning stage. The sensation that all of this is over that began so long ago for this mind was the beginning of the falling away of the self that seems to be the experience unfolding so clearly now. Perhaps in the end this mind will realize that there is nothing to be written because the experience of the self is not real."

(By *self* I meant *person*.)

I sought detachment, and it often brought me peace, but more and more it was ultimately uncomfortable for me. I wanted to be detached from the pain of ego, but I found I lost what I thought of as me in the process. As a person, I had boundaries that defined me. A recurring theme in my journal at this time was my discomfort without them.

(Dialogue 20150718) *"Feelings are to Existence what the body is to Being and what thoughts are to Mind. They are the bounded substitutes for boundless Existence… Not-feeling scares me because it is an experience of Boundlessness."*

I realized that true peace was no-feeling. Of course it is! It made so much sense, but I continued to resist this. I wanted it both ways, to feel *and* to be at peace—to be a person and to be Spirit.

I went on to write a great deal about my conflict over No-feeling versus feeling. I did not write about the Love and joy that came with not feeling, or the liberation that was Boundlessness as I would have done in the past. I was not feeling them as I had done in the past, and I didn't seem to notice. I had forgotten.

Beside the growing sense of desolation, I did have interesting new experiences. One day when a question for Spirit arose in my mind, I found *I* answered. This was startling. I had changed places. I was not the questioner but the Teacher. I recalled that a year before, when Ginny died, I had been both that which was grieving and that which comforted the griever. I was mentoring a part of myself. Clearly, the boundary between Spirit and me was now sometimes gone.

I was very disoriented. The interesting experiences, while welcome, felt foreign, too. I didn't know how to see myself. I didn't know how to look at the person still here or what to do with her. And this time it would turn out to *not* be a short-term shift in self-concept. It went much deeper than that.

As time went on, I felt done with ego, but not out of pain and frustration with it. I simply felt it was over and I was ready to be Spirit. This was new.

(Dialogue 20160107) *"...I want the real shift. I'm done with this other stuff that goes nowhere and is not a real change. I don't say this in frustration. I simply see there is nothing left here for me. I am done spinning in place. I don't sense anything standing in my way. I don't feel any fear about this, again because it's not about becoming something. It is about letting Something be. And that does involve something else falling away but I feel done with that."*

(Dialogue 20160111) *"...All I can see now is how it has all been spinning in place. Error/correction of error. Same coin, different sides. The real shift would be <u>another</u> coin..."*

Error/correction is the Atonement. I also saw past it—to the other "coin":

(Dialogue 20160121) *"There's...a deep vision I get that I can only describe as it's about God returning to God. This vision is like seeing a healing take place in Being. Except I also see that it's something like it <u>would be</u> like God returning to God if it was really possible for God to not be God. It seems profound. But I also see the profundity is also itself a temporary thing only experienced at a level where it seems possible that God has left God.*

...Neither the seeming-separation nor the seeming-healing

are real..."

While I filled my journal with confusion over ego's persistence in my mind, I often ended with the same conclusion: It didn't matter. Only God is real, and God is untouched by anything that seems to happen apart from It. I felt the truth of this so deeply, it never failed to lift me out of my obsession with what occurred in my conscious awareness.

I found I could use the idea *this is past* to lift myself out of an upset. It dovetailed with my sense that I made the decision for Truth long ago and had only been watching this unfold since. Both experiences reinforced my sense that I was done with the world. (Originally, I interpreted the awareness that I made the choice for Truth long ago *personally*—as *a* Son of God—and thought I made it unconsciously as a teenager. But I was actually tapping into the awareness of *the* Son of God, that the idea of not-Truth was undone by Truth's All-encompassing nature as soon as it arose.)

So used to feeling myself as an *instrument* of Spirit, I had to adjust to the awareness that I was, and had always been, an *expression*. I was not "used" by Spirit to, say, teach to bring about the Atonement. My mind, my teaching, etc. were *manifestations* of the Atonement—of Spirit.

While I had learned to commune with God in meditation with no agenda *in the moment*, it turned out that was part of a larger goal of mine—to realize God. So, as the line between Spirit and me blurred, for a couple of years taking time to meditate felt awkward. I felt *There*; what was I meditating *for*? Then I realized meditation was happening organically. I meditated because it was time to rest in Truth. I truly had no agenda now.

5

Experiencing something as new that I had experienced before would characterize much that was to unfold in the coming years. It was a sign that whatever it was, was sinking in deeper. In October of 2016, the awareness that I had no self-concept rolled around again as though it was a new realization. This time, I felt it explained much of my growing discomfort, and I felt unmoored.

I also felt "unlocalized" more often. In centered moments, I felt everywhere.

That month, I was caught up in a sexual fantasy for a couple of weeks, reminding me of the type of distraction that occurred when I was translating the *Course* into plain language. Then suddenly, I began to write a romance novel. I was embarrassed because I suspected this was ego trying to fill the void left by not having a self-concept. But sometimes I sensed more might be going on.

(Dialogue 20161023) *"It feels like things are being rearranged inside me and all I can do is watch and let it."*

(Dialogue 20161024) *"...It feels like a last, dying grasp at something. Perhaps it is the ego pursuing a story in the absence of a story for this self. Perhaps it is trying to build a new self-concept as a writer of fiction. Perhaps it is both of these. I don't think it is really anything organized, just desperate. Yes, certainly a whiff of desperation about it.*

There's an underlying depression or grief it is trying to mask, too. I have these moments when I see it. Something is falling away. Or, more correctly, already has. There is a huge shift that has occurred and is rising to conscious expression.

I have long sensed an ending."

I wrote romance novels when I was younger, but for decades had no interest in writing fiction. I developed plots for novels to entertain myself when I cleaned houses, but no longer cleaned houses. But now I wasn't simply feeling like writing again. The way this surge of creativity came to me made me feel again that I did not know who I was anymore. I thought the nature of the creative burst might represent something else.

(Dialogue 20161029) *"…I've also felt the Vision of the Holy Relationship is very close. There have also been moments when I've glimpsed this is all about something else…This surge of creativity, of sexuality, of inchoate longing is the desire for the Vision of the Holy Relationship…"*

(By *Vision of the holy relationship* I meant *spiritual Vision* or the *real world*.)

(Dialogue 20161030) *"I think the writing is serving these purposes:*
A way of releasing creative energy as I go through whatever transformation this is
A means of some pleasure during the discomfort
A way to keep the surface of my mind busy as a lot of processing goes on underneath
If I look inward I feel something is being dismantled. But I also have moments of feeling something is breaking to the surface. These are not exclusive of each other. The surface and all that is on it cracks as the breakthrough occurs…"

This burst of creativity would turn out to be short lived, and I put aside my notes for the romance novel.

I was also aware that for a long while I had been in an emotionally dry place. This was an aspect of The Barrenness and God-as-desolation and not simply a lack of feeling emotional satisfaction. I just did not know how to describe what I felt. But I did have a clue it was not just something emotional lacking. I recognized I didn't have anything to replace ego, and that the only thing that could was the Vision of the holy relationship. But I did not feel I needed a relationship to experience spiritual Vision.

I did examine my personal life, but I could not find a problem. I loved Jessie very much and was happy in our marriage. My life coaching practice was never what I considered full, but that was certainly not the source of the *lifeless* place within me. Anyway, I knew nothing in the world could offer me fulfillment. I did not understand the exact nature of my discomfort, and I could only let it be and expect to understand later what it was.

I had a long-time client who asked me now and then to quantify my peace. For quite a while I told him I was 85% at peace. The remaining 15% was a hard nut to crack and I didn't know what it would take. I did not know I had maxed out peace in ego-consciousness and I was, basically, breaking through what remained of ego.

Sometimes I felt there was something in my mind I could not see. I thought of this as a "black box in the corner" of my mind. I felt this was something I would probably have to face one day. Later, I would equate this with the 15%.

I knew my discomfort was ego. But why wasn't it falling away despite my feeling done with it? I missed the significance of *feeling done with it.* I granted too much significance to its continued appearance (and would for a long while). It was *being undone*; I only had to watch.

Any comfort I had during The Barrenness was in the awareness that only God is real and that nothing changes this. This awareness made the constant ego blather in my conscious awareness less and less significant to me. But at the same time, its contrast with the discomfort only highlighted it.

(Dialogue 20161101) *"I think I thought that when I reached this point it (ego) would fall away because I was so ready and there would be minimum discomfort. Obviously I must be ready. And I cannot say that this is the most uncomfortable I've ever been. I have resources I never had before. But it certainly is very uncomfortable and more uncomfortable than I've been in a very long time."*

I was to grow even more uncomfortable as time went on, but I accepted this as part of some unknown passage I expected to understand later.

As well as feeling at times *unlocalized*, or abstract, the material world felt *nebulous* to me. One day it dawned on me that the nebulous sensation was seeing and feeling the unreality of the material world. I had somehow expected that I would one day *see* it was not real, but I did not expect it would mean a different *experience*. Of course, that made no sense, because I would have to be in a different experience to see this. But it attested to my desire to experience things differently while still experiencing them the same.

I came up with a metaphor for my confusion:

(Dialogue 20161207) *"It's like all I've ever known is being dry. That feeling of dryness was what I defined as reality. Then I have another experience, one of being wet. And since I'm not used to being wet at first I don't trust it. But in time I come to accept both experiences. However, there's a subtle unconscious belief that the proof that I have accepted being wet is reality is when it feels like being dry. But of course that can never happen because if I'm wet I'm not dry and when I'm dry I'm not wet.*

This is what I was doing with the concrete and the Abstract experiences. I have been waiting for the Abstract to feel like the concrete before I'd accept It as Reality. Which of course now seems absurd."

Soon after this, I began to feel like a "ghost in the world". I likened this to being like Bruce Willis's character in *The Sixth Sense* who (spoiler alert!) interacts with the world throughout the movie but is revealed at the end to be dead.

It would be a long while before I would correctly identify these experiences as *being* Spirit. But I *did* correctly feel that I would need to have experiences of Vision to shift further away from ego. Because as far as I consciously knew at the time, Vision was the only experience I had *as* Spirit. And then I felt Vision drawing closer.

(Dialogue 20170117) *"Something that has been happening for me the past couple of months is finding my mind back in the room I had in that dorm-like house in Manoa... back in the Emily/Holy Relationship days. What I recall is the Vision and the joy I experienced...And what I saw yesterday was that if I return to that state of mind now I know I will not be leaving it this time. I may vacillate for a while, but unlike then I am not starting out. This is the end-game. And I think it is knowing that, that makes me hesitate. There will be no going back this time."*

Of course, I was not *hesitating*. It was unfolding. I soon tuned in to what was to come over the next few years:

(Dialogue 20170228) *"...I feel there is just a thin veil or membrane between me and spiritual Vision. I am staying open to It but what comes up is that I will be 'leaving' while still in the world. It's like a long good-bye instead of just going... And then I seem to see it from the other side and realize that it has already happened. It has already begun: I am already 'dead' and I just have not accepted it. Again, that feeling like I'm interacting with a world I've already left..."*

(Dialogue 20170422) *"Yesterday I went off in front of Jessie about my frustration at the slowness of my mentoring business. Tons of 'friend' requests on Facebook but no clients, blah, blah. Income way down, etc. We discussed me going back to housecleaning part-time...Anyway, I became aware of a shift. At first it seemed superficial and just related to making this external change. But as the day went on I began to feel that something is trying to emerge in me. The word 'rebirth' keeps coming to mind."*

I flashed more often on being done with the world and I would feel and think *"Then I'm dead."*

Well into 2017, I felt certain the self (person) was gone, but I did not characterize what this meant beyond the self-concept being gone. I was uncomfortable because I could not clarify my new experiences, something I was not used to. I felt I knew my mind well and clarity always came in time, but it was not happening now. I thought maybe this was because I was standing in a new place in my mind.

In the summer, I had vivid dreams and found I was devising plots in my mind around them during the day. I was not certain what this was, as I had not been certain about the burst of creativity a year before. But this time, I did not judge what was occurring. I was more accepting and willing to see where the ideas went. However, I did not bother to write them down.

Quietly there came another new experience. I found a delicious Spaciousness in my mind in the evenings as I played a word game on my laptop. I had a sense of a vast, open, liberating space in my mind. Of course, I knew the game was not the source of this experience, but I came to equate it with The Spaciousness and looked forward to playing it whenever I could. The Spaciousness was a lovely offset to the discomfort I had been in for so long. Little did I know it heralded the rebirth I had been sensing.

B. THE HOLY RELATIONSHIP

Beyond the body that you interposed between you and your brother, and shining in the golden light that reaches it from the bright, endless circle that extends forever, is your holy relationship, beloved of God Himself… at its center Christ has been reborn, to light His home with vision that overlooks the world. (T-22.II.12)

<u>6</u>

Although I used the pronoun *I* for all that was written before this, I no longer feel that was my life. She who lived it is gone—although she never was. When I awaken from a dream, I realize the figure in the dream was only an idea of me.

I think of she who fell away as *person-Liz*. She was my experience that a person in a body in a world was my reality.

As recorded, I long felt her end approaching, although I did not know at the time what exactly was ending. Her ending overlapped with what I now understand were emerging experiences of myself as Spirit.

Person-Liz would not be totally gone until the moment I call *The Break*. But *transition-Liz*, the stranger who would take her place (and also not last), showed up for the first time in August, 2017 when the Golden Light of Love broke into the delicious Spaciousness I had been enjoying in my mind.

One of the plots I had fashioned out of a dream in the summer of 2017 stuck with me. I played with it in my mind until it no longer resembled the dream. It persisted strongly, and I finally decided that the only way to get rid of it was to resolve the ending and bring it to a conclusion. So, I did this one Saturday, letting it run in my mind as I went about the chores of the day. I continued with it when I woke up in the middle of that night and into the next morning as I mowed the lawn.

I should have sensed what was coming. Historically, I only wrote a novel when I could clearly see the beginning, middle, and end. And as I mowed, I knew I was to write it and began it that day.

(Dialogue 20170814) *"Totally scrambled. There's been some shift. Things are not the same within. Yesterday I found myself writing that book!... It's like I watched the writing from a distance. I was not taking dictation; it just came easy...I just have no idea what's going on in this mind. I can only watch and ride... Yesterday was like a non sequitur from what went before. All that happened last week, all that I ended thinking about Saturday...— boom! Went in a totally different direction on Sunday, thank you very much...I feel like something is being done to me, through me, and without me and all I can do is watch...Couple of thoughts. One is that this story coming through me is the way that love is being expressed through this self..."*

The novel blazed in me with a Golden Light of Love, an experience I came to call *The Golden*. Sometimes, I felt my mind was being hijacked. Other times, that maybe I was losing my mind. Ego, which had not been directly threatened for a long time, attacked viciously. It was much like when I translated the *Course* into plain language. I felt crippling inadequacy, guilt, and resistance, but then I would simply stop judging and settle into writing what came each day. I tried not to draw conclusions about what was occurring and just watch and ride, but it was difficult because I could feel this was happening in the context of something larger. I grabbed for anything familiar to hold onto.

I had always loved writing and enjoyed writing fiction when it was part of my early life, but never like this. I felt creative in a way I had never experienced before, and I was sure this was because the Inspiration was Spirit. I felt I was expressing Spirit, even though this did not come through in the story. I had experiences I heard other writers talk about but had never experienced myself. The characters were three dimensional and very real to me. I loved them as my children. I felt their feelings as I wrote about them, which could be uncomfortable, and yet was always somehow enjoyable at the same time. The imagined places in the story (it is set in Las Vegas) were vivid in my mind, especially Erika's home (which is still so clear to me I swear it must exist somewhere).

Because of the Love that inspired it, the book was like a living thing to me. It so filled my mind that it was with me everywhere I went, especially the characters, who were my companions throughout the day. I found I knew what their thoughts and reactions would be to what I faced. I was inspired to incorporate into the book everyday events and ordinary objects that I came upon. When I wasn't writing, I often had to stop what I was doing to make notes for the novel.

I never felt so alive! I wrote what I enjoyed reading, a character-driven story of personal growth. It was like I was the writer of fiction I fantasized about being as a young person but had put aside as my life went in other directions.

The book is littered with symbolism I would eventually discern, as though I was sending myself coded messages through it. Erika, the love interest of the protagonist, Ally, symbolized God's Love to me. I was deeply aware that the story, which was about Ally coming to feel worthy of Erika, was an allegory (*Ally*-gory, get it?) for my own coming to feel worthy of God's Love. (To this day I am in love with Erika and get a goofy smile if I talk about her.) My chest burst with almost unbearable Love, and I was sexually aroused when I wrote any scene involving connection or love between the characters, whether the scene was sexual or not. I had never given much thought or credence to chakras as spiritually significant before, but writing this book I became so aware of my heart, solar plexus, and sacral chakras I felt I understood how they were conflated with spirituality.

I was aware *A Good Woman* read like an ordinary romance and would not affect readers as it had me, but this did not detract from my enjoyment in writing it. I was confused, however, by what it was and what its value was, if anything. I was experiencing *expression* rather than *purpose*, which had been the shift in seeing I had been in for quite a while. Repeatedly, I brought myself back to "process, not product" regarding the book. This was not about outcome, but the expression of Love, no matter the form produced.

For quite a while, as I withdrew my projections of meaning onto the world, I had an experience of it as a stage full of scenery and props but with no story giving it meaning. It had become neutral and two-dimensional to me. But now, as The Golden blazed in my mind and I carried this story of Love with me everywhere, I felt the world was in me. I felt about it, in fact, just as I did about the book. I was the Author and everyone and everything was my beloved creation.

My sense of being had expanded. I no longer felt a boundary between me and the world, which was a lovely experience, but frightening in what it represented: My mind was undergoing a wholesale change. In my worst moments of disorientation, it felt like I had entered the funhouse mirrors of my mind. I doubted what I was experiencing was spiritual and feared The Golden was a mental aberration or possibly a sign of a menopausal mental break.

With all of this came a disconcerting change in personality that showed up now and then. This was the first appearance of what I would later label *transition-Liz*. She was relaxed, confident, light-hearted, and dynamic, the latter two traits being unfamiliar as the Liz I was used to was pretty much a stick-in-the-mud. When I felt this "stranger within", as I labeled her, my body language was different, too. My facial muscles relaxed, and I stood straighter.

I could not call up this new personality at will. It just showed up, usually when I was with others. Then I would wonder "Who *is* this?" Once, my sister, E, gave me a sharp look when I said something with uncharacteristic lighthearted wit, so I knew I did not just imagine that I was showing up differently.

I was afraid the story I was writing would stop coming to me, because I enjoyed writing it. But I was also afraid it would continue because I did not understand what was happening. These new experiences were fascinating, but I was terrified. I often sensed they were *only the beginning* of something significant. So much so that I sometimes thought the book might only be a side effect of something trying to break through.

(Dialogue 20170819) *"...But the golden feeling, I think, is about Real Perception. It is about Love. It's like that is trying to break through some blocking membrane and it can't quite make it but this story is what comes through instead. Maybe the membrane is like cheesecloth and the Love can't squeeze through whole and intact so what oozes through is some residue—the novel."*

Worrying about my sanity and distrusting new experiences was not how I would have wanted to feel when Love finally came to my conscious awareness, but at the time I was not sure that was occurring. It is easy to believe ahead of time that a shift to Spirit-consciousness will be recognized for what it is and be joyfully accepted. Just as it is easy to look back and remember only the Love and enjoyable creativity and forget the doubt and fear. I had no instruction manual that said, *"this* will happen at *this* juncture, *this* is what it will *feel* like, and *this* is what it will *mean."*

However shaken and confused; however much I vacillated between crushing inadequacy and attacks and Love and wonder, I eventually did settle in and roll with what was occurring:

(Dialogue 20170820) *"...I need to trust the process, yes. It's new and unexpected and different but I don't feel I'm off the rails."*

I certainly questioned if the book represented unfulfilled desires on my part, but no. As well as being happy in my marriage, I had no interest in being involved with someone new. I had long felt that if something happened to Jessie, I would not pursue another relationship. If it were to happen it would have to come to me, because I felt whole in myself and had no reason to seek it—or anything, really.

Anyway, falling in love is fun in fiction, but I always found it stressful in actual life. I had no desire for the drama common in the early stage of a new relationship. And I certainly never wanted to be in Ally's perceived situation through much of the book: in love with someone who did not return her feelings. I was happy to be past such hellish things.

The Golden and the writing brought a sense of renewal and seemed to bring life where I had been feeling barren and it was more than enough. I felt, in fact, that perhaps my *happily ever after* had come and it was with Love Itself. I hoped it would continue and wondered if writing fiction was the life-change I had sensed would occur in my mid-fifties. However, I had a feeling it was just part of something greater going on.

Jessie was uncomfortable because she was used to me being available to her when I wasn't with clients, and now my office door was more often than not closed to her as I needed long stretches of uninterrupted time to write. Ah, now the shoe was on the other foot! Jessie's games absorbed her, and I only interrupted her if I had something important to discuss with her. I often lamented that I missed sharing with her the everyday trivia that form the connecting web of a domestic relationship, because when she did have time for me, I had to use it up with significant matters.

But overall, as always, she was supportive, even if she did not understand. I explained how my writing came from an unexpected, intense burst of creativity that was somehow related to my spirituality. Not fully understanding it myself, this was hard to get across to anyone else, much less someone who did not understand my path. I told her I had been running from something for three years—since Ginny's death—and now I had no choice but to face it. She said it did not sound like me to run away or to be in denial.

This was generally true, but I was facing ego's undoing, an aspect of nonduality that she did not understand. To her, ego was God-given, and something to tame, not transcend. She had no concept of a shift in consciousness.

I recognized The Golden was the Vision of the holy relationship, the beginning of the real world. I was dismayed because it seemed the resistance to Love I recognized at the time of The Mansion/shack Insights had not changed in three years. I spent a lot of time and words in my journal analyzing this. I still believed there was something for me to do to get beyond this resistance. But now I know the resistance was a meaningless show of ego, no matter it made me uncomfortable.

As the direct attacks from ego diminished, depression crept in when I wrote, and I could not understand what it was. Each time I wrote, it hovered in the background and grew as the day went on. I looked at it from my usual formula of *depression=anger=fear=guilt*, but I could not seem to hit upon the source of the grief.

(Dialogue 20170825) *"...The depression (fear) does not affect the writing. Nothing in the writing, process or story, depresses me. But something about the process occurring, I think, may be causing the depression. The Golden is not affected by the writing or the depression, but I sense It is the cause somehow of the writing."*

I could only accept the depression and continue to write. Some days, however, it became oppressive, and I had to stop writing for the day. Eventually I learned to write with it hovering in the background.

(Dialogue 20170825) *"...Obviously I am not thoroughly depressed. I carry it around, but I do not see it as me. I feel it, but I don't identify with it. Something in my mind is depressed/fearful.*

And what part would that be?..."

I still *felt* ego; but I was not *identifying* with it. But I did not grasp the full significance of this. I no longer identified with what I had made of myself. The authority problem was corrected.

The Golden had come into the vast Spaciousness of my mind, so beyond the novel, I found my mind quieter than it had ever been. I was afraid, but I valued The Golden. It was the Vision of the holy relationship I had wanted since Emily. And about the holy relationship the *Course* says:

The holy relationship is the expression of the holy instant in living in this world...The holy instant never fails. The experience of it is always felt. Yet without expression it is not remembered. (T-17.V.1).

So, I was concerned: What would happen when I was done with the novel? How would the holy relationship be expressed without it?

<u>7</u>

Back in February of 2006, just as I began my Dialogues, I was thinking about the mystical holy relationship. I felt long past Emily, but I wanted to extend the awareness of my Self that began with her. I realized I would not have to start over. Any mystical holy relationship that came would be a continuation of what began with her. However, I felt that whether the mystical holy relationship was with Jessie or another it would "wipe out" the relationship I had with Jessie. The mystical holy relationship is Christ to Christ, and we had a practical holy relationship, not a mystical one. So, whether a mystical holy relationship was with her or another, it would not be the relationship we had.

But I also felt I did not require another to experience Oneness. When I acknowledged I still experienced Vision after Emily was gone, I realized the holy relationship was with Spirit. She had only been a symbol for me. I felt my relationship with her was simply the "doorway into" Vision. From then on, I expected that if I experienced Vision again, I would experience it everywhere—I would see the real world. So, it would not be a *relationship*, but Spirit-consciousness.

My experience of The Golden as the holy relationship only reinforced this expectation. The Light was with me as I went about my days, and simply glowed brighter when I wrote. However, I was to discover my expectation was mistaken regarding a mystical holy relationship with another but correct in that Oneness cannot really be said to be a *relationship*.

To teach and to stay in front of potential clients, I wrote articles each week that I put out in a newsletter and blog. An informal group of regulars posted at my blogsite on and off over the years, sharing their experiences, asking questions, and commenting about my articles or each other's posts. One of them was a woman named Hannah, whose sharing I often found rambling and incoherent. I found her writing lax, as she often didn't use punctuation, uppercase letters, and did not correct typos, and this only made her harder to understand. I also felt she overshared, leaving herself vulnerable to attack.

Moreover, this Hannah person seemed to rely a great deal on synchronicity. She saw coincidences between people, symbols, events, words, etc. as meaningful. This can be tricky, because one can interpret "signs" as they wish but decide that the universe is sending them a message. I felt that if a message *seemed* to come from outside of me through another or in symbols, the true source of the message was Spirit *within*.

I often saw connections and coincidences, more so as I advanced spiritually. I felt that as everything is interconnected, seeing this more often came with being more aware in general. I took synchronicity for granted, and mostly just enjoyed it. Rarely was I prompted by Spirit to pay attention to it.

But I was not sure how Hannah used synchronicity. And adding this to what I felt was her incoherence, if I thought of her at all over the years it would have been along the lines of *that kooky woman at my blogsite*.

Forty years old, a *Course* student for ten years, and a commenter at my blog for six, in July of 2016 Hannah contacted me by email for mentoring. She wrote:

"I actually have no idea what we will talk about. Questions that arise always seem to be answered fairly smarty these days, and the answers seem to be pretty much narrowing themselves down to a few focuses, but I trust you and im [sic] *really curious, I have no idea what the talk will bring about!..."*

She lived in Australia, so when we met for the first time the next month, we used Skype. She came to our first session frankly terrified. It is not unusual for clients to be nervous in our first meeting, as they intuitively know that speaking with me, they will face themselves. But no one had ever been this nervous. She could hardly speak.

However, my notes show we did get some conversation in, and she felt I gave her permission to accept how her life was unfolding at the time. It was six months before we met again.

Initially, I had mixed feelings meeting with Hannah, which was not usual for me. I generally enjoy my clients and look forward to speaking with each of them. Rarely do I have a client who is resistant, intellectually combative, or even egotistical, and they don't last long. Some are so depressed or self-pitying it is impossible to reach them. But even when a client is difficult for one reason or another, I only meet with them for an hour at most, so I do not feel strain. I simply do not look forward to meeting with them the way I do with my other clients.

But while I enjoyed much about Hannah—she is very bright, quick, and funny— I was uncomfortable because I found her to be what I thought from her postings at my blogsite: Inarticulate, with a mind that seemed interesting, but that I often found opaque and difficult to follow. She spoke in a kind of shorthand and used words and symbols in ways I was not used to. Just listening to her, I felt I was flailing, because I was never certain I understood her. I was married to someone who had ADHD and who often started stories in the middle and used words and symbols inaccurately, so I had learned with Jessie—and clients who also had ADD or ADHD—how to listen to and ask questions of people whose mouths could not keep up with their racing minds. But the skills I used with them did not take me far with Hannah. They only seemed to make matters worse.

It did not help that she had a heavy accent, often used Aussie-isms I was unfamiliar with ("I was at the servo in the arvo and that mate of mine I was telling you about rocked up in her ute..." *Huh?*), and that our Skype connection was usually poor.

In our first call, except for a moment when I thought she looked like Emily Blunt, whom I found cute, she manifested so much fear I found her unattractive. This was not usual for me either, and added to my discomfort. There are many people I do not find attractive, but that is something different from finding them *un*attractive. One is neutral, the other is negative. However, the *un* wore off over time and eventually I simply did not find her attractive.

Her nervousness and tension diminished over time, but she often could not speak, find the right words, or would lose her train of thought. She told me, each time, that this was not like her. I took her word for it, but nervous and inarticulate was the only way I knew her.

After a while, I felt that my not understanding her had to be due at least in some part to a limitation of mine, because others at my blogsite seemed to understand her when I could not. I also learned that she looked at synchronicity as a way in which she communicated with herself—or her Self communicated with her. She was not *reading the signs* but reading herself and she understood that.

I enjoyed her enough, though, that eventually I did look forward to our calls, even though I was concerned I would not understand her and that our Skype connection would make it worse. But I did not give her any more thought than I gave to any other client or blogger.

An empath and sensitive, Hannah also experiences precognition, often sensing what will unfold in the future for herself as well as for others. This was not something unusual to me, because my sister, E, is the same. So, I did not dismiss her when she told me that she felt we were meant to be more than mentor and client. She felt we were supposed to have a relationship on a more equal footing, but she did not know how to characterize what she felt beyond that.

I did not feel this at all. She was no different to me than any other client. But I told her that if she wanted to be friends, I could do that. I had a client before who had become a friend, and I knew of life coaches who coached their friends. It was a matter of being focused on the issue at hand in mentoring sessions and being a friend and not so much a mentor outside of a session.

She did not say so at the time, but Hannah felt *friends* was not quite what she felt we were to be. However, she was not clear on what we were to be, so she accepted my offer of friendship. For my part, I felt the friendship was something for her and not for me. We continued to meet only for our sessions, and I still did not give her any more thought than any other client.

My records show that we met a dozen times in 2017 as mentor and client before she emailed me toward the end of August—the month that the mystical holy relationship returned for me as The Golden Light of Love and I began *A Good Woman* —to tell me that she was ending mentoring because she had developed romantic feelings for me.

Unknown to me, Hannah had been having Golden experiences of her own. She had an episode where for a while she looked out at the world and saw her Love reflected back to her. Also unknown to me, Hannah had found things about me attractive for a while and had sexual dreams about me. About a month before she cancelled our sessions, she had one where we were making love in a void and we blended. She could not tell where one body ended and the other began. It was beautiful, deeply intimate, open, and trusting, and went far beyond sex.

In our sessions, she had shared that in her thirties she realized she was bisexual and went through the coming out process. So, I was not surprised that she *could* be interested in me romantically. But I did not take her feelings seriously, because I felt she didn't know me from Eve. I explained to her that this was probably just transference, a type of projection people go through with counselors of all sorts—therapists, life coaches, mentors, clergy, etc. As the client begins to feel good about themselves, they project this onto the counselor and can sometimes think they are in love. This had occurred with me a couple of times before with middle aged men, and it passed quickly.

Hannah respected this point of view and even trusted it, but she cancelled our sessions. We had not yet pursued our friendship outside of them.

My records show we met a week after I recorded receiving her email cancelling, so she must have gotten back in touch with me. As I told Jessie, I felt awkward, but was willing, as I knew Hannah's crush would pass. The gentlemen who had experienced transference with me had mentioned it only briefly in passing and seemed relieved once I explained it to them. It was never mentioned again.

However, I knew Hannah was likely to bring it up as she was learning to be open and honest with this type of thing. So, I decided I would be honest, too. I felt a little awkward, but I also felt her feelings were her responsibility, not mine. If we continued meeting and I felt her feelings were an issue, we could discuss it again. This is what I told her when we met.

But I discovered a whole new Hannah on that call. She was relaxed, open, and engaging. In fact, on a later call I felt a brief jolt of dangerous attraction and thought, "Oh, now don't be *appealing*."

As an empath, Hannah expects others can feel her as she feels them. She explained that much of her manifest discomfort in our calls just before she told me about her feelings was due to her being afraid I would feel her feelings for me. I explained that while I am intuitive, I am not an empath, and I rely on words and body language to read people. She had been so guarded in her body language it looked like the fear she had in our first calls. So, no, I did not pick up her attraction to me at all.

She told me that she felt it was safe to be honest with me because she knew I was happily married, and it could not threaten my marriage. She wanted to continue to meet with me, despite her feelings, and she felt that now that she had been honest, she would be more comfortable, open, and relaxed in our sessions, which she was. She also wanted to continue to be friends. I told her I still thought she was experiencing transference, that it would pass, and that I would work and be friends with her unless one of us became uncomfortable.

Our friendship took the form of email exchanges, and I had gotten to know Hannah enough by this time to be interested in her opinion of the book. But I had not told her about it because I felt there were some things in it that resembled her situation with me, and I felt it would be insensitive to ask her to read it, even though in subtle ways she had made her way into the book. (The word *petrichor*, for example.) But in either an email exchange or on a mentoring call, Hannah asked what kind of love stories I liked, and this seemed so out of the blue that I could not help but feel that she picked up on my involvement with one at the time. So, I told her about the book, and I first mentioned her as a friend in my journal on October 11, listing her as one of my pre-publication readers.

Jessie, too, would be one of my readers. When we met twenty-four years earlier, I had just submitted a romance novel to a publisher. I was rejected, but Jessie read it. She found it dry.

What Jessie noted about *A Good Woman* was that all but one of the characters were nice. Yes! It is an idealized love story; it is feel-good escapism. It is an expression of Love. But I somehow felt this was, if not exactly a criticism, an indication that it was not to her taste.

Those two works of fiction were the only books of mine she read.

<u>8</u>

I was so consumed with what was occurring with The Golden and the novel that nothing else had my attention for long. I struggled to understand what was going on. I spent a lot of time analyzing the meaning of the book in my life as well as the themes and symbols in it and what it all meant about my mind. All of this would turn out to be completely off the mark and, frankly, a waste of time, effort, and mind power. My journal from that time reads as more blathering on about ego and guilt and overcoming them. I did not see that I was far past all that.

Part of my discomfort at the time was a sense that I was done with the world and was just spinning in place. Certainly, I knew The Golden signaled some important shift, but I was confused by how strong ego still seemed to be, and why I continued to run with it. For a long while, I made the mistake of thinking that what arose from it was something to be undone before it could fall away. But I finally did question this:

(Dialogue 20171005) *"...Do I really have to visit all these judgments and feelings of lack and guilt and fear? Are they really what's hedging me in and preventing me from accepting Spiritual*

Vision?"

I also had my first insight about the grief I felt when I wrote:

(Dialogue 20171005) *"…Earlier I asked if I'd been grieving. But I suspect it was just resisting."*

I could only try to understand what was occurring in my mind in the context of what I thought I already knew. I was not wrong about a big shift occurring, but I was way off in understanding it. However, sometimes I sensed what was going on.

(Dialogue 20171016) *"Every time I feel Love wanting to expand through me into the story (the world?) I hit this limitation: death. There's no getting away from it. And now I want to open to another way to see it but I'm afraid I'll see…that maybe my whole life would be shaken up. But I guess I have to face that. I can't pretend I haven't seen this."*

As I edited *A Good Woman*, The Golden faded from my awareness and I missed it, but I also suspected it was partly integrated. I felt that there was something about the holy relationship emerging, but I was not sure if it was something about the holy relationship itself or something to do with an obstacle to it. For a few days, I flashed on the room I rented at the time of my holy relationship with Emily and recalled the occasion when all I could remember was Light sitting across the table from me after she and I had spent the day playing board games. At the same time, I saw the hearth in Erika's house in *A Good Woman*, out from which I always saw The Golden pouring. These two spaces felt the same to me, as though they were linked by a wormhole in spacetime that bypassed the thirty-three years between them. The thought *closed circle* came to me when this occurred. It was, after all, the same Light, and It is Timeless.

I already had another book in mind, its origins the book that had come to me the year before *A Good Woman* in that first mysterious burst of creativity. But while it was another story of a woman coming to accept love—it would turn out to be a classic coming out story—when it came time to write it, I felt none of the same chakra-opening bursts of Love.

Sometimes I wondered if I was writing just for the sake of writing, as this new book did not come the same way. But I enjoyed writing it, even though depression hovered as I did so. The Golden was not in my conscious awareness, but my other new experiences writing fiction remained, and I loved the characters as my children.

But what had happened to the holy relationship? I felt it had come to stay with The Golden as I wrote *A Good Woman*, but now The Golden was gone. How was it to be expressed now? I thought that maybe writing was a way to stay open to The Golden.

I grew more comfortable with the idea of being a writer. Unless I wrote a best seller there would be no money in it, but my life coaching business, which had always ebbed and flowed, had gone into deep ebb, and never flowed again. Maybe this was why.

My second novel, *Towing the Moon*, came easy at first, despite depression in the background when I wrote. I had come to see the depression was a form of resistance, and I found that by merely accepting it, I could write despite it. A frontal attack from ego came later, and I questioned whether I was to finish this book. I put it aside a couple of times, only to return to it each time.

While I accepted and enjoyed the writing, I didn't need it. The part of me to which it would have been important as a self-concept as well as an occupation was gone. I had no self-concept to massage, express, fulfill, or alter. And as for enjoyment—it was nice to do something I enjoyed, but it was not necessary to feel whole.

What went through my mind was, "Why now, when I

don't need it?" In ego, I was in lack, and the purpose for everything in my life was to make me whole in some way. But as Spirit, I am Whole, so I need nothing from a material life. It is merely a coinciding appearance. The questioning came from the fading ego point of view.

I was confused by the writing coming on the heels of The Spaciousness. I had felt, for a long time, that I was moving away from the world. I felt done with it. I felt I was expanding and then, to write, I had to contract. My mind had been free of the world, and then was suddenly filled with very worldly thoughts and feelings. I felt wrenched back to something I had willingly released. I could not reconcile this contradiction and wondered if I had gotten something about my path very wrong.

I had a sense of loss, but I was not sure what I had lost.

9

I had moved away from identity-spirituality and had dropped ideas like a Higher *Self*. But now that The Golden had come and I recognized it as the holy relationship, I recalled seeing my Self in Emily.

(Dialogue 20171122) *"...I wondered—is that Self the same thing I experience as the Golden? That I often felt as I wrote the book was emerging?..."*

I sensed The Golden heralded a big shift and the feeling that something was trying to emerge intensified as I went along. But this recognition of The Golden as my Self was the first time that I had a real clue about what was going on. Unfortunately, it got lost in my day-to-day confusion about The Golden and the novel.

It was at this time that I first mentioned the idea of a

hybrid-mind in my journal. I felt I had moved past my own split-mind and tapped into the *universal split-mind,* or what the *Course* calls the *Son of God.* This was another way I expressed my sense that I was shifting to Spirit, although I was far from labeling it so at the time.

My sense of loss began to crystalize:

(Dialogue 20171126) *"Two or three times today I experienced a fear that I can only describe as a breathtaking sense of losing my humanness. This is, I think, the fear that underpins that fear I've had on and off for a while that choosing Truth now would result in being 'dead in the world'. It was like choosing death while the body is alive...*

... I used to comfort myself with the thought that I'd still exist without the self. But now I experience that and it is not comfort. There is a sense of a loss there is no return from.

I've also seen that the (ego) fears my continuing on without it. Which I find interesting because why would it matter to it? It's done either way.

Ah! Perhaps because if it is gone through the death of the body it feels it has succeeded in destroying 'me'. But if I go on without it, it proves I don't need it..."

This insight preceded an episode of feeling like I was flying without a net or hurtling downward through open space. I was so terrified that I could not look directly at this. But I was also aware that it was too late, and I could only ride out whatever was to come. It was out of my control.

I continued to feel I was a ghost in the world and done as a self, even as I wrote *Towing the Moon,* confused to still be writing.

At the end of February, I wrote in my journal about midlife issues coming up, mostly to do with a sense of limited time left. I did wonder if my creative burst was a midlife crisis—and perhaps The Golden was an aberration—but I didn't feel in crisis. I felt my mind was in a transformation of some kind. Even so, I asked myself what I wanted the time left in this life to be about, and the answer was immediate: The holy relationship. By this I meant Vision—the real world. But this question arose after the answer was already unfolding.

(Dialogue 20180226) *"Again, I just watch all of this. I do not have to make anything happen. It is happening. This is what is different from past shifts/transformations. In the past I felt I had to do something. I didn't. It was then as it is now. I'm just feeling it move through me, but it's not about me making something happen..."*

I felt that like most people who ask themselves this question in midlife, I harkened back to a happy and satisfying time of my life when I answered with *the holy relationship.*

(Dialogue 20180226) *"Oh, such joy to be finally back here again! I am sure there will be rocky parts, especially at the beginning, but I am willing to go through them because they will pass and the outcome will be rewarding. Been there done that partly, anyway. I mean this specifically about the holy relationship but also about shifts to other stages that were always rougher in the very beginning."*

(*Rocky parts.* Oh, how naïve that sounds now!)
I continued to revisit my holy relationship with Emily.

(Dialogue 20180308) *"...was feeling the Light upon me like from back then and it went through my mind, 'Now your <u>real</u> work begins.' Oh, thank You very much. Whatever that means."*

But I did recognize Vision was forgiveness and had a preview of what I was to see almost a year later in a quite different (and totally unforeseen at this time) circumstance about my former material life:

(Dialogue 20180311) *"...Then my mind goes onto life and choices made and not made and possibilities, etc. And I realize Vision wipes it all out. It's all of a piece and Vision erases the whole piece. That's forgiveness and it's right here for the taking. There are no problems to solve or errors to correct."*

Despite recognizing at times that I was in a process that I only had to watch unfold, my journal rambled on with the usual attempts to find my obstacles to Vision and Love. One seeming obstacle was feeling "I'm too small", as at times Love seemed to overwhelm me and I felt I couldn't take It in.

(Dialogue 20180314) *"The fact is, I won't exist as I am. It is not 'Liz will receive Love'. It is the mind will be Love. And that's a wholly different experience..."*

Feeling too small was ego. But it still felt like me—although clearly not all the time anymore—and I still felt it had to be overcome. Sometimes, however, I recognized that the insights I had about my psychology or obstacles were the *effects* of the shift I was in and only had to be seen and were not meant to *cause* the shift by motivating me to do something about them.

As always, Spirit was right here, in my unconscious. So, I was aware I understood much more than rose to conscious awareness only now and then. This is why I came to feel my conscious awareness was the least significant aspect of my mind.

10

As well as sensing the timing of larger things unfolding in me and in my material life, I often sensed, even if only briefly, if someone was going to be significant to me, as I did with Emily and Jessie. With each, it was upon first meeting them. But I had no such experience with Hannah, even though I had known of her for a few years at my blog and had known her for over a year as mentor and friend. Before that, the only thing that may have been recognition was when I saw her full name in my email indicating that she had posted at my blog (she wrote under two names), and I felt a teensy niggle that I could not identify. At the time I figured it was just that she had an aesthetically pleasing name.

And even though she came more fully into my life at the same time as The Golden, the writing, and the sense something larger was going on, it never once occurred to me that there might be a relationship between those and this new friendship.

Hannah and I bonded over *A Good Woman*, even though she *was* triggered by parts of it. But she worked through that, and our friendship grew over the next months, into 2018. I felt a satisfying intellectual and emotional connection with her, and enjoyed her wit, intellect, and charm, even though I still did not always understand her mind.

I tend to find people more attractive the better I know them, and this occurred with Hannah, too. But I was not particularly attracted to her. It was funny to think, however, that I had once found her *un*attractive.

Her love for me was warm and inviting, and I was surprised to sense the strength of it. (I was to learn that as well as being an empath, Hannah has a strong mind that sends as well.) It reminded me of my mother's love, which was just there, and did not have to be earned. I had not asked for it, after all, and I wasn't looking for it, so it was a nice gift to simply receive.

But I became entangled in blurred lines between our professional relationship, friendship, and her romantic love for me. While I enjoyed the gift of her love, I wasn't sure about the morality of accepting it when I did not return it. But she assured me that, while she had some rough moments, she wanted to love me without making claims.

That was fine for her part, but I was not certain about mine. I felt it was spiritualizing ego for her to try to make her personal love for me unconditional. True Love just is and is wholly apart from the material experience. So, It is not directional, and is neither conditional nor unconditional. Only ego sets conditions for love or strives for unconditional love to attempt to be Spirit-like. Of course, this fails, leading to martyrdom and reinforcing guilt. I felt it was best to accept ego as it is, with its limitations and conditions, without judging them, which only makes them real.

But Hannah had a somewhat hippie upbringing, which, I felt, leads to a lot of beliefs and approaches that attempt to spiritualize ego. So, she did not agree, and I let her follow her own path while I wondered if I should let her go. I did not wonder too much, however, and told myself her feelings for me were her business, not mine. I wrangled much more with whether we should continue in our professional relationship. She left that up to me.

We began to have more and more synchronicity between us, deepening my sense of connection with her. Synchronicity and intuitions were natural to me, as they had been part of my relationships with my mother and my sister, E, and were aspects of any intense or long-term relationship I was in. I took these experiences for granted where most others, like Jessie, thought them remarkable. Of course, they were natural to Hannah, too.

During my marriage to Jessie, I sometimes experienced strong emotional responses to other women early in my friendships with them, one of them romantic. Each time, I didn't take it seriously, and felt it would be brief and pass, and I was correct. So, as I felt my connection with Hannah grow, I told myself it was the same as those other experiences. But it was not. This time I felt my marriage was threatened.

But the feelings themselves were not different, so it could only be that *I* was different. However, I did not look at this. Instead, I felt I was in a weakened condition with everything else going on within me, and therefore I should not take my feelings seriously this time as well. I reasoned that just because this time something felt different, it did not mean it would not pass as the others had.

It still did not occur to me that this new relationship could be part of the shift going on. I resolved that if I came to feel there was a real threat to my marriage, I would let Hannah go, as I valued Jessie and my marriage above all.

In the middle of March, I considered how I always had it in the back of my mind that the Vision of the holy relationship would come again for me. But, again, I still thought it would be only a general experience, not include a specific relationship. And I felt it *had* come as The Golden, which, though I was not experiencing it as I had, I felt was not lost.

Then, while thinking about Emily and the holy relationship, I suddenly wondered if I was to Hannah what Emily had been to me, a first holy relationship that I did not share with her. I have no record of thinking of Hannah in terms of a holy relationship before this.

In early April, new and intense experiences continued. When I wrote, I felt "I am the book!" I recalled feeling this with the first novel as well. This was like feeling the world was my creation and was in me. I felt fully myself when I wrote. I felt in a new world, not the book's world, but where the book came from within my mind.

Of course, I was not actually *the book*, nor was it my *creation*, as the *Course* uses that term. I knew even as I had these early experiences of Oneness that I did not fully understand them. They were brief and intense, and I could not get my mind around them. But as I got used to and was in these experiences longer, I realized I did not feel One *with* objects, but I felt Oneness *and* there was an appearance of a world. So, I was the Source of the *Love* (Oneness, Unity, Wholeness) extending from me as I wrote, which was a coincidental appearance enveloped by my Extension. Oneness—the real world—was my new world.

(Dialogue 20180403) *"…I'm thinking how this whole thing with the book is so strange and unexpected, and it occurred to me that the first holy relationship experience was strange and unexpected at the time. And I'm laughing at this, 'yes, it was' when it goes quietly through my head: 'This is the way back to it.'"*

Way did not refer to *means*, but to what was unfolding in front of me. I *was* on my way.

I knew that Love coming into my awareness was "the real going away". My life as it was, was over. I was experiencing the "real shift" in consciousness, not just the "shifts in place" that I had experienced before. But then I had a shift about the shift. I had been focused on the books and The Golden, but felt I wasn't seeing something significant. And then I saw it.

(Dialogue 20180406) *"I think the promise I felt at the beginning with* ACIM *and the holy relationship is being fulfilled. I've learned not just a nicer way of being in the world. I've learned the way to leave it. And when I'm there, there's no sense of loss, there's no sadness. There's no sense of leaving something behind, like going from one world to another. If I think of loved ones, there's an awareness all that is not real. And I <u>see and feel</u> that. It's a lifting out of nothingness to What is…*

… It feels beyond the experience I have called holy relationship, Vision, the Golden, True Perception, Real World, etc. Who knew?! I know I felt this at the beginning. But somewhere along the line the Vision became the expected goal. I thought that when the

Golden came, that was it. But then I got stuck. Nothing more happened. I have spun in processes and insights, and became aware I was getting nowhere real with them. I tried to emphasize the Golden, but that seemed more of the same. <u>This shift is beyond all of that.</u>

I am leaving. <u>And that is breathtaking</u>...

... And the Golden was the signal I'm ready. I mistook It for the goal. It was a symptom, a leading indicator, the canary in the coal mine (though this is rather grim), as it were.

I was about to write, 'I say I'm ready, but I don't know exactly what I'm ready for, do I?' And I was reminded of ACIM about this stage 'You thought you learned willingness, but now you realize you didn't know what you were willing for.' Or somesuch. Close enough..."

I had briefly got caught up in my state of consciousness and lost sight of its Source, the real significance of this shift. This is what I sensed and felt, rightly, was corrected.

(Dialogue 20180407) *"After yesterday's shift on understanding the shift, my mind has been quiet. I feel such relief, because now I see more clearly what happened and how things fit. And I have had all day that feeling of humility.*

So what's changed? My relationship to everything, it feels. I don't really know what it's going to mean day to day, moment to moment. I don't know if the feeling of going will mean the body falling away or just the ego. I also have no expectation that it is soon. It's just this is what that big shift three and a half years ago meant was starting. It's what the Golden was about. I have been dealing in effects and missing their cause. And I'm relieved now because I knew I wasn't seeing something. I just couldn't see it until I saw it!"

I know something in hindsight that I was nowhere ready to see at the time. Obviously, Sight of the real world occurs in consciousness, so Seeing the real world could not be the source of feeling I was "going away." But its Source, Christ, is the Bridge between consciousness and God, so Christ is the End of consciousness. So, it was not because I shifted *consciousness*, but because I shifted *identity*, that I felt I was leaving, and the shift was so traumatic for me.

Three days after the shift about the shift, I better understood The Golden—and the shift.

(Dialogue 20180409) "*...And then I had a thought that made me gasp: What if the Golden didn't 'break into' my mind but I rose up to It but have not fully realized this?...*
...Is that Christ's Vision?...
...I've had glimpses and there was the holy relationship. But this is being lifted to that level, not just passing through..."

(Dialogue 20180415) "*I'm trying to characterize how this shift is different from what has come before. It is so different. I found myself thinking of my first experiences of Vision. And all that have followed have been the same. It's as though what I saw was a view of where I was headed. But this new view is from that place. It's as though I used to flash on a distant hill, but this view is from that hill looking back to from where I came. And it's a different view of it. Instead of seeing the Light I'm looking out from the Light on what I used to see without It.*
Is this not Christ's Vision? And what I had before was a Vision of Christ."

This was the first time in *years* that I thought in terms of *Christ*. Unconsciously, I returned to identity-spirituality, as I was aware I was not just seeing differently, but had shifted to a different Seeing—a different place in my mind.

11

My journal—Dialogues— began as my conversations with Spirit about my spiritual process. I often wrote in it for clarity; to sort things out. In time, I recorded spiritual insights, shifts, experiences, and understanding. It was never a diary of my material life. Jessie, who was so central to that life, was rarely mentioned. Our relationship was well established by the time I started the journal, and we did not have issues in our relationship that crossed over into my spiritual life.

But this changed as I found I was again experiencing a singular expression of the mystical holy relationship. It felt to me the boundary between my inner and outer lives was gone —an experience I would not fully understand for well over two years.

(In email sent to Hannah, 20180423) *"I think (wow, massive déjà vu) I would like to fire you as a mentee and just be friends with you. And something more that I am unsure of. I think you may be a mighty companion. But I feel you are in my life now for a purpose... I think we may have a Holy Relationship, which I have many times suspected, but, again, I am never sure when I am projecting. I suppose I would say I have a holy relationship with you whether you are aware of it or not...I've been too massively confused about everything and untrusting what I've seen/felt, so I haven't said anything earlier."*

The previous month, I suspected Hannah had a holy relationship with me, but I did not feel it with her. Now, I discovered that it might be the other way around. This type of projection would characterize much of my relationship with her.

As my holy relationship with Hannah eased slowly into my awareness, I was confused by various personal feelings for her. I was concerned I was projecting feelings from the characters in my books onto her. I could not separate out my material feelings from the holy relationship.

As remarkable as this realization about a new holy relationship would seem to have been, my journal for the rest of that day and the next two is filled instead with issues that came up as I finished *Towing the Moon*. However, I continued to see the boundary between inner and outer was gone in other ways.

(Dialogue 20180426) *"I am the book! No wonder I feel it as I do... And somehow, in a way that I don't understand (thus the confusion and resistance), <u>therein lies the Love</u>!*
...Somehow, I feel more fully alive in it. I disappear into it. Or, is it, there is no 'I', so it feels 'disappeared'? I am pure conduit. No! <u>I am the book</u>!..."

(Dialogue 20180427) *"...When I began AGW I felt the whole world lived in me. This is the same thing. There is no 'I' in the world. I am the world! But I experience it through writing. The boundary of the 'I' is gone...."*

(Dialogue 20180428) *"...Earlier today I was writing to Hannah about our holy relationship and how it was different from what I experienced with Emily in that with Emily I had that experience of recognition, of looking in a mirror and with her (Hannah) it is more a dropping of boundaries between our minds. Extension! And I realized that 'I am the book' is very close to the experience I had with Emily. But, of course, the Golden, Hannah, 'I am the book', all blur together for me. They are part of one experience..."*

I had a couple of sexual dreams about Hannah, which I took to symbolize our Oneness. She wished they meant more to me, but she accepted that they did not. In the meantime, I was surprised by how natural the holy relationship was this time.

(Dialogue 20180429) *"...It's so fascinating to me how the holy relationship seeped back in with no fanfare. Well...the Golden was pretty dramatic, and it's all part and parcel of the whole experience I'm having. But Hannah...when did it happen exactly, you know? It was just there, and it's like, oh, yes, of course. It's remarkable how unremarkable it's been. So natural and effortless... None of the fear (unconscious guilt) of the first time. None of the shock. Because, well...I've been there in a way ever since, haven't I? I just grew more and more aware of it until I was ready for it to more fully show up again. Ah, full circle! Promise fulfilled."*

That night I wrote that I dreamt I wanted to get physical with Hannah and I pursued her around her house, even though Jessie was there. Hannah was uninterested, however, and I couldn't tell if it was because I was married or if, now that I was there, she realized she was not attracted to me after all.

I thought the dream may have had to do with not yet having told Jessie about my holy relationship with Hannah. The Unity of a mystical holy relationship is far more intimate and satisfying than anything an emotional relationship can offer. If I described this to Jessie, how could she not feel threatened? I wasn't sure how much I would explain. When I first met Jessie, I tried to make my holy relationship with Emily clear to her, but she did not understand. It is not possible to *convey* Oneness; it must be experienced.

Yet, I would not keep something as significant as this from Jessie for long, no matter how hard to express. The longer I waited, the more it would seem I had something to hide. I waited for the right moment to tell her to arise organically, but it was on my mind all the time.

What seemed like an issue for my marriage, however, was only part of something much greater occurring. Later that evening I wrote:

(Dialogue 20200430) *"...There has been such a complete break in my life in the world that it no longer seems to me that where I am now continues the narrative I was in before. Yes, I've said I've come full circle, etc. But I feel such a huge shift occurred that that life is gone. It got me up to the point where this shift could occur, but it is not related to the shift...it is since the Golden that I feel I have changed greatly. I want to say I'm a different person. But I'm not sure it's a person I feel different as. This mind has changed greatly more like. The self-concept fell away and the self is falling away..."*

The episode I refer to as *The Terrible Conflict* had begun.

The next day, I read an email from Hannah in which she responded rather friskily to my dream, and suddenly I was not confused about my feelings for her. I acknowledged my in-every-way attraction to her, all of which felt part of the holy relationship. The whole relationship felt *given* rather than formed the usual way, an experience that would expand later. Suddenly, the dream seemed to have been a premonition. (It would turn out it foreshadowed not just my interest in Hannah, but her eventual response.)

I could not help but notice that situations I had only recently wrote about in my novels—and *never* wanted to live out—were showing up in my life. Certainly, there were parallels between Hannah's situation with me and Aly's with Erika in *A Good Woman*. And now I was in a position like Mary's in *Towing the Moon*!

Hannah and I felt our spiritual and material experiences of each other were one thing and could not be separated. This was in line with my overall feeling of the boundaries in my mind being gone. Yet, I felt the holy relationship (by which I meant awareness of Unity) was the priority for me and, while I acknowledged my material feelings for Hannah, I did not want to pursue them. Frankly, they were not particularly strong. I felt *within* Love with Hannah rather than *in love with* her. I valued my marriage.

But I did acknowledge that I felt my other life was over and that I was in a new world with Hannah. I put it that I felt "on the ground" with Jessie and "in the ether" with Hannah. So, I set boundaries with Hannah. Some light flirting was okay, but we would not engage in any overtly sexual banter. She said she accepted our spiritual-only relationship and that it was enough for her, although she could not separate out the material and the spiritual herself.

A couple of days after acknowledging my feelings to Hannah, I took Jessie out to dinner for her birthday. I was preoccupied during the meal as I considered how to tell her about my holy relationship with Hannah. But I was nagged by something just out of my grasp. It did not seem to be the holy relationship or even that I was attracted to Hannah. I wanted to be clear on whatever it was before I spoke to Jessie.

Dinner over, I waited outside the restaurant while Jessie went to the restroom. And while I waited for her, it hit me what was bothering me: Ever since I recognized the holy relationship with Hannah I had been hearing in my mind, "Here's your new partner; get to know her." I was bothered because I felt I had another *partner*.

It was absurd to feel this in so short a time, but it was part of feeling the relationship was *given* and of being in a new world with Hannah. My partnership with her was simply here, already established. It did not have to be made. It was a relief to find what had been nagging me, especially as I was clear it was exactly what I felt. But it was also difficult to see.

I realized, however, that this was the way to explain the holy relationship to Jessie. Now that I was clear, I felt I could keep it light, like this was no big deal. So, when she came out, I informed her, casually, of my holy relationship with Hannah by telling her that I felt I had a spiritual partner in Hannah.

At the word *partner* a look crossed Jessie's face that must be what someone looks like when they are hit in the head with a baseball bat. It was fleeting, but I registered it, and somehow her being so rocked signaled to me that something much more significant was occurring than I was willing to accept. Later, I would look back and realize that this was the moment I knew our marriage was over.

Jessie asked me to explain, and I did my best. As always, she wanted to be supportive, because she wanted me to be happy. Our conversation continued in the car as I drove us down the strip mall parking lot to a bookstore Jessie wanted to wander through. We sat in the car and talked for a while. I acknowledged to Jessie that my spiritual connection to Hannah came with a physical and emotional attraction, but I explained that this was not particularly meaningful to me. I thought those feelings were probably symbolic and would pass. I was happy with Jessie, and I wanted to be with her.

This situation was not entirely without precedent in our marriage, and Jessie acknowledged this. She had had an emotional relationship in one of her online games with another gamer through their avatars. I was a possessive lover, which Jessie liked about me, as it made her feel secure. But this came at a time when she felt it would facilitate some healing for her and, with boundaries that made us both feel secure (the same ones I established with Hannah), I agreed. That relationship ended after a few years, having served its purpose for Jessie.

Polyamory was something Jessie and I had discussed theoretically over the years as the issue came up in books or movies. But it was not something either one of us wanted to pursue. Jessie had been in a three-way relationship when she was young, and it had not gone well. However, she felt that she was more comfortable with blurred lines in relationships than I was. I tended to be single minded and focused, and I didn't spread myself around emotionally. So, while our arrangement was not out of her comfort zone for herself, she was uncomfortable because she knew it did not come naturally to me.

She was also threatened because she knew Hannah shared my spiritual path, which was most important to me. But she said she hoped to connect with Hannah someday. She felt she was in a relationship with Hannah now, too.

Our marital boat was rocked, but we felt, although this was unprecedented, we would make it through this together, as we did everything else. We knew we would talk about it more in coming days and went into the bookstore, glad to have something to do as we both had a lot to process.

12

I so wanted to feel some relief for having put everything honestly out there but, in fact, I felt much worse as I walked around the bookstore. Who was this happening to? This was all so unlike me that I could not find myself. I didn't want another partner; I didn't want any kind of three-way relationship.

But while this was true, it was not the real issue, and I knew it. I would rather it was! I sensed my conflict was not to be short term, and it could not be resolved by being open, because it was not about my material life. I felt I had stepped further into something I did not understand, and it was only just beginning. And whatever this was, it was taking me far from anything I understood and was familiar to me. It was totally out of my control, and I had no framework for it.

I knew this shift was to do with Truth, and that I was going to discover things I did not yet know. I was overwhelmed. In a way, I felt that I—or what I had thought I was—was obliterated by whatever I was entering. I no longer felt anything familiar within that I knew as *me*. It is hard to convey the sense of having entered *a completely alien landscape within myself*.

I was certain I was experiencing the spiritual shift I had always wanted, but it was nothing like I had expected, and I was dismayed. The joke was on me, because it was coming at a much higher price than I had anticipated—*me*.

I wrote in my journal that I was willing, only because that had always been my posture, but, really, she who had been willing was *gone*. I was something unrecognizable to me that had no choice but to endure what was to come, because I could feel the movement of something big that was going to run no matter what. I knew resistance would make it even more difficult, so I breathed deeply and accepted and tried to stay open. But I was, if not afraid, *extremely* uncomfortable—and comfortless. This was a disappointment, too. I wished I could feel joy in this shift, but simply did not.

In the next days, I felt I was being dismantled within, as though structures in my mind were being broken down. In my discomfort, instead of simply watching it unfold, I was, for quite a while, too quick to label, characterize, and draw conclusions about each new experience. My journal is filled with efforts to fit all the pieces together before I even had all the pieces, because I was desperately hoping each new piece was the last piece. I did not like the sense that I was only at the start of a huge, uncomfortable shift, the length and end of which I could not see. I had such a sense of pressure at this point, I thought changes in my personal life were being rushed to prepare me for something coming. I thought that Hannah, and maybe some others, were part of a support system being put in place for me.

Jessie continued to be supportive.

(In email to Hannah, 20180503) *"...Jessie and I also discussed 'our marital boat is rocked' and we both feel it is not tipping over. It's more like we're shifting around on the boat and causing it to rock temporarily. She is such a blessing! A true partner. I am blessed. This morning she asked how you felt about me referring to you as a partner. She wanted to make sure you responded in a way that met my needs, the dear!..."*

Jessie joked that if we somehow came into money, she hoped I would not take off for Australia. She acknowledged she considered leaving after I referred to Hannah as a partner, as her security was her highest value, and our new situation was undermining it. But she decided to stay and see where this went. I felt, and assured her, that the shifting I felt was within me. I did not feel a need to change my material life.

I felt strongly, but did not express to Jessie, that I was already with Hannah in a new dimension. Hannah expressed that she, too, experienced our Oneness not as *joining* but as *already so*.

I felt with Hannah in the same dimension from which The Golden came. In fact, I noted as I formatted *A Good Woman* for Kindle that I suspected the reason I wasn't experiencing The Golden as I had when I wrote it was because now I was in The Golden. Love was my new Context.

I desperately wished the shift was just this "arranged partnership" I felt with Hannah, and that the only consequence was how it challenged my relationship with Jessie. How small and simple and manageable that seemed! But I could not escape the feeling all around me that something more significant was only beginning.

And then I saw something that totally rattled me: Hannah was my future. This came in a kind of nonmaterial Seeing that was not totally unfamiliar, but which I was used to pertaining only to my inner life or to the long-term unfolding of my material life. I was rattled by what I saw and *that I saw it*. Again, a boundary was gone, and this Seeing seemed to be part of the new State I was easing into. But was I seeing what was to happen or was this some new kind of fantasizing? It came to me as these things had been coming, in my sense of being within a huge movement. It was not like any fantasy.

This Seeing—both the Seeing itself and what I saw—led me to feel at times that I was going down a rabbit hole. Who saw things like this about, and then reported them to, someone who was a virtual stranger, as I did to Hannah? I had a horrible sense of disorientation that I could only ride out.

I felt not just that Hannah was my future, but that *I*

would be going to *her*. And she, too, saw me there with her. This was a type of Seeing that she was used to. But since I could not think of leaving a valued wife and happy marriage, I could only assume Hannah was some *distant* future for me.

On one hand, I felt I was not yet the Liz I saw with Hannah on the material level. But on the other, I already felt so thoroughly with her it was as though there was no difference between the present and the future. It was like spacetime was one of those structures in my mind breaking down. The Unity of the mystical holy relationship is *always*.

My conflict intensified as I felt I was living two lives, one material and the other in Spirit. When I was in one, the other felt unreal. I tried desperately to reconcile them and thought for a time I was not to do so and was meant to live two irreconcilable lives. I thought maybe this was the way I was to experience my mind without its former boundaries.

I continued to experience the absence of boundaries between my mind and Hannah's. I was very confused about her in my life, but I also felt she was a gift given. Where I used to think of a holy relationship as for a purpose—for the two in it and/or for the world—I saw it was now a natural expression of my new State. If I was involved with someone, I would have a mystical perception of a holy relationship. Yet, I still felt I didn't *need* it. It was so new to me to be in a state of abundance without a purpose for it that Jessie said it was as though I had a cake with which I was happy and now I found it had frosting, too.

13

A friend of Jessie's had a coupon for a complementary night at a lodge at Mt. Charleston that she was not going to use. She gave it to us for our twenty-third wedding anniversary, which had just passed in April. So, a little over a week after I told Jessie about Hannah, we went up to the mountains, a 45-minute drive from the middle of the city.

I was in a state of constant low-grade anxiety and was longing for the dry emptiness of The Barrenness of the previous four years. It had been uncomfortable, sure, but familiar. It was also identifiable, even if I had not been certain what it represented. But now I was not only having new experiences, I didn't recognize who was having them. Nothing was familiar in me. I looked forward to having time to process in a quiet, natural environment.

At the mountains, I had the first of what felt like *thunderous* insights into what was occurring. These produced a stunned sensation, as though someone had banged a large gong right next to my ear. They felt profoundly significant.

These happened in the Context of a Great Presence that I felt over and all around me. I called this *The Hugeness*. I knew this was Spirit in my mind, but I could understand why some, historically, felt this was a physical visitation from God. I did not expect anyone else to feel what I did, yet it was so powerful I was still amazed they did not. I was nearly overwhelmed.

The Hugeness was to come and go for quite a while, always signaling an insight or clarification, and I wondered if it was to be my new normal. (It was not.) Of course, The Hugeness was the entirety of my mind as I came out of denial. My sense of being was expanding. But at that time, what I felt was "a becoming", like I was shedding skin as something in me emerged.

It was refreshing to be up in the mountains in so much quiet, even with The Hugeness. I felt a respite from the chaos my mind was in, since for the first time in a while I was able to turn inward into a clear mind that was like a long well-lit room.

I felt distant from Hannah, and I told Jessie that my material feelings for Hannah were "shallow rooted". I didn't know her. My feelings for her had not grown in the usual way. I grappled with who she was to me and why she was in my life.

I explained to Jessie that my personal feelings were no longer significant to me anyway and they no longer motivated me to act. She did not understand this and thought I was denigrating myself. But I left it at that, as I had no way of explaining in a way she could understand movement that came from Wholeness rather than personal need or want.

I wished I had a couple of more days in the mountains—preferably alone so I could simply feel and process. But we returned home.

(Dialogue 20180511) "...Feeling far from Hannah... Have questioned whether this is some weird midlife crisis, etc. Did not think so...questioning if I've been misunderstanding my feelings for her, misleading her. Then I find myself laughing at something she wrote and there it is: The tiniest joy niggle in my solar plexus where the Light and Joy pour out. Oh, it is so not like being in love. I saw a commercial the other day that reminded me of what that joy is like when one is first in love, and compared it to what I feel with Hannah and it is like a lamp to the sun. And, frankly, just different. Not whole, like this Joy with Hannah, my playmate in Light and Love. <u>I so do not understand this!</u> But here it is. I meet her in the Joy. And though my personal feelings may be shallow now, they are there. And I feel...dammit, I don't know how else to put it... they come from the future. <u>What the hell does that mean??? How can this be???</u> Is spacetime really collapsing? Or am I having some kind of mental breakdown and taking this poor woman along for a ride??? (I know she would say she could not be taken for a ride. But, still, it's hard when I do not know what is going on with me.)..."

This began intense and disorienting vacillations between ego and Spirit that went on for quite a while. And nowhere in them would I find myself or anything familiar to hold onto.

I also began to feel ego's resistance to Hannah as a symbol of Love when I spoke with her or would even consider speaking with her. I recognized this, as I had been through it in my holy relationship with Emily, although it took a different form. With Emily, I heard "Get away from her!", and although I understood ego as something apart from me for the first time, I continued to identify with it. Now, ego was something held in suspension in the space of my mind rather than me.

(Dialogue 20180511) *"...I felt earlier that feeling again of certainty that I can trust that this is not to be painful. Any of the darker or negative feelings are just faulty thinking. I don't mean this like I'll go through pain but the outcome will be joyful. I mean, even what I'm going through now is not meant to be painful. It is only because of my own faulty thinking. So I can trust that the negative feelings are a mistake..."*

Occasionally during this episode, I heard in my mind "soft unfolding for all" in relation to Jessie and Hannah and me. At the time, I took it to apply to what was unfolding immediately. But now, in retrospect, I see what was being described was my entire experience of ego winding down and Spirit emerging. I was uncomfortable with how long it took, and ego did not break down gently or quietly, but now I see that, because it was a *process*, it was softer than a sudden shift would have been.

14

With Hannah I did not keep to the strict boundaries I had set. I did not feel good about myself in this. I also discovered that I was correct in my suspicion that the person in the middle of a three-way relationship was inherently in a selfish position. I felt very selfish.

I was not just someone I did not recognize; I was often someone I did not like. Yet I had nothing else! Not when it came to the person or ego. I trusted I was in Spirit. It was the Context in which all this was occurring. I felt that. But I could not access Spirit as I once did, by turning to It for guidance. There was no longer a *me* to seek guidance. I suspected I was shifting to Spirit as my Identity, yet I was not manifesting that yet, and was stuck somewhere between where I had been and Where I was going.

Jessie seemed to settle down. We made an appointment to see her therapist together, but she decided she wanted to speak with her alone. Jessie also wanted to have some kind of acquaintanceship with Hannah. She felt that if something bad happened to me, it would be awkward for that to be the first situation in which they connected. She expected one day she would Skype with Hannah. Hannah was amenable to this, but I did not know how I felt, largely because I did not experience them at the same level. It didn't feel to me that my two worlds could blend.

As much as I felt Hannah was my future, I lost my sense of connection to her if I thought of the future because I had such a strong sense of our relationship as *here/now*. When I expressed this to Hannah, she said it's like we're more than inevitable; it's like we've already happened.

At one point I asked her if she ever felt uncomfortable as the "other woman" and she replied tentatively, "Actually, I feel Jessie's the other woman." This, and moments on Skype when I had a deep recognition of her, confirmed what I felt before and was growing stronger: The Golden marked the end of one life and the beginning of another. I was in a new life, not a continuation of the other.

(Dialogue 20180514) (*Oz is a nickname for Australia.*)
"*...What about Jessie? My fear is that Jessie was the partner of the mind that was self-identified...the one with the story that ended with self-identification. Although I can say I don't feel done in this classroom. I have felt done with the life I had. But is my relationship to this classroom, therefore Jessie, going to change? Or has it*

already? Has it in these last years without me realizing it? I live in terror of losing her and hurting her. That's what some of my anxiety is about. Or do I project my terror of the holy relationship onto this idea? Is it just the idea of sacrifice and has no merit? I don't feel when I am with her that we're over. I only fear that is where all of this leads.

Sometimes I think I'm not jumping all in because of the fear of losing Jessie and all that is familiar because I'm to run off to Oz or something. Although, there are other obstacles, too. Practical ones, like money, occupation, emigration rules. But, no, going to Oz doesn't seem quite right, either. Gentle unfolding. Sometimes I get the sense that, as it unfolds and becomes more clear, I will look back and laugh at these fears and go, 'Of course it wouldn't happen that way.'"

In the middle of the month, I was balancing my checkbook when it came over me how un-portable my life was; how bogged down it was in attachments, responsibilities, obligations, and just *stuff*. In a clear flash I saw I would leave my life behind and take the bare minimum with me and start as fresh as possible. It was a refreshing thought but came a little too vividly for my comfort. I laughed it off.

C. THE TERRIBLE CONFLICT

A mind and body cannot both exist. Make no attempt to reconcile the two, for one denies the other can be real. (W-96.3)

15

The Break was such a shock to me that I did not write about it in my journal when it occurred. It so stunned me, I wanted to ignore it. My first reference to it in my journal was oblique, on May 27, 2018, in an excerpt I pasted from an email I sent to Hannah. But that was days after it occurred. This kind of avoidance and denial was very uncharacteristic of me, as I had for so long practiced radical self-honesty in my journal. And certainly, I had for many months been recording all sorts of new and shocking experiences. My unwillingness to write about The Break attests to how significant it was for me.

What I remember is I was sitting out back on the patio one morning reading the news on my laptop. My situation with Jessie and Hannah was running in the back of my mind. Suddenly, I saw Hannah and felt hurled upward in consciousness and outward toward Australia, and heard in my mind, "Truest wife; truest partner."

But. I. Have. A. Wife.

My mind rent in two. The person I had thought was me was now completely gone, although I did not fully realize this until later.

Since I don't know the exact day The Break occurred, I don't know if the following journal passage was a hint of The Break to come or if, afterward, this is how I slyly referred to it:

(Dialogue 20180517) (About Hannah) *"...It's like I'm connected with her from the inside out rather than the outside in. I don't remember ever feeling this with anyone before. Sometimes it takes the form of 'she's my real wife', which sounds wackadoodle. This does not come to me in any romantic, la-di-da, fantasy way. Nor is it a feeling of a 'soul mate'. It's just a feeling. I do wonder if it's just what the mind does with the spiritual connection of the holy relationship. It has to try to make sense of it on its level..."*

I knew I was shifting to what I called at the time *Higher Awareness* (Spirit-consciousness) and at The Break I felt it complete. I felt fully in a "new world" or reality. My conflict, in essence, was over, because I now had only one reality, and that was Higher Awareness. Oneness spread across the boundaries of my mind and enveloped my material experience. It was my new Context. What I had seen as my material future with Hannah was indeed now.

But I could not acknowledge this; it was too huge. So, The Terrible Conflict worsened. I pretended what I experienced at The Break was a metaphor: *New Love, New Life, New Land* represented my upward shift in consciousness—that's all!

(In email to Hannah, 20180519) *"...I realize this anxiety I have around you is like I'm facing the worst fear of my life. I recognize it's the fear that is at the heart of all fears. And then I see it... <u>I no longer exist as I used to</u>. It is the fear of death...I'm dead. Just as I wrote last year in my articles, I am dead and seeming to walk around in the world still and just not realizing it..."*

A little voice would show up now and then saying, "I was not supposed to come along." Ego felt it was not supposed to be here when I awakened because that meant it was aware of its own dying, and it was terrible. I felt I was experiencing a "living death."

I was to go through stages of recognizing and experiencing this death, but of course ego never came to accept it. Instead, I went from feeling this death as my own to feeling *something in me* was dying. And that something slowly diminished for me.

On and off for a couple of years I carried with me a feeling I called the *death pall*, a feeling that death was all around. This was clearly ego's view of what had occurred, but I could not shake it simply by recognizing this. However, recognizing this "death" I came to understand the grief that had accompanied my novel writing. The holy relationship signaled the end of ego. Still later, I came to see this was not true grief. Grief is the healing process we take to acceptance after a loss. But this grief never processed out, so I called it *pseudo-grief*. In time, I simply thought of it as one way I experienced ego.

In sorting out what I felt were the different aspects of my mind, I tried to place my material feelings for Hannah. Although I felt they were "given" and "rode in on the Light", I did not know where they fit in with my new experience. I did not want to deny them, as I had never found it useful to deny feelings. But I also did not want them, as I was with Jessie and Hannah was across the world.

Hannah talked about seeing me there in her home with her, but I clung tightly to the shift being "upward not outward." I made a sign saying this and posted it near my desk to remind me when I became too focused on Hannah and our material relationship. I desperately resisted any sense my material life was changing with the shift in my experience of existence.

Having read through my journal, I find I had always been self-centered and arrogant, and during this time I was particularly so. I was caught up in my own processes as though they were the be-all and end-all of existence (which, of course, they were for me). I felt something huge was happening to me and that others were there to support me. While I was aware that Jessie and Hannah were going through their own rough things, I took it for granted that what was occurring for me was more significant, or at least that I was in the lead. I felt with Hannah that, having experienced the holy relationship before, and being what I felt was more advanced, I was to "bring her along" so she could catch up. I wondered how it would unfold for us with me more advanced than she.

Later, I felt that I had it wrong and that, being more advanced, it was my place to serve others, particularly Jessie and Hannah. This was just another kind of arrogance, of course. It was all super-charged ego.

Hannah came to feel that since I was not going to her that perhaps she was in my life only to be a catalyst for change. Perhaps our holy relationship had served its purpose and was over. She withdrew for a while.

I then withdrew from our relationship myself, because I felt I needed "to figure out how to be with being dead without any other distractions right now." I did not know if we were ever to come together again, although I had been having sensations like "she is my most natural wife" come over me, and I had heard a couple of weeks before that "she is a fact of your life now." Then Hannah sent an email ending it between us. She felt she was "drowning."

I grieved Hannah leaving my life, but I couldn't shake the sense of our holy relationship firmly in my life as an expression of the Oneness that was my new Context. However, I wanted to focus on my new awareness, and I felt that maybe not having contact with her would be useful. I was sure we would reconnect, perhaps in the distant future. I felt, in fact, that we had just completed "Phase One" of our relationship.

But Hannah had not been the source of the shifts I experienced, so her going did not change anything. I was so different now that I wondered how I was to relate to my life and Jessie going forward. For her part, Jessie felt that "something big" was coming.

Hannah reconnected a couple of days later, and I felt Love go out to Love in joyous recognition of Itself. I expressed this to her, but she felt it was too much. I was not going to her, so she set boundaries to honor her grief. This was difficult for me, because it was painful to not express these joyous experiences, but I understood and respected her boundaries.

I did not know who I was or who was acting in this new life. I figured this confusion was ego. About Hannah, I felt disoriented and often thought, "Who is this woman and what is she doing in my life?" I wondered if these were, in essence, the same experience. If Hannah was my new material life as Spirit, I would not recognize her from ego.

16

I felt that ego had fallen away, perhaps all the way back when Ginny died but, if not, certainly at The Break. However, I still quite obviously thought with and felt ego—or some semblance of it. Were these just habits? I wasn't sure of the difference between ego being here and ego habits being here.

Although I did not *call on* Spirit as I transitioned to It as my Identity, It still sometimes arose as a distinct Voice when I wrote in my journal.

(Dialogue 20180523) (Spirit in bold.):
"Then what's gone? What is that gap you feel? You're just stuck with habits of thinking. If self-id is gone, there is no ego.
But why do I fear if self-id is gone?
It's just a habit; a shadow. You're unlearning. You're untraining your mind.
Even this is old thinking—'me' and You. Now it's usually just 'this mind'.
You're close to the bottom of the ego, beyond Which is Truth. These are its darkest, deepest thoughts and beliefs. You're familiar with them. They are not consuming you, are they? You don't really believe them. You're undoing them. Finally."

Eventually, my sense that ego was gone, and I was simply undoing the habits of it, was validated through other sources. I shared my experiences with readers in my articles and with clients who asked about them. One client shared with me that she heard from a teacher who had awakened that when ego falls away it takes a while for its momentum to wind down. She likened it to when you stop peddling a bicycle and yet continue to roll forward. And a reader shared with me that in *A Course of Love*, another book dictated by Jesus which many feel is a sequel to *A Course in Miracles*, he says:

"[E]ven though the ego is no longer with you, the pattern remains because what you learned, and the way in which you learned it, remains." (D:Day3.24)

In discussing the effect of the holy relationship, the *Course* says about sin (guilt, fear):

You see it still, because you do not realize that its foundation has gone...Only the habit of looking for it still remains. (T-19.III.8).

And about overlooking appearances:

One of the most difficult temptations to recognize is that to doubt a healing because of the appearance of continuing symptoms is a mistake in the form of lack of trust. (M-7.4)

But if ego was winding down, it seemed to have wound up first! I often felt I had entered the funhouse mirrors of my mind as I felt horribly surreal disorientation. Mostly, I trusted that this was ego's distortion, and in the long term this was validated. Looking at the shift from its point of view, it *was* surreal.

(Dialogue 20180527) *"...It is quite possible I'm losing my mind, and dragging Jessie and Hannah with me.*
 It is quite possible I'm going through some weird mid-life

thing, and dragging Jessie and Hannah with me.

It is quite possible I'm going through some weird menopausal thing, and dragging Jessie and Hannah with me.

It is quite possible it's all or some of the above..."

However, it seemed to me that what felt shock, loss, and surreal disorientation could not be ego, so much as my mind where ego had been. I came up with a theory that what I experienced was not actual ego anymore, but the part of my mind that had overlearned ego. (This would dovetail with the quote from A Course of Love.) I referred to this as the *ego-identifier*. I felt this was the "black box in the corner" of my mind or the 15% left to be undone to be in complete peace. It was, in essence, the part of my mind where ego had run deepest. (Think of a scab falling off. It falls off first where the cut was shallow and last where it was deepest.)

As I define ego as *identification with the person*, that was certainly what had been falling away for years and fell away completely at The Break. The person was still here. I still experienced her. But she was not me anymore, so it felt as though I had lost me.

There was much I went through with which I consciously wrangled due to the ego-identifier's doubt but felt I *did* understand. The body's sight and ego's judgments and interpretations were what usually occupied my conscious awareness. But Spirit uses another Seeing, and this Seeing was now rising to my conscious awareness, bringing understanding with it. However, repetitive entries in my journal about ego winding down as Spirit emerged indicate how much I did not trust this yet. But I did trust the shift in consciousness, even if I did not yet trust how it showed up. I clung to the new Context I was sure was here, even when I was not feeling It.

For a long while I was like a person in their first snowstorm, seeing the snow on the ground and feeling the kind of cold that only comes with snow, yet not trusting that the frozen water falling from the sky was part of it.

Spirit had been here person-Liz's entire adult life. If I was not shifting to It now, the only alternative was to accept that I had built a life around an illusion, and I was now losing my mind. Eventually, doubts became so strong that I felt I needed a test to be sure I was *not* losing my mind. I realized if I was functional and could meet my responsibilities, I was sane. And even in overwhelm, I still did what had to be done, if not as efficiently because I was distracted, nearly so.

Ego *winding down* refers to habits of ego feeling and thought responses falling away or being undone. (Sometimes, I referred to these habits as the *echo* of ego.) When ego is gone, Spirit is free to *emerge* from behind it, joining with Itself (the other 85%, in this metaphor). That was my sense of expansion. But as I said, it seemed as though ego was *winding up* first. Apparently, I had to emerge *through* the dark box in the corner, reclaiming that part of my mind every step of the way. So, beginning with The Forgetting, I was back in ego and felt lost to myself.

In the long Dark Passage to come, I would see that my biggest issue was lack of trust in *myself*. Over time, my experience of Spirit shifted from Something within me that still seemed *other* to the Strength within me to Which I could turn. But while I identified with a person, there was a gap—me *and* Spirit. Now, the gap was gone, yet I was to feel weaker than ever.

When I embarked on a spiritual path as a person, I was taught to not trust myself, because I used the ego thought system. I had to learn to recognize, and trust, Spirit. Now I was Spirit emerging through what remained of ego. It is no wonder I could not find anything that felt like me, as I did not recognize myself as ego anymore and, lost in the last vestiges of ego, I was not in touch with myself as Spirit!

As the residue of ego is ego (just as the smell of peanut left in a washed peanut butter jar is peanut), I continue to refer to ego habits or the ego-identifier as ego. I still feel, though, that my theory about the ego-identifier was a valid characterization.

Much later, I realized it was the ego-identifier's point of view that something in me was *dying*. It was Spirit's view that ego was *winding down*.

17

I had moments when I felt certain I was to stay in my life as it was with Jessie, but at other moments I felt so completely with Hannah that I couldn't figure out why I was still physically with Jessie. One day as I wondered why I wasn't leaving Jessie for Hannah I heard, "Because it is not needed." Did that mean ever or just for now? Or was that response simply validating my sense that I was with Hannah already and I didn't have to concern myself with our material relationship? It was, after all, effect and not cause.

Material change was not *needed* for my shift in consciousness, but was my shift in consciousness *leading to* material change?

I grew more aware each day that I was in Spirit-consciousness, it was my reality, and that I was with Hannah, no matter how it appeared at the material level. I felt so truly with her that it did not feel *necessary* to be with her in person. I knew she felt this, too, but still struggled with my not being physically with her.

But although I was satisfied, and even joyous, with how things were with Hannah, my conflict continued. I pushed against *The Wave* that I felt lift me at The Break. I would only acknowledge the *upward* part of it and insisted that the *outward toward Australia* feeling was just a metaphor. I could not understand the necessity of a material change when I was wholly *There* and satisfied. I again resorted to a sign near my desk to remind me "upward, not outward" to undo what I felt must be ego trying to make a change at the material level.

The reminder did not undo my conflict.

As far as *upward* went, I sometimes had an almost physical sensation of being hoisted up, as though by my armpits. This sensation would come and go for over two years, especially when I experienced Vision or higher miracles.

I insisted to Hannah that if she just let it, our situation could be wholly satisfying to her, too. I felt that we could come to see our not being physically together as a "mere technicality." But she still saw me there as well as wanted me there. And she felt that if she could not trust a Seeing that she had always trusted, then she was lost. "Then who am I seeing?" she asked in true bafflement as I insisted I would not be going to her.

I considered that maybe she *was* seeing someone else in her visions. I knew this would be difficult for me to face. But what other scenario could there be? I felt she was my *future*, so maybe there would be someone for her until our relationships ended naturally and we both found ourselves free. (On my end, that would have to be Jessie's death, as I could not imagine either of us leaving.) Hannah said that if she did get involved with someone else, they would have to accept who I was to her.

I envisioned a situation where we would be together in Spirit—the way that was truly real to us—but "on the ground" with others, at least for the time being. There would be Love all around. This was out of character for who I had been, however I was willing to grow in that direction.

In fact, I was *desperately* attempting a bargain with The Wave. I would grow the person in *any* direction, if only it meant she wasn't gone! The movement I felt was not just carrying me out of my current material life. I felt it carrying me *out of material life altogether*.

It washed over me at times that what was occurring in my material life was "small potatoes" relative to the shift in my consciousness. I saw and felt that material life was now incidental for me. I was no longer living in it. I was no longer a person.

18

In my joy and confusion and conflict at this time, I also took the first steps into darkness. One day I thought about how I was never to die, just exist differently, and it went through my mind, "Different *is* death." Where I expected relief, instead I found intense resistance.

(Dialogue 20180530) *"...It would be like telling a person 'you're the ocean now, but, hey, you continue to exist.' How could someone who was so identified with being a person understand being an ocean? How would you make that shift?"*

This was the start of *The Dark Passage*, a baffling experience of encountering and experiencing every dark thought and belief and feeling of ego, as well as reliving its attacks in ways I had not done in many years. This was all wrapped in terrible fear that took the shape of horror and dread. I never doubted it would pass, but I did not know what it was, I felt completely lost in it, and I did not know how long it would last.

For a few years before The Break, I had thoughts that my life was over, and now those thoughts became some version of "This means I'm dead." At first, these were only thoughts. But as time went on, they were accompanied by shock, horror, and intense pseudo-grief.

Try as I might to hold onto the life that I had and to fit Hannah into it, my awareness that the outer shifts only signaled something significant occurring within led to a disconcerting sensation that my mind was not suited for Spirit, and that it would need to undergo substantial changes. I understood this would be a long process completely out of my hands.

Yet, I was frustratingly aware that I was already in my new State and just could not access it. I felt it all around me. The new signs at my desk were "Be at mind" and "Upward, not outward. Vision, not behavior. Mind, not body". I made reminders for myself because I felt, correctly, that I was erroneously caught up in material changes that were not the point. My *only* reality now was mind (consciousness) and the material world only effect. Throughout The Dark Passage, I felt thwarted in attempts to access my new Context, which I felt *right here*, as my conscious mind was consumed with what had passed and processing the shift occurring.

One day, while cleaning the shower at home, I was in this sensation of being now in mind *only*, and I felt, mildly, "I am already gone". And then:

(Dialogue 20180601) *"...How do I describe this? It's the flipside of the 'I'm already gone' sensation. I saw and felt that I am spirit/mind. I <u>experienced</u> myself as spirit. <u>I have already transitioned</u>. Thus the feelings of being a ghost in the world. Thus the feelings of being unable to locate myself because I'm everywhere. Thus the feelings of...so much along these lines.*

...the 'spirit' feeling was my existence <u>not as a body</u>..."

I froze in place for several minutes. I remained in the crouched position I had been in scrubbing the shower door, staring at the floor, one hand on the door, the other on the wall so I would not fall over. Then I stood and stared into space for several more minutes.

(Dialogue 20180601) *"...Ever since I have been gobsmacked. Some things fell into place in my mind immediately. There was some joy. But mostly this mind has gone stunned-quiet...I can't even get this mind around the implications of this. But it explains the 'already there' feeling with Hannah. I am spirit, not body."*

This was my first recognized experience of immortality. I realized that this, not death, was what ego truly feared. Immortality was the "mystery" beyond "death". I realized, with joy, that *the only death was ego*. Not its passing—but the experience of ego itself was death as it was Life-less.

Beyond the obvious, experiencing myself as Spirit was significant because it replaced my experience of myself as a person. Before this moment, I had no recourse to thoughts of being dead and gone. I had nothing to replace the person, although I had every reason to know I was transcending to Spirit.

The new and unusual experiences since The Golden—really, since I felt like a ghost in the world and "someplace else"—could now be put under the heading *I am Spirit*.

Because I was Spirit, I felt I was expanding into and being lifted up to my Self.

Because I was Spirit, Vision and Seeing were more real to me than what the body's eyes reported.

Because I was Spirit, it felt more real to me that I was with Hannah than with Jessie.

Because I was Spirit, I didn't feel guilty feeling Hannah was my truest wife. The person of Liz was gone, and Jessie had been *her* wife.

Because I was Spirit, *I* was the Context in which the winding down/emerging occurred and, even in the darkest dark, I knew this. I still had two experiences, but I knew one was real and lasting and the other false and finally passing.

My previous experiences of Spirit were in the context of ego-consciousness and identifying with a person. I had been a Spirit-centered person, my mind split between those thought systems. But after I rose to Spirit-consciousness, I experienced ego in the Context of Spirit. It felt like an idea—powerfully experienced, but still only an idea—suspended in my mind, rather than a part of me. My habitual identification with it could not take hold without attachment to a person, and certainly not with Spirit to replace the person.

19

As June began, Hannah and I grew closer. She realized she had an "unexpected sort-of-wife". I crossed the boundaries I had imposed. We did nothing sexual online together, but I would feel her come over me physically and sexually at times and respond in kind. It was unexpectedly satisfying. This was a wholly new experience for me. We exchanged text messages acknowledging these moments, initially without being overtly sexual. But that didn't last as boundaries slid away.

But we also had problems in material communication, which would become characteristic of our relationship. I shared with Hannah what I thought the issue was from my side and asked for a different approach. She did not change, so I modified *my* approach. But this made no difference to what I felt was disjointed communication between us.

I continued to have disorienting moments when I wondered who she was and what she was doing in my life. Once, I heard "Just love her."

This disorientation persisted well into writing this memoir. I recognized Hannah spiritually, but personally I could not figure out what she was doing in my life. Why this change? It was hard to not grant it significance as it occurred simultaneously with the shift occurring. I was concerned that if I disregarded it, I was misunderstanding it. Yet, I repeatedly saw and felt strongly that the only shift that mattered was occurring in my mind.

Jessie was solid in her own spirituality. Over the previous year, she had made and deepened friendships in her twelve-step program and had a trusted group of mature women friends, something she never had before. And now her friends and therapist were telling her that she should be angrier with me than she was.

This led Jessie to some honest self-examination. She had

her bouts of jealousy, especially when she heard through a door a tone of voice that she said I used only with Hannah. It reminded her of how I was with her early in our relationship. But these passed.

She wished she could experience Christ with me as I did with Hannah, but she knew this was not possible. She was careful to monitor herself for self-pity or martyrdom. She felt that her path was to serve others, and that she was serving me by allowing me to have this relationship.

I explained to her that my relationship with Hannah did not come from lack. It was not from need or want. Nothing was missing in my relationship with Jessie. It was an expression, or effect, not a cause. I used the idea of *The Two Pictures* from the *Course* (T-17.IV) to explain to her my shift and how my relationship with Hannah was different.

Basically, in ego the emphasis in relationships is on the frame, or form, rather than the picture, or content, ego. This is to distract you from the guilt and fear and hate that are the real content of special relationships. But in Spirit, the emphasis in relationships is on the Picture, or Content, Spirit. The frame, or form of relationships, is insubstantial and overlooked as the Picture dominates your attention.

I pointed out to Jessie that she and I began with a special relationship, but over the years we each shed a lot of ego and became aware of our Wholeness in our own way. We had a practical holy relationship.

Jessie had always made it clear that her goal was a spiritualized ego, as she felt ego was God-given. And as she walked away from this conversation, I had a vision of her in which I seemed to see her reaching her goal.

Later that day, I went to tell her that I was going to take a nap, and when I turned away it came over me that "I have already left this marriage" and I was hit by a wave of grief. But I would only take this to mean that our marriage was not what it had been. A week before, I had seen our relationship was spiritual now. I felt this reiterated that. I dared not think it meant *only* spiritual now. (Actually, *everything* was only spiritual for me now, but I had yet to understand this.)

Despite resisting the end of my marriage to Jessie, I felt strongly that I would be with Hannah one day. The feeling was so matter-of-fact, so *of-course-how-could-it-be-otherwise?* that I could not deny or resist it. In fact, I felt I was already living it. But how could this be, unless I was truly Seeing, both our Oneness in Spirit and how our relationship would unfold in time? This was a lot to accept.

But I also feared I was *not* Seeing.

(In email to Hannah, 20180607) *"…I'm so afraid I'm seeing a metaphor rather than what will unfold in time. There was an episode of the old Dick Van Dyke show where Laura's old boyfriend comes to visit. He wrote her the most beautiful love letters in college. When he arrives she learns he's become a priest. She goes back and reads the letters and realizes they were to God, not her. I've feared this. The effusive, solar plexus-blowing Love I share with you—are you just a symbol of that Love?…"*

It washed over me that *it made absolutely no sense* to change out one woman for another. All relationships are the same! Their content is, for me, Spirit or ego depending on what *I* bring to them. This was never determined by the other.

This was true, but on the other hand, this was exactly why it did not matter if forms *did* change. The Content never changed, but the material world did according to what expressed the unfolding Atonement.

What occurred at the material level was not *for* or *about* me anymore. Really, it never had been. The sense it had been had only been ego's storytelling. And as I no longer identified with the person, those stories made no sense to me now. The material world was only a passing appearance.

But I only felt that and did not understand it yet. My journal is filled with the contortions my mind went through as I tried to understand my new relationship to the person of

Liz and the material world. My identification with the person was only newly gone and I was premature in my conclusions. I hated to think I was only at the very start of a long, uncomfortable process. But I was.

20

While The Dark Passage and ego's ramped-up resistance began at this time, I also had new experiences that were startling, always fascinating, but were unable to fully unfurl yet.

As I shared, when The Golden Light of Love broke into my mind, I experienced the world *in* me, and I felt a creator's love for its creation. The feeling of Oneness extending in my awareness was not wholly new to me, but I had only glimpsed it before. Now, it was intense, and I understood it was my new reality. But, though joyous, it was too powerful for me to want it to be sustained. And, in time it, and the material creativity that rode in on it, faded.

But that was just the start, and the experience evolved. With the holy relationship and Hannah, I felt I was in a story that was coming from me, that Liz and Hannah were merely characters, and that I could step back and watch their Love story unfold, like I would a play I wrote. I called this experience *The Author*. When I felt this, no matter what occurred, I had a sense of lighthearted enjoyment that was clearly not due to what was appearing. However, as I felt the same sense of creation I had writing novels, I sometimes wondered if I was making it all up.

An aspect of The Author experience was that I did not feel anything deeply or, if I did, it was in the moment and passed not long after. I thought this must be what it is like for a method actor, feeling the appropriate emotion for the immediate scene, but not carrying those emotions for long into life off stage. This experience was more subtle than some of my early, intense experiences, but just as disconcertingly new, and certainly an indication that I was in a new reality. I wondered if shallow feelings would pass or if they were my new normal and I would acclimate to them.

(They would turn out to be my new way of experiencing the material world as I rest in the real world [Oneness]. I am still acclimating to it. I imagine that on paper it sounds lovely, and it is in its way. But if I had imagined this before, I would have imagined feeling it *as a person*. I did not know anything else. I had no idea how wholly different it would feel to be Spirit. So, it is not the experience itself that is disturbing, it is the absence of recourse to my former experience, which I always had when my mind was split, and the awareness I will not be returning to it.)

As well as my feelings being disconcertingly shallow, I did not feel I was deceiving Jessie with Hannah, although my intellect said I should. But I felt my relationship with Hannah occurred in a different Place from my relationship with Jessie. Of course, this was because person-Liz was gone and Liz-Spirit had taken her place, but I was not acknowledging that yet.

But I did wonder if feeling this way was a moral cop-out and I was deceiving myself. Does everyone feel this way when they cheat on their partners? But I did not feel that I was *justifying*. I clearly felt in another realm with Hannah. It was my honest experience that these two lives did not intersect, but I didn't grasp the implications of this.

21

For Hannah's birthday, we went online together via Skype and, beginning with the Dutch Masters, looked at art together by sending each other images or links and discussing them. I consider this our first (and only) *date*. We had a lovely time and drew closer. But soon after, she said she had to step away for a while.

I had told Hannah that I felt wholly with her now and saw us physically together *eventually*. I felt so certain that we would be together at some point that although I had thoughts of letting her go, I could only think in terms of *for now* instead of *forever*. For some reason, I had in mind a 4–5-year timeframe before we would be together, but with no idea how it would unfold. But one evening when she was gone, she and Australia suddenly felt imminent, and my several-year time frame felt ridiculous. But I continued to cling to it.

She reconnected a couple of days later.

Mystical holy relationships are difficult. The *Course* makes this clear, and I knew from my experience with Emily that it is the most threatening thing to ego because it undoes specialness when you recognize your Self in another. I felt that while Hannah's conflict *seemed* to be about my not being with her when we both saw so clearly that I was to be, that her real conflict was the holy relationship. I asked her to lean on me as I knew what to expect in a holy relationship. However, I missed that her central conflict was that my not going to her meant that she could not trust the Seeing she had always trusted. She was lost without it.

Within a day of her return, Hannah sent an email saying she had to let me go.

(20180614 email from Hannah) *"...i kicked into a place of greater clarity, more honesty. which is that i simply do not want this anymore, i really do want to get over you, (im so sorry) it is simply too hard for me where i actually am, plus i truly do not believe that what you are seeing is actually us in the future but the last vestiges of something else masquerading as a true vision, clinging to what is a shift into True Vision for you now. im so very very sorry. it really deeply is necessary that i get over you for my own peace of mind..."*

That evening, as I grieved, I had the strongest feeling

that I was to gather all our emails and what messages I could harvest from Skype and put them in my Dropbox cloud. This was not a sentimental feeling. I did not hold onto things like that. Historically, I was more likely to delete to let go. But I did as I felt moved to do, although I could not understand it.

The next day was what Hannah and I came to call *The Terrible Friday*.

I went on Skype to leave her a text message and discovered that she was writing to me. We ended up messaging back and forth for two and a half hours. In the process, I felt I discovered missed cues in our relationship, as I had been so caught up with what was going on with me. I realized I had ignored some things she said in what I felt was ego petulance, because I had learned to ignore that kind of acting out with Jessie. I promised to do better and to pay more attention.

But in the end, this did not seem to be the issue for Hannah. She was saying goodbye and was only writing to bring us both clarity. She intended to go during the entire exchange. As there was no opening for me, I told her to say goodbye and mean it, which she did.

Then, as I grieved that day, it got strange.

(Dialogue 20180615) *"…Something seemed to have shifted in this long exchange. Deepened. For one thing, I became even more certain of us, though she still ended it. It's kind of a 'Yes, okay, now I see us' feeling I don't really understand. I do feel more clear myself…really, there is a quiet that was not there before the exchange…"*

The certainty and quiet were baffling. They did not have to do with anything we discussed. How could they, when what became clear to me about my behavior was not her issue with me? These were just the beginning of experiences that revealed I was, indeed, in a different consciousness using a different Seeing. Later that day:

> "...It's as though the self was finally what it is supposed to be in Liz and Hannah's relationship. It's not as though she deliberately or even unconsciously wasn't being that. It's that it was just time for her to show up. She's not the Liz that will be, but the beginning of her.
>
> *Crimeny, am I really writing this shit? Who the fuck says shit like this?*"

And still later:

> "...I think I just felt that 'Part One of Liz and Hannah' has passed..."

I felt this with a joyous uplifting sense of, "Yes! This is what is *supposed* to happen." I was experiencing material life as a play, and it was as if that morning was an important "scene" in it. All my common sense said we were over, but something in me—something more real to me—was joyously twirling around because we were supposedly advancing in our relationship. How could I feel this? Was it real? Was I losing my mind?

I felt that we could never be truly over. I felt this as a fact as solid as my Self. I was sure this parting would not be forever, but for a significant time nonetheless, so I still grieved. It was not lost on me, either, that I had written a parting in *Towing the Moon* that was temporary but grieved as I wrote it, knowing the characters would feel it as loss. Sometimes it seemed my novels were previews, not of details, but of experiences I was to have.

Since I still felt that we were together in the holy relationship—which was, really, the whole new Context of Oneness that I now found myself in—I wondered how to still be with Hannah without being in physical contact with her. But it happened spontaneously anyway. Whenever I slipped into Spirit-consciousness, I felt her There.

When this occurred the following day, I felt her come rushing through the ether at me. It was as though she was in the room with me, and I heard her say in my mind, "I'll be back, you know." I felt I *did* know this, but that it referred to a distant future.

This experience was significant because it was a variation on how I felt her as my Self. I felt it was Hannah-Spirit who came to Liz-Spirit, sort of different "flavors" of the One Spirit. It was Me and Me. And this time I felt I *stepped up into* Spirit-consciousness rather than that I was *hoisted*. This experience I would come to feel was our real relationship, and I would think of it as our relationship *essence*.

Later that night I felt her come to me again and call me by her nickname for me, "Minty". These events were later conflated in my mind as one event, which I came to refer to as *The Minty Moment*.

22

I had decided when Hannah went away before that I would not tell Jessie about Hannah's comings and goings, as I expected this would occur often and Jessie was concerned it hurt me. But this parting seemed definite, and I was grieving, so I told her about Hannah's email letting me go. But after we Skyped our final goodbye, I told Jessie, and she was not surprised that we had connected again. Sometimes I suspected she sensed more than she shared.

Jessie's Liz was gone, and I wondered if what I was becoming would suit her. I had been saying I felt my former life was over, and now for the first time I thought in terms of the whole person of Liz being gone. But despite this insight, I still clung to it being correct for me to be with Jessie now and with Hannah in the future.

I felt parting with Hannah was necessary and a part of our development toward each other. Of course, I did not share this with Jessie, but I did tell her that I felt Hannah would be gone for a couple of years. She said, resignedly, that she thought she would be back much sooner than that.

So began what Hannah and I came to call *The Terrible Week*. For me it is so called because as much as I tried to allow the grief and move on, I felt horrible tension. It was another situation in which I expected to feel some relief but did not. I was not used to being so wrong about what I was going through!

That week, my mind twisted all over the place to explain what was going on in me. Hannah was gone, but I still felt in a new reality with her. I grieved her absence but could not get rid of the sense it changed nothing and we were still together. I could only imagine some distant future together to explain this.

I tried to convince myself that I felt so awful because I was grieving, but I knew that was not it. The Terrible Conflict did not end when Hannah left, and not just because I felt it was not a true end for us. It seemed that with her leaving my life could spring back to what it had been, but instead it highlighted that that life was over and what I had been in it was gone. The Wave that lifted me at The Break still had me, with or without Hannah. I clung desperately to the vestiges of the life out of which it had lifted me like a shipwreck survivor to the boat's debris.

At the beginning of that week, there were moments I felt I was visiting Hannah, or she was visiting me. I didn't want to intrude, so I let those moments be and didn't pursue them. But a couple of days into it, she came over me strongly, and I had an urge to check Skype. I discovered she had blocked me. This was a blow, but as soon as this reaction passed, I felt, again, the rightness of this so that our story could move forward. I felt we were just "starting the future."

I was also proud of Hannah for setting what she felt was a necessary boundary.

Seeing continued with these intuitions about Hannah and the sense that nothing had changed despite her being gone. I say *Seeing*, but I rarely saw images. It was *knowing* in a new way. I both knew only Oneness was real and knew things about the future. And it was this certainty that disconcerted me. I told myself it was stress inducing because I did not know if I could trust it. But really, I *did* trust it. I knew it was real. I was uncomfortable with both the new Seeing and what I saw.

Three times during The Terrible Week it came to me that Hannah would contact me soon, one of these thoughts being as specific as during the coming weekend. These came as ordinary thoughts, so I didn't take them seriously. However, I still felt moved to record them in my journal.

As always, I had insights that previewed what was to come for me, but I missed their significance at the time. For example, I wrote in my journal that my inner dismantling and the dismantling of my material life were the same thing. This was the first time I thought of my material life coming apart.

But though Hannah was gone, I wondered again why I would give up Jessie, a good woman I valued, and the life I treasured with her, for a relationship that I knew would be "a mess". Because before she left, I had begun to see that Hannah and I might not be compatible in many ways. I was aware those things were not the basis of our relationship. Spirit was, so things like personal compatibility were not relevant. But I knew our egos would use those things to drive us apart. A holy relationship can be difficult precisely because the two in it are not brought together by their own personal psychology and desires. Ego is cut out of it.

However, this was moot, as Hannah was gone.

On Saturday, a week and a day after my final exchange on Skype with Hannah, I went about my chores as usual. While shoving clothes into the washing machine, it occurred to me that there was no reason for Hannah to ever contact me again.

Done with the laundry, I went to my laptop in the nook to check my email and there she was, in an email titled "in Love and in doubt".

I was *gobsmacked*. I really had not expected to hear from

her. I glanced at the email to get the gist, which was positive enough, and slid to the floor. I curled up in what I called the *egg position*—hunched over my bent legs, hands on the floor, head on my hands—a posture I was to take often in overwhelm.

I knew then that all that had been happening was real and existence as I had known it was over. The overarching Context of Oneness I felt around me; the experiences as Spirit; the Visions of Oneness with Hannah; the new Seeing; the feeling of a whole, complete new life given; the new experiences of time; the lighthearted experiences of Author—Hannah's return validated all of this. There was no denying anymore that it was real.

I wasn't even sure of Hannah at this point. I could not see a resolution for her dilemma, because I was not leaving Jessie. But the details did not matter, because what was real for me was the inner shift that I could no longer deny. Hannah's absence and return made it clear to me that my conflict was not about her and Jessie. I had tried to make it so, or to make it an inner life/outer life conflict or a Higher Awareness/ego conflict. But that was my old split-mind, and those boundaries were gone. I had only one Reality now.

With Hannah back, Jessie—who was not surprised—reiterated her boundaries. She surprised me, though, by saying that while she considered herself polyamorous, she thought that I was "more mature than that." So much for her position that polyamory was more evolved.

But was this polyamory? I didn't know how to look at anything anymore and just listened to Jessie. I was confused to still be in a life I felt more than ever had passed.

When I thought about the moment weeks before when I felt I had already left the marriage, I realized that was not quite accurate. I was not the person who had been in that marriage. She had fallen away, taking that whole life with her. I felt that even if Hannah had not reconnected, I would not remain in the life I was in. I had come to think of it as the *old life*.

Three nights after Hannah reconnected, I spent a couple

of hours with her on Skype. I was still confused about her but felt carried along on a strong current. As I left my office, I was surprised to find Jessie at the door. She said quietly, "Tell me you are never going to leave me for her." I realized I could not and told her so.

Jessie said she didn't know if she could go on with me. Her most important value—security—had been undermined by my answer. I felt the ground beneath us crack in a hundred directions and begin to give way.

I went to bed to not sleep, and she went to her office. In the morning, I faced myself in the bathroom mirror and knew that I could not reconcile my old life with the new life that had come. *That* was The Terrible Conflict I had been in. I went down the hall to Jessie's office and told her this.

I have only one entry in my journal for June 27, 2018:

"Left Jessie this morning."

D. THE DISMANTLING

The death of specialness is not your death, but your awaking into life eternal. You but emerge from an illusion of what you are to the acceptance of yourself as God created you. (T-24.II.14)

23

It was hard to believe. A friend of Jessie's would say, "There were three things in life I thought would never change: death, taxes, and Liz and Jessie."

The Liz I had been had felt the same. If someone had shown her a glimpse of a future without Jessie, she would have thought Jessie died. But, instead, *she* died. And I had to take apart her life to get on with mine. That's what it felt like: I was cleaning up after *someone else*.

When I tearfully told Jessie I could no longer reconcile my old life with the new one that had come, her response was compassion. She could see my conflict and thought, understandably, that I was having a mental break of some kind. Of course, I was, but not what she thought.

But Jessie would say a few times in anger that no one's spirituality would lead them to leave a happy marriage. Given her belief system, I certainly understood her point of view. And, given her belief system, I knew she could never understand mine. How could I explain a death that did not involve the ceasing of a body? There was much I was still confused about, but I was certain about this. The person I thought I was, was gone. I felt her end coming a long time before she fell away completely at The Break. And I had struggled to hold onto her life ever since.

In attempting to explain, I told Jessie I felt she was the former Liz's widow. She felt this was further evidence I had lost my mind. But eventually she would say, "I know my Liz is gone, because she would never have left me." *Exactly*.

Oh, what a blessing that in the previous year Jessie's own spirituality had deepened and she had gathered around her a group of strong supportive friends. Of course, I didn't feel this was a coincidence. *Soft unfolding for all.*

After leaving Jessie that morning, I ate breakfast and walked the dogs as usual. I was in shock, but finally relieved. But my relief was not complete. On the walk, I felt movement toward Australia flow unhindered as all obstacles were gone. I went further into shock. *This was going to happen.*

When I got back, I told Jessie and she said, crushed, "Oh my god, you *are* leaving me for her." I tried to explain that no, I was leaving her *and* going to Hannah, but I knew this was too fine a distinction for Jessie. It sounded disingenuous, but it was how I felt. This was not a continuation. The other life had ended before Hannah. She was only the sign a new life had begun.

I left a message on Skype for Hannah telling her I left Jessie. I didn't want to assume she still wanted me there, so I didn't ask her until we spoke that evening. She nodded a slow yes, seeming in shock herself. On one hand, her Seeing was validated. But on the other, she had to adjust to what my going to her meant to her life.

I made the necessary round of calls to family and friends. Everyone was shocked, but initially supportive. My sister, E, said she and her son, J, had discussed in the past year how I had changed toward Jessie. I do not know what they saw, because I had not been aware of any change in behavior. Jessie, too, said she had not been aware of anything.

E was stunned, however, to learn about Hannah, and that I was going to Australia. I never did quite feel polyamory was going on, so I had not told anyone about her. I was waiting to see what unfolded between her and I and Jessie before sharing it.

Having experienced when I came out how people are generally supportive when given unexpected news but can change as the news sinks in, I knew some initial support could dissipate. And some of it did, most notably my friend, N. She would come to say I was no different from the middle-aged men who left their wives for other women, no matter I couched it in spiritual terms. In her disappointment with me, she fell away for a while.

Supportive or not, everyone thought I was having a midlife crisis or a mental breakdown or both.

When I eventually shared what was going on in my life with my readers and clients, I was mostly supported, but there were a few who were upset or disappointed in me. Some, like Jessie, thought my leaving a happy marriage could not be the effect of Spirit. They were angry and unsubscribed from my newsletter and blog. Others stated what I shared scared them, but they took the opportunity to look at their fear with Spirit.

Some told me how they had left or made drastic changes in lives they had found untenable. This is not what I had described, of course, but I took what they shared in the spirit of support they intended.

As I continued to share my experiences, a few, who were both clients and readers, so knew me personally, felt a mystical shift in themselves, as though they were riding along in my slipstream in consciousness.

It was interesting to see how sharing something like this in my own life made others feel they could share their secrets and private thoughts with me. I was to hear from some who were not happy in their circumstances but had not told anyone until they told me. Still others felt free to tell me what they had thought all along was wrong with my marriage to Jessie. The latter was revealing and disappointing, if somewhat amusing, because I did not leave because I was unhappy, and I thought I had made that clear. In fact, I felt it was a key point that the former Liz had ended as happy and whole as one could be in ego-consciousness. Her life had come to completion.

On the bright side, I received a beautiful email from my brother. And my sister, C, supported me by calling to check on me, coming to help with the yard sale, and giving me a place to stay between selling the house and leaving for Australia.

There was really no one I could talk to about what I was going through. I did think of a couple of spiritual teachers I knew, and eventually did speak as friends with one. She shared with me the story of her own teacher, who also left a happy marriage after a woman he had dreamt of as his wife showed up in his life.

For my family, it was not the divorce, but my going to Australia that brought up their grief. After all, the divorce was amicable, and Jessie was to still be part of the family. I felt my leaving brought them a taste of the death of their Liz that I felt occurred.

In bitterness one day, Jessie told me I would end up alone; no one would be able to be with me. She knew how important commitment had been to her Liz, and pointed out that my word meant nothing now. I would never be able to commit to anyone again, not even to Hannah. I had already thought of this, and agreed, and had discussed it with Hannah. (Who did not agree, *commitment* being one of those concepts of which we had different ideas.) Although Jessie and I had both said at the beginning of our relationship that our spiritual process came first, I did not realize at the time that this meant that I could not commit to a person. This had been my mistake.

24

The former Liz's life had to be dismantled. I was to divorce Jessie and we were to sell the house.

As my life coaching practice as it was and the royalties from my books did not bring in enough money for me to live on, I needed my portion of the proceeds from the sale of our home and some minor investments for the coming…whatever. I did not know! But I did feel I was never going to have to worry about money. I would always have what I needed to do whatever I was to do.

The Dismantling occurred with remarkable logistical ease. Of course, it was painful, but The Terrible Conflict was over, and that had been worse. I was no longer resisting The Wave that lifted me at The Break and was carrying me into the new life. It was to do it all for me.

In the course of The Dismantling, I grieved Jessie, the Liz who had been with her, their marriage and material life, but this grief was mild. Most often my feelings went no deeper than if I was watching a sad story—which is exactly what I felt I was doing. It was not, after all, my life I was leaving.

Instead, I felt thunderous pseudo-grief that it took me a while to sort out from any true grief occurring. Going forward, it was an ever-present undercurrent when it was not consuming me. It would characterize The Dark Passage.

Pseudo-grief showed up more and more with Hannah. In fact, I could not speak with her without it arising. Sometimes it was so intense I had to back away from her for a while. I surmised ego resented her as a symbol of Love and as a symbol of the changes occurring. Later, I would realize pseudo-grief was simply the experience of ego's resistance without any covers. It came up any time ego was triggered.

I felt that, now that Spirit-consciousness had come, despite all that was occurring in my material life, I should be happy. This expectation and resulting disappointment only added to my confusion and discomfort. It was another form of ego's resistance. I was in a process. Happiness was to come as ego wound down.

And sometimes it was here. When it came time for the yard sale in which Jessie and I sold off most of what we had accumulated in twenty-four years together, I spent three days in deep Serenity. It carried me through one of the toughest parts of The Dismantling.

The most difficult part of The Dismantling was watching Jessie's devastation. I had pulled the rug out from under her entire life. She would tell me later that I had cost her a wife, a best friend, and one of her dogs (she kept Rory and Joey went to my sister, E), but that the worst part was that I had taken her home from her. That was her security.

Even later, when she was settled on her own, she would tell me that she could stand what I did to her, but not to Rory. He was not happy in an apartment without a yard. However, she was happy to have him. He was, after all, the dog she had always wanted. It turned out I *had* been raising him for someone else, just as I had felt when he was a puppy.

But, except for an occasional and totally understandable angry outburst, Jessie was civil to me. We had a lot to sort out and we partnered in divorce as we had in marriage. She is probably the most fair and decent person I know. In fact, she continued to be so solicitous toward me that her friends told her she needed better boundaries with me. I told her the same.

Either before or soon after embarking on my spiritual path I read Peace Pilgrim. She was an American mystic who felt moved to walk for peace for 28 years. She carried nothing but the clothes on her back and a few items in her pockets. She "walked until given shelter and fasted until given food." It terrified me at the time. What if I was called on to do such a drastic thing? Well, moving into the unknown after ending a whole, good life felt like my drastic thing.

Sometimes I wondered (hoped?) if I would wake up one morning and discover this had all been a dream. I could imagine saying to Jessie, "I had the strangest dream about this client I have occasionally. She lives in Australia. We became friends and then…"

The Dismantling whittled my material life down to a 5x5 storage unit in Las Vegas and what I could get into the few suitcases I was to take with me to Australia. Here was the bare minimum that my material life would become that I had seen in a premonitory flash a few weeks before.

25

Not long after I left Jessie, I had a kerfuffle with Hannah when I felt she was not there for me during a particularly difficult time. I handled it as I always had done in relationships in the past, which was explain why I felt hurt and state what kind of support I wanted, with the intention of discussion going from there. But this did not go well with Hannah, who felt I was trying to change her. I was taken aback. But as she was involved in a family event at the time, I let it go.

But, again, I found myself feeling I was somehow "off" in approaching things as I had done. Something wholly new to me was occurring, and I wasn't seeing it. I had felt this about so much since The Golden.

I felt I did not have to consider the usual things; I did not have to *make* a relationship with Hannah. It was *given*; already here, whole and complete. I felt I could take it for granted, as I would a relationship I had been in long term.

Actually, a key thing was happening here, but I could not see it or understand it for a very long while. What I felt was Whole, and I didn't need anything from my relationship with Hannah. There was no right way to act or right approach to take to our material relationship. I felt as Spirit feels, which is that what occurs in the material world is irrelevant. What I felt was a whole new experience of *indifference*. But ego was still spinning too much for me to accept I could just let go of the material experience.

It would be a long time before I stopped approaching this relationship as I had relationships in the past. All I knew then was I felt I was in a whole new world, and I was all out to sea, as

I didn't recognize or understand it. But it was also exciting because I felt something *real* was finally occurring. This was *the* shift, and this holy relationship was proof of this. I was curious to see how a mystical holy relationship would be expressed.

I used the word *learn* for what I had to do with my new experiences, but I did not feel *learning* the way I had as a person. The person was not growing or developing, or if that happened, it was incidental, and I did not experience it as me. I no longer felt it was *necessary* to grow the person. In fact, I had felt this when I thought I was to grow into an open marriage.

Perhaps *discovering* is a better word for what I experienced as my new State emerged in my awareness. I felt, after all, that I was now in a State that was given, and I was walking into a life that was "readymade."

I also felt it was not exactly complete to say I was in a new *life*. Obviously, that was occurring at the material level, but I felt that term did not describe what was significant to me, which was the shift within. But *within* was also not quite correct anymore! The boundary between inner and outer was gone. This was a *shift in consciousness*—but this did not feel like a complete statement either.

It would be over a year before I landed on the most accurate way to describe what I felt. I have discovered reading my journal for this memoir that I described it long before The Break. I was in a new *experience of existence*.

Consciousness, life in the world, and *existence* are synonymous, but I felt *consciousness* was better applied to how I saw, *life in the world* to the person's material circumstances, and *existence* to my most fundamental sense of being, which had been as a person and was now Spirit.

For decades I had occasional, momentary shifts in consciousness, but I never imagined what it would feel like to be Spirit, except to experience love and peace and joy. I certainly never considered feeling immortal.

I had been describing my experiences in my articles for years, and that it would take me so long to find the best way to convey my new experiences is indicative of the substantial change that occurred. I was in a wholly new State that I had to let emerge and unfold to discover and describe. Even when I could feel the difference between my former and new experiences distinctly, I could not convey the new experiences until they crystalized in my understanding in their own time.

To start, experiences of my new world were buried amid my shattered old world and were disconcerting in their strangeness. For the time being, they showed up most clearly with Hannah.

(In Skype message to Hannah, 20180716) "...And I was thinking how close I feel to you...and I went to think 'falling more in love with her all the time', but it didn't fit. What my experience is, is realizing my love for you all the time. A Love that is always here is being uncovered more and more. Just as with Truth. And again I thought of those experiences of familiarity with you...and the feeling of walking into a life already being lived...

Ah! Another way to put that. It's like the outer life is catching up with the inner. I heard before 'Here's your new partner. Get to know her.' And I was all 'WTF???' at the time. But the more I do get to know you as a person, the more I am aware I already do know you on another level. It's close to deja vu, but not exactly like it. It's not that intense 'I've been here before'. More just a 'this is already so' on some level."

I felt that I was going out not just to Hannah, but to her family as well. She made for me a chart of her rather extensive living family tree, complete with relationships past and current that resulted in children. It took no effort for me to memorize it.

The sense that I was heading into a readymade life, one that I felt I was already living on some level, grew stronger as I no longer opposed it. It brought to mind an episode of Star Trek: The Next Generation with the curious title, *The Inner Light*. Jean-Luc Picard wakes to find he is in someone else's life and ends up living it out before he again wakes up to his real life.

That was how it felt for me at the time. But later I would realize I had it backwards. The existence I had been in was not my real existence and the one I was awakening to was. Needless to say, this was very disorienting.

26

Hannah did not have the range of experiences of us that I had. She had experiences of Oneness with me to begin, briefly felt we were already so, and knew I was to be with her, but reported nothing more. I wondered what this meant for how our material relationship would unfold. I felt that our relationship was perhaps for her what my relationship with Emily had been for me, the "doorway into" Vision. But she was more advanced than I had been at that time. (I had just entered Undoing and I felt Hannah was classically in the middle of the misery of Sorting Out.) So, even though Oneness was my new State and something she had only yet glimpsed, I thought maybe the gap between our levels of awareness would not matter too much.

Still, my awareness of Oneness with her meant I felt an intimacy with her that she did not yet feel with me. It was awkward at times to feel a stranger was a partner!

When I was getting ready to write about what was occurring in my life in my newsletter and blog, I did not know if Hannah would be comfortable with me using her real name, especially as she was known at the blogsite. I thought of using the letter X for her, but that seemed lurid. So, I thought maybe Z, then felt I should just give her a pseudonym, and *Zelda* came to mind.

I suggested this in an email to her and received back a blast of shock. It turned out the name Zelda had great synchronistic significance for her having to do with things she had seen around her eventual life partner. In fact, much that she had seen over the years to do with a future life partner pointed to this time of her life and to me, including such things as her partner being a foreigner. So, while this was the kind of Seeing Hannah trusted, to watch so much come to fruition after so much time meant Hannah was dealing with out-of-the-norm experiences as well.

Obviously, mine was not the only material life to be disrupted, either. Hannah had lived deliberately alone for seven years, and I would be coming into her space. I also reassured her I had no intention of going out to her and jumping into her bed. I was not ready for that. I wanted to get to know her first. I joked I would court her from her spare bedroom.

Between *Hannah's Return* and my leaving Jessie, I had with Hannah the most beautiful moment outside of experiences of Oneness. On a Skype call, she saw that fear is not real. I watched as she totally got this and positively glowed.

It was a true moment, but, as these things go, one that would be covered by fear again as she resumed the process of undoing her identification with ego.

She began to have doubts. What if her feelings were only a metaphor? What if she was misleading herself and me? I reassured her that I was not going to Australia for her or under a personal motivation or to find something. I was riding an irresistible Wave I was a part of and was a part of me. She and Australia were an effect, not a cause.

But Hannah expressed fear in different forms more often, and of course I had my doubts, too. Within a month, Jessie and I had sold all our stuff, cleaned up the house, had it on the market, and were in the process of a divorce. It had become very real very fast. It was no wonder we had our doubts.

I still sometimes wondered if I *was* only having a midlife mental break. My family continued to think so. Jessie said she expected me to crash and burn, but when I got back, she would take me in as a friend. My sister, E, thought I was probably being scammed and Hannah was luring me in with sex so she could steal my money. (A *looong* game for so little money!) My sister, C, told me to not be too embarrassed to come back if things didn't work out with Hannah and I spent all my money. She said the family would say "I told you so" but would still love me and help me and give me shelter.

I could say this time of internal and external upheaval took all the trust I had to give, but, really, I was beyond trust. I was riding The Wave and it had me and it *was* me and I knew I would ride it to the end, wherever it took me or however crazy it looked.

A month after I left Jessie, Hannah told me, in despair, that her romantic feelings for me were gone. She had been in love with me for a year. We had been involved for almost three months.

I thought: *Fear.* I figured, *okay, we'll work through this.* But she was so different toward me after this that I knew, fear or something else, this was not a passing thing. Gone was the warm, powerful love that I could feel through the computer. Gone was the Hannah who was interested in me and wanted to get to know me.

She was never to return.

27

I had experienced fear of Love often on my path and I usually recognized it. I had felt depression and grief and anger, for personal reasons and over my path. But I had glimpsed experiences that I could call *dark* only rarely. Until The Break. After that, a dark feeling of death and horror and dread hovered around the edges of my mind. I felt this mostly as an undercurrent of low-grade anxiety, until Hannah told me her romantic feelings for me were gone.

For a while, we churned over her lost feelings together. She could not understand what happened. She didn't know if she was sabotaging something beautiful, or if the feelings she had for me for a year were "a mirage". She felt terrible; sometimes she felt she was losing her mind. She wanted those feelings back but could not make them return. She was to grieve their loss for a long while.

Sometimes, in trying to figure out what happened to her feelings, she would express how I was missing certain things she wanted in a life partner. She said that if she could not have all she wanted then she would rather be alone. But at other times, she would tell me it was nothing about me or anything I had done or had not done that caused her feelings to disappear. She could not explain what happened.

In any case, it seemed the dream I had that began our romantic relationship, in which I was chasing her around her house and she was uninterested now that I returned her feelings, had been a premonition.

I had a theory as to what was going on with Hannah, but I did not share it with her at the time, as she did not seem in touch with what happened.

To ego, a life partnership is meant to be a special relationship that validates ego, not expresses Spirit. To ego, a partnership that is only an insubstantial frame around Wholeness, like a mystical holy relationship, is the same as no partnership at all. Either way, it resists and grieves a sense of loss. In fact, it would prefer that there be no partnership than that it express Spirit, because then it could still hold out hope that a special relationship could come along for it to use for its purposes. The *Course* explains this:

Now the ego counsels thus; substitute for this another relationship to which your former goal was quite appropriate. You can escape from your distress only by getting rid of your brother. You need not part entirely if you choose not to do so. But you must exclude major areas of fantasy from your brother, to save your sanity. Hear not this now! *Have faith in Him Who answered you. He heard. Has He not been very explicit in His answer? You are not now wholly insane.* (T-17.V.7)

I was experiencing just this resistance myself. Ego was screaming at me that this relationship was a sacrifice, even before Hannah's feelings fell away, because she was not the "special one" it would choose for me. So, I wondered if Hannah's romantic feelings fell to the same resistance. She could have a holy relationship with me, but ego in her needed to keep the door open for a special relationship with another.

I tried to be understanding but vacillated between compassion and anger. I felt her material feelings had opened the door for mine, and now hers were gone, and I was in exactly the situation I never wanted, with unrequited feelings. Once I said to her, "Damn it, Hannah, we could have had it *all!*"

But sometimes I also felt relieved. I was way too unsettled in myself to want to be involved with someone else. Also, a part of me seemed to accept what was occurring without judgment. In fact, both Hannah and I felt about her romantic feelings falling away that nothing was wrong. It was, I knew, as always, ego making me unhappy. But it was spun up and I could not get past it.

I certainly considered not going out to her, but I still felt clear that I was going to Australia. Perhaps I was to go, but not to her? I played with this idea, but I could not escape the feeling that there was no Australia without Hannah. We felt more real to me than anything appearing. This was, of course, our *essence* I felt, as I had in The Minty Moment, but it seemed to extend to our persons.

Maybe I was going to her, but later? After all, before I left Jessie, I felt Hannah was my future. But, no, The Wave was carrying me there now. Hannah's romantic feelings were gone, mine were not, but I was still to go. Ego was not happy with me.

For a while, I had some hope Hannah's feelings for me would be found under fear, as mine had been with Jessie. But towards the end of August, I accepted they were not going to return.

And one night soon after, I went to the darkest place of pure rage. For a long while I called it *The One Dark Night* because I hoped it would be, although I sensed it was not wholly undone. It would turn out to be just the first of many experiences of the dark heart of ego. (I continued to refer to it in my journal as *The One Dark Night*, but sarcastically.)

That night, I experienced anger to a breadth and depth that I never had before. It was **Hot. Red. Rage.** I doubted God's existence as I had never done. I went over my entire former life and saw that, over and over, I wanted or expected things, and when they didn't happen, I simply spun an excuse in Spirit's favor.

In fact, I realized I had made up Spirit. I had duped myself for decades.

I had thoughts like this before, on and off throughout my path. But never at this depth or with this force of rage or disbelief and distrust. It was the darkest dark. It was the purest *awful* there can be. If there was a hell, I was in it. If there was a Satan, *I* was Satan.

I spent hours in this deep, dark, furious darkness. And then…It lifted, and I went on.

But I did not feel anything had been resolved. (Frankly, ego was correct that things had never gone its way. My relationship with Spirit was never about getting my way, but rather Its guidance in my mind and material life.) I wondered if the red rage was just repressed, although I had not worked at repressing it. In fact, I had egged it on to its furthest edge. I hit bottom with it. No, it was gone because, as dark as it got, it was not real, and I knew it. I had experienced the deepest dark of ego and came out of it untouched.

I was to come to doubt that I had truly seen it was not real, because this episode did not dispel the dark fear once and for all. It persisted as an undercurrent, and I would descend into its depths again. But I *had* seen truly. Each time I descended, I saw it in another form, and each time it had no real effects. This was the true forgiveness that the *Course* teaches.

Now I had grief over Hannah's feelings being gone, upon the grief over my dismantled life, upon ego's pseudo-grief. Feeling that I did not know myself grew with the dark fear. I had shifted consciousness, but where were Love and peace and joy? Was I mistaken and this was something else? But I felt I *did* know what was happening. I had shifted consciousness, and I was only facing an interlude I had not known to expect. I clung to this awareness, and I tolerated the darkness because I felt it occurring in just a *part* of my mind.

28

I would spend three weeks alone in the empty house. To save on the power bill in summer in Las Vegas, I moved myself into the master bedroom. I put a futon mattress on the floor and used a dinner tray and boxes for a desk, and pretty much lived and worked there, making forays to the kitchen for meals.

My sister, C, said I could stay with her, but I longed for time alone. I would take up her offer when the new owners came to take possession of the house a month before I left for Australia.

But while I basked in the solitude, it was an extraordinarily difficult time. I was almost a total stranger to myself, I was dealing with unexpected dark fear, and I felt I was living with the corpse of my former person in a house that she had loved. It was empty of *stuff*, but full of twenty-one years of memories. Hannah was different, and it seemed to me our communication problems were worse. Spiritually, I felt I had nothing. Spirit was no longer separate, but I was not exactly in touch with myself as Spirit, either. Meditation was merely processing the turmoil within.

But…the only way out was through whatever this was. So, I held myself together and breathed my way through, hoping something I could recognize as me would be there at the end. I was grateful for the mental endurance I had acquired through years of cardio and strength training. I could tolerate a lot of discomfort.

Part of feeling I did not know myself during this time were the petulant, needy, petty, and just plain juvenile thoughts and feelings I experienced. I felt I had been an insensitive jerk to Jessie, and I continued to say and do things to Hannah that left me apologizing far too often. It was like ego had regressed to a pre-Spirit-centered-person state. For someone who did not like drama, I was to spend a couple of years with ego creating drama where I felt there really was none. But ego lacked a personal flavor, as though it was generic now.

I could not stop it, however. When I tried, it just seemed to flow around me. I could only watch.

I not only did not know who this person was showing up, I did not like her. But I can't say I actively *dis*liked her, either. I was not comfortable with the person, but also not guilty about her.

My first interpretation of this episode was that because I no longer identified with the person, I no longer unconsciously curbed ego to show up as a mature, decent human being. This may be true, but as time passed and I got further away from identifying with the person, I felt she did not belong to me anymore. She was in the flow of the universe, playing a part in the expression of the Atonement and this mind was just the Space in which this appeared. Who was I to judge her?

With all that was going on within me and in my material life, I longed for simplicity and to be left alone to process. I craved a small apartment, with a little bearded Jack Russell terrier I would name Tom, anywhere in the world over going to Hannah. I wanted the shift to be over, but I knew it had only begun and The Wave was to carry me to Australia.

So, when Hannah took some time away to seriously question whether she wanted me to come, I still went ahead and applied for a visa and was immediately granted one. As expected, she soon reconnected, and we decided on my going in early October. This gave me time to take care of logistical matters and to decompress a bit, and Hannah time to say goodbye to her solitude.

Insights came a mile a minute during this time. I understood I was not seeing my relationship with Hannah correctly. One day, I felt strongly I was to let go of everything I ever learned about relationships, going all the way back to my mother. This seemed to fit with "just love her", with feeling the relationship was *given*, and feeling I did not have to *make* the relationship.

But I often disregarded my intuition and approached our relationship as I had relationships in the past. Usually, this was just the running of my own thoughts along certain lines —like being Hannah's victim—even as I felt those lines were no longer appropriate, valid, or authentic. Sometimes, it broke through into my behavior with Hannah, and this led to drama. I could feel a contrast between my no-longer-valid approach and my new State, but I could not access my new State and stop the no-longer-valid approach. Like the dark fear and the childish ego, it seemed to have to run its course.

It was a relief when it came time to leave behind the physical remnants of the former life and go to my sister's condo. I felt as though I had spent those weeks alone in a graveyard. At my sister's, I began to decompress, processed a great deal, and turned toward my new life. I did not miss the old life at all. Sometimes, memories came, or I expected to see a dog at my feet or on the furniture, and I would feel a little grief, but I felt no longing. That life was over, and I could focus on what was new in my mind and life. I felt carried high on The Wave.

Yet, I did wonder why my material life had to change. I was confused, because I had just been growing aware that the material experience was the least significant aspect of consciousness when my material life went through this upheaval. I wondered if I was misunderstanding something and there was some relevance to it after all.

From the start, the shift in my mind was more important to me—and *felt* like the more significant occurrence. But the material changes surprised me, allowing ego to get a hold. At first, before I left Jessie, I thought ego might be trying to take over the process by insisting on material changes. And it *was* meddling, but not by being the source of the material changes. It confused me further by focusing on the material changes as at least as significant as the internal shift.

It would be a long time before I had this all sorted out, but the *sense of significance* granted the material shift *was* all ego. The material transformation was merely an effect of my internal shift, like a tidal wave after an earthquake. And like all effects, it had no effect on the cause. The internal shift went on, completely untouched by it.

29

As my departure for Australia neared, I sensed that being with Hannah in person was going to be different from being with her online. It came over me quite often that we did not really know each other, and it was best to go to her with an open mind.

I also discovered I did not know what she really looked like. Over time on Skype, I deduced that if I threw together Emily Blunt with Laurie Metcalf and threw in a dash of Gene Wilder, I would get a close approximation to Hannah. But she had shown me many pictures, and she looked so different in each that I could not formulate a cohesive idea of her. In close-up photos, her eyes were so large she reminded me of a Margaret Keane painting. But at a distance, her eyes were small and beautiful. (She was aware that she photographed so varyingly, so this was not just my perception.)

When she switched from her laptop to her phone for our calls, the phone's screen distorted her face, so it seemed longer and her forehead, eyes, nose, and mouth loomed larger than they had appeared from the laptop. I missed the Hannah of the laptop! But one day she placed her phone on the kitchen counter (*bench*, in Australia), and stood back by her sink as she spoke with me, and I was floored. She was shorter than I imagined, although she had told me her height. But more than that, she looked so different altogether that I realized the laptop had not given me an accurate look at her, either. (We had already discovered that our cameras distorted skin tones. On my laptop her skin looked porcelain white, but she told me it was olive.) I made a conscious effort from then on to keep an open mind about who I was meeting, both in personality and body.

It was disconcerting to me that I felt relief when Hannah and I took time apart. When we connected, the pseudo-grief rose up, and ego resented her as the symbol of the shift in me. This went on quite apart from my willing intention to go out to her. I knew this conflict was within me and not with her. Yet, I still sometimes took it out on her. And even when I did not, she would empathically feel what I felt anyway.

I faced the same resistance to Love I had felt in my first holy relationship, only this time I felt I would move past it. Resistance was not my entire experience of the relationship, and it felt like something suspended in me rather than what I was. Yet it was an annoying burden that often affected my behavior. The problem was, I did not yet have anything to replace my identification with ego. I was only at the very beginning of a transition to Spirit as my Identity.

In the *Course*, while discussing Helen and Bill's switch from a special hate to a holy relationship, it points out that it would not have been merciful to have done it slower, as ego would then have the chance to reinterpret every step. Well, I was not granted the same mercy for my shift in consciousness! Ego came along the whole way, distorting my experiences, and interpreting every step as shocking, death, and loss, both before and after The Break. I can say for certain now that after The Break it *did* wind down, becoming less real and significant to me, but for over two years it was not clear it would.

Although the time between dismantling my former life and going to Australia felt like a respite, the death pall hovered. So often an insight about the shift or my new Seeing would occur and I would feel *this means I'm dead*, and the pseudo-grief would land on me hard.

For a brief episode, I felt an awareness beneath the sensation of *this means I'm dead* pushing through. But I couldn't grab it. Then one day it emerged: *This means I am not a body.*

This sensation expanded and I knew, as I had months before as I cleaned the shower in my former home, that I am Spirit. I have no beginning or ending. I am immortal; I am eternal. This time I was not gobsmacked. It was simply a breathtaking fact.

To ego, of course, death and Spirit are the same thing. But Spirit is supposed to show up after the body falls away.

The death pall was an ongoing undercurrent, but I felt far better at my sister's than when I was in the trappings of my former life. With that practical busy-ness over, my mind was free to process and be present.

E. NEW LOVE, NEW LIFE, NEW LAND

Prisoners bound with heavy chains for years, starved and emaciated, weak and exhausted, and with eyes so long cast down in darkness they remember not the light, do not leap up in joy the instant they are made free. It takes a while for them to understand what freedom is. (T-20.III.9)

<u>30</u>

I took each family member out to lunch in turn to say an indefinite goodbye. This included Jessie, who was to remain a part of my family, as she had been for twenty-four years. (Oddly, she chose the restaurant where I told her about Hannah on her birthday. Neither of us commented on this.) My sister, E, asked sarcastically how I was going to get to Australia. I knew she was referring to my fear of flying. In fact, although certain by this time that I was going, I did not know if I was going to go in peace or managing anxiety. As the day of departure drew near, my fear did rear up, and I went to the doctor for a low dose anti-anxiety medicine just in case. Knowing I had them took a weapon away from ego.

In fact, I felt quiet and centered the day I left, and I never needed the pills. My initial flight was delayed, throwing off my whole itinerary, and I spent quite a while with a clerk at the airport as she redid it. In an interesting twist, I was rerouted through Hawaii. It was as if I was to touch parts of my old life as I left it. But despite this hiccup, I was completely at peace and just watched it unfold. I had no deadline, after all. My only concern was letting Hannah know about my later arrival.

And through nearly twenty-four hours of travel and layovers I was calm, centered, present, and thoroughly enjoyed myself. I went with the flow, like I would on vacation.

My three flights were uneventful. The only real sleep I managed was a couple of hours on my last flight, from Melbourne to Perth. Only then did I think about where I was headed and feel a little nervous about meeting Hannah. Who was she and what were we headed into together?

In Perth, I discovered my luggage was lost. My bags had gone to Sydney rather than Melbourne, as Sydney was where I was originally supposed to first land in Australia. They had not made it to Perth yet. So, I had only my backpack as I made my way down the escalators, scanning the crowd for Hannah.

She spotted me before I saw her. When I recognized her, I felt, *Yes, of course that's her*. She was familiar but, as I had come to expect, she did not look like she had online. She was smaller and softer. But my feeling of recognition came from someplace else anyway, just as it had when I first saw Emily.

We both wore wide grins as I approached her. "You're shorter than I expected!" were her first in-person words to me. I asked her if that was okay, and she laughed and said "yes" as we embraced, and I was engulfed in the sweet scent of her coconut shampoo.

It was night when I landed. So, in the dark, Hannah took me to Fremantle, a suburb (*neighborhood* in the US) of Perth, to see where she had spent her early childhood. I dipped my toes in the Swan River.

We stayed a couple of days with her mother and uncle in his apartment in Perth before heading to Albany. The first night, I thought I was hearing a neighboring baby cry. But as it persisted, I thought it must be caterwauling felines in heat. The next day Hannah explained: Crows are ubiquitous in Perth. Perthians don't even notice them.

When I saw Hannah that first morning, I felt a nearly-impossible-to-resist magnetic pull to her. I had never felt anything like it. Not embracing her was like trying to hold back The Wave, but I didn't know if it would be appropriate. As she no longer felt for me as I did for her, I was careful how I approached her physically. I did not want to be creepy, especially as I knew I didn't have to act on my feelings for her to sense them. Until I learned her boundaries, I was to let her initiate any physical contact.

Instead, *she* stepped forward and hugged me. She had told me that as an empath she sometimes confused others' feelings for her, for her feelings for them. I found this disturbing. Did she hug me because she felt the pull, too, or did she feel my pull to her? Or was the pull not there for her in any way and she was just being friendly? I felt too much to ask.

In the next couple of days, I said hello to the Indian Ocean, only my second ocean, as I had lived in the middle of the Pacific and visited its eastern edge in California. We went to the zoo, where I wanted to hold Hannah's hand, but restrained myself, again not wanting to be creepy. I felt swathed in Golden Love, but we were strangers and awkward, although friendly, with each other. We had a short visit to gorgeous King's Park, which had great views of South Perth and the Swan River. Perth reminded me a great deal of San Diego.

The capital of Western Australia, Perth is the only big city in the vast state. So, the 250-mile drive to Elleker, a suburb on the east side of Albany, was pretty much country, forest, and small towns. It was all beautiful and refreshing to me coming as I did from a desert city.

We detoured up to one of those small towns, Katanning, to meet Hannah's best friend, and—surprise! (to both of us)—Hannah's father.

Hannah's home in Elleker was in pure country, complete with paddocks, fields, horses, cows and, of course, sheep. But I was not to discover this until the morning as we arrived in the dark. Hannah's nephew, who was looking after her home and cats while she was fetching me in Perth, had a delicious dinner ready for us. That night I looked up at the stars and for the first time *felt* I was in the Milky Way and part of a vast physical universe. I had always lived in well-lit places and had never seen a sky like it.

The next day I discovered the sunlight in southern WA is *golden*. Hannah and I chuckled over this. She had been in other countries but had not noticed. (I thought perhaps it was just the season, as October is spring down under, but it would turn out to be golden year-round.)

The following evening was our first time alone and it was the closest we were to get physically. I felt again that irresistible tug toward her, and we could not stop embracing. I kept disappearing, by which I mean boundaries melted again and again as I expanded into Oneness.

Hannah said she wanted to be closer but wanted some things to fall away so she could be "all there." I said what I felt clearly—it wasn't time.

I had gone to Australia believing Hannah's romantic and sexual feelings for me were gone. And but for her words that first night alone in Elleker, nothing ever occurred to make me think or feel otherwise. But nearly a year later, when I was about to leave Australia, Hannah revealed to me that during our stay in Perth she had to restrain herself from going to my bed. Alas! But by the time I found this out, I had no regrets, considering what followed between us. To have become sexually involved at that time would have been disastrous.

31

It took me ten days to recover from jetlag and the time change. Hannah had made for me a comfortable space in her guest room. She took me around to meet her family and friends, all lovely, loving people, and to some of the nearby sights and scenes, including several beaches on my third ocean, the Great Southern. (Most Australians live within a half hour of a beach. The Outback, which covers 70% of the continent—and no, I didn't see it—is largely uninhabited.)

For the first few weeks in Australia, I had two lovely

concurrent experiences. One was what I call *The Hereness*. I was amazingly present. It was similar to, but not as complete as, The Serenity I experienced for those three days around the yard sale. I felt like an island of peace around which time flowed.

(Dialogue 20181019) *"...I am content in every moment. I never have a moment where I wish I was doing something else. I also do not have to fill every moment and am content to just be sometimes, with thoughts flitting by as they do..."*

This was eventually to give way to time and death and darkness. But I knew this was my inevitable destination in my new State.

The other was *The Enchantment*, a lighter, livelier version of The Golden. This was the State I was in as well as how I experienced Hannah. This experience diminished to a milder day-to-day experience of Oneness, so it has never fully left me. And to this day, I am enchanted by Hannah, no matter what occurs between us or what other feelings intrude.

I once shared this feeling with one of Hannah's (many) sisters and she said, "Yes, she *is* enchanting", so I have never been certain how much of my enchantment with her is due to her personality or to our Oneness. That it persists no matter what else happens between us leads me to think it is an expression of the latter.

During this time of Hereness/Enchantment, I had several experiences of feeling *she is me and I am her* about Hannah. These were not dramatic experiences. They flowed into and out of my awareness quietly and naturally.

As time went on, I was to have experiences when I would look at Hannah's body and know it was mine. I did not feel ownership, possessive, or even that her body was familiar to me. I simply felt, matter-of-factly, that her body was as much mine as the body of this person.

A mild feeling of disappointment often followed my

various experiences of Oneness with Hannah. I understood this was ego's disappointment that she was not the someone special it would have chosen for this experience. How could I experience Oneness with *her*, when ego could not find that special something that would "save" me, or even anything familiar in her person to justify it? This was the question behind the feeling, "Who is this woman and what is she doing in my life?" that would dog me for over two years.

Ego felt that since Hannah was not special, she could be anyone. Which is exactly right! The answer to why *Liz and Hannah*—or any two who experience the Oneness of the holy relationship—has nothing to do with supplying individual egos' sense of lack or satisfying individual personalities' psychology. It is an expression of the unfolding Atonement.

To each who walks this earth in seeming solitude is a savior given, whose special function here is to release him, and so to free himself. In the world of separation each is appointed separately, though they are all the same...

...The plan is not of you, nor need you be concerned with anything except the part that has been given you to learn...The ark of peace is entered two by two, yet the beginning of another world goes with them. Each holy relationship must...learn its special function in the Holy Spirit's plan, now that it shares His purpose. (T-20.IV.5-6)

Hannah's bedroom was the largest room and just off the kitchen. As I was an early riser, I woke her each morning as I made my breakfast. She graciously switched rooms with me, giving me not only the largest room, but the one with the best view across the paddocks, where kangaroos could sometimes be seen hopping in the mornings or early evenings. (But it was quite a while before *I* saw any!)

One morning as I sat at my desk, which I had set up to look at the view, Hannah came into sight in the paddock just across the driveway outside my window. She had showered and dressed to go out. Yet she was dragging a cloth piled high with yard debris behind her and singing off key at the top of her lungs as she made her way to a pile meant for a bonfire come autumn. "Who *is* this woman?" I asked myself, totally captivated. And how did I get to be there with her? I felt so blessed—and so baffled.

Hannah is the most beautiful woman I have ever spent any length of time with. Physical beauty was never important to me, as I had learned in school that the best looking kids were not necessarily the best people. And, as I shared earlier, anyone I liked got better looking to me with time. Only twice before Hannah did I have the experience of being around physical beauty that I never tired of looking at: My nephew when he was a young child and my parents' springer spaniels. But where they were more classically beautiful, Hannah is not. And this is what, to me, makes her all the more captivating. Symmetry in faces bores me pretty quickly. I prefer a face that varies and so keeps me interested, and that is Hannah's.

Hannah moves me as no woman ever has. To the end of my time with her, I felt the best part of each day was the first sight of her and the first sound of her lovely voice. She also smells wonderful. But while all of this was delightful, I didn't need it. I was whole. The physical beauty of Australia and Hannah added nothing to my life. I enjoyed them when with them and did not miss them when they were not around.

I felt all the things for Hannah a lover would, yet I still felt it more accurate to say I was *within Love* with her than in love with her. After she told me she no longer had romantic feelings for me, I felt some things fall away for me, too. I was never certain what they were, but I did find a certain blessing. When we were involved, I wrote to her of longing for her. But now I did not feel that for more than passing moments. As much as I delighted in the sights, sounds, and smells of her, I did not ache for her. I felt no lack.

(Dialogue 20181019) *"…I feel so blessed by Hannah, yet I*

do not have to be with her all the time. It's all of a piece, our being together and our being apart. It's not really that I am okay either way. It's just whatever is happening is what's supposed to happen so our being together and our being apart are the same. This is impossible to explain, but it's part of the holistic experience..."

This was a relief! It took the sting out of unrequited feelings. But boy was ego resistant to this. I spent the first couple of months with it churning on how these *personal feelings* meant I was making her *special*. I sensed this was not true, but I was to go far down that road before I was certain.

Although I sensed they no longer applied, there were habits of thinking like this that I fell into again and again. It was as though I was stuck in vast machinery to which I had once been attached, and, although free, I had to make my way out of it. In the meantime, it chugged along as usual around me. My mind automatically took the approach that there was a lack to supply, some thinking I had to fix, obstacles or blocks to undo, or there were things to learn to grow. I spent two years in this machine, trapped in this thinking, seeing and feeling it was erroneous, with freedom in sight, but unable to extricate myself any faster than what was naturally occurring. Because ego *was* simply winding down and I did not have to do anything but watch.

I was reminded of the Period of Relinquishment, when for months I was stuck in the habit of following myself instead of Spirit, even though I knew I had truly shifted to following It. That, too, was a winding down.

32

The Hereness passed and I could not have been more in ego, even in the Context of The Enchantment. I arrived in Australia with real and pseudo-grief and anger right at the surface.

So was ego's resistance to the holy relationship, defensiveness, and the dark fear.

It did not help that I was in menopause and my hormones were swinging wildly. This made me outright volatile at times. Some women do not like to acknowledge how much their hormones affect their thoughts, moods, and behavior. They think doing so is making an excuse. But I always felt it provided a helpful (and factual) *explanation* for my feelings and behavior when I knew hormones were in play. I took responsibility for their effects, took care of myself, let myself off the hook, and warned others.

So, I knew when I had physical symptoms as well as a certain familiar down, tearful, or volatile mood that more was going on than ego's resistance. Either way, I did, mostly, have control over my behavior. But I did not have to express anger for Hannah to empathically feel it. She was disappointed in me, even though she had seen my anger before I went out to her and had expressed concern about having that energy in her space.

Ego prodded me to be upset about her not having feelings for me anymore when I felt I really was not upset about this. It attacked her and wanted me to feel I was being asked to sacrifice, but I did not feel this. Nor had I felt it about my former life passing away, although it seemed to "cost" a great deal. I understood I was moving into my Self, and it was not just that this was more valuable to me. It was Truth and I knew it. But that I could see ego's ideas no longer applied did not stop them or the painful, angry emotions they caused. I felt ego's thoughts and feelings of lack and fear overlaid my awareness of Wholeness, but I felt that awareness was here.

For several months, I returned again and again to questioning why my material life had to change. It seemed to make it significant when I sensed it was not. Each time, I came to see the other life had been person-Liz's and this was now Liz-Spirit's material life. There was nothing more to it than that. Only ego tried to make it into something more.

I did not understand why ego was so loud and strong as I shifted consciousness. Of course, it made me doubt I *had* shifted consciousness, but never seriously or for long. I felt in the grip of a process because of it, but it was not a process I had expected. So, I was very confused.

I could see the falsity of ego, but I felt it running over me as it had not done in a very long time. I had been aware of my Wholeness in my previous life but—it now seemed—as a distant thing. Now I felt within Wholeness as a part of me ran on with thoughts and feelings of lack, and these dominated my experience for a while.

I said more than once to Hannah that I did not understand why we were to be together at that point, as I felt no one should have been around me in that condition, and most certainly not an empath. I had nothing to hold onto but the awareness that this was occurring in a larger Context (Wholeness) that I could not access but in Which I believed and trusted—most of the time.

Hannah could not feel the Context I did and all she saw was pure ego. She felt I mischaracterized my experience, and that ego had not fallen away, as I had been saying, because I continued to manifest it. This was a source of conflict for her with me for a long time.

I found I could not convey my overall experience to her and had to accept that she could not see the larger Context. Sometimes, she did say she sensed a deep peace in me. But I was not experiencing this at all, so perhaps at times she *did* tap into the Context I could see but not feel.

As I was dealing with so much darkness and confusion, I asked her to support me by looking toward the Light in me rather than always pointing out ego. This is how I thought a holy relationship was expressed, both from my own experience and the *Course's* prescription to Helen and Bill for handling conflicts. Oneness was our Reality, but the holy *relationship* it inspires is expressed as a practice, with or without the experience of Oneness.

But Hannah felt we were to "keep each other honest". I told her that if I was deceiving myself, I would hit that wall soon enough. I trusted what was unfolding, and I did not have any choice anyway but to let it happen. There was nothing I had to do. The Wave had me.

What I wanted with Hannah was to share, describe, and explore my experiences—both ego and Spirit—to better understand them. How was Oneness expressed as a holy relationship but as mutual support? I understood she was not having my ongoing experiences of Vision and Seeing, but she *had* experienced our Oneness. I also knew we would not be *perfect* at supporting each other, as she pointed out I did the same to her that she did to me (attacked her ego). But, for me, that's where forgiveness came into it. Neither of us felt seen by the other.

But Hannah did not agree with my understanding of how to practice a holy relationship. (In fact, I would learn much later that she does not think there is such a thing as a holy relationship between two people, so certainly nothing to *practice*.) So, as she was telling me I was wrong about my experiences, undermining my trust in them and myself, and reinforcing my doubts, I poured my thoughts into my journal instead. I stopped looking to her for support and shared less with her.

Her rejection of my request for help came when I was swamped with so much conflict and confusion and inner turmoil that I could only lump it in with everything else that was not unfolding as I expected. It is surprising that I was not shocked or dismayed by her response. To a large degree, I took it in stride, as I had her romantic feelings falling away. Either some part of me did not need these things or knew how things were to unfold and was not surprised. Probably both. I was to see much later that on some level both Hannah and I know exactly what our relationship is and how it will unfold.

In retrospect, I am not certain what her support would have given me anyway, because her lack of support did not affect the process of ego winding down and Spirit emerging in any way. The material experience is pure effect and does not cause anything. But these rejections were sure fodder for ego when it rolled around, even though I knew I did not really feel deprived. I always knew I had no real conflict with Hannah. I experienced ego's conflict with me. But that did not stop me from projecting onto Hannah when I was in ego.

Hannah and I also had things in common, of course. This was nice, unless it was something we did not like in ourselves, in which case we projected and attacked it in the other. We both have strong minds, hide in our intellects at times, and are fiercely independent. I realized I sometimes encountered in Hannah what Jessie complained about in me.

Hannah did admire my ability to forgive and just accept the flaws and dysfunctions of my person. But she could not understand why, if I saw they were not me and were not real, I did not fix them. Putting aside that we did not necessarily agree on what was a flaw or dysfunction, to work on them I would have to make them real to me! I felt if there was something about the person that needed to change, I would be moved to make a change or find a change occurred.

Hannah told me she grieved her romantic feelings for me falling away. (I was sure she was also relieved as I had turned out to be a disappointment.) She felt her synchronicity signs had pointed to me being her partner, but she thought she had seen a *romantic* partner. So, either it was a coincidence that they pointed to me and her romantic partner was still out there, or the signs had pointed to a holy relationship instead of a romantic one. She feared the latter.

With her disappointment, grief, confusion over synchronicity, and other issues, Hannah soon went into a dark place herself. I call this *The Time of the Daggers* as it came to feel as though knives were flying at me, even in her silence. This is what I meant when I wrote earlier that her powerful mind not only receives but sends. She did not have to openly attack me; it was in the air. And when she did openly attack me, look out! I felt pummeled and pushed back against the ropes in my weakened state only to later realize, *wait—she's not right!* After a few of these episodes, I trusted myself and either stood my ground or walked away when she was on the attack.

I sometimes thought of leaving her home to stay in Albany. She would later tell me that during this time there were only a few hours one day when she seriously thought she might ask me to leave. But neither of us made a move and I spent the whole year with her.

The Time of the Daggers passed, but Hannah remained in a deeply uncomfortable place in herself. Finally, in the new year, she had a significant shift and someone like the Hannah I knew before her feelings fell away showed up. (This occurred on an incredibly significant day for me—to be shared later.)

I still found her mind to be opaque, but I discovered that, given days or weeks of her discussing a certain topic, I would eventually form a picture and understand her. But we continued to have communication issues.

I had the impression our personal conflicts were not as significant to me as they were to Hannah. I felt this was for three reasons. One was that in my previous life I had reached acceptance that personal relationships were inherently conflicted, and she still struggled with this. The second was I felt my conflicts with her would resolve when my conflicts with myself resolved. (Which could only mean ego wholly gone.) I was much more occupied with the ongoing conflict in my mind than its effects. The third was that, since the shift, more than ever the material experience was incidental to me.

I do not want to give the impression that Hannah and I were in ongoing conflict with each other. As students of the *Course*, we each took responsibility for our own thoughts, feelings, and behavior. In fact, I felt Hannah often took this too far and repressed when she should have expressed. And for long stretches, Hannah and I got along very well and enjoyed each other, no matter we were both caught up in our own intense processes. Overall, my time in Australia was enjoyable and full of Love with her, her family, and friends, despite feeling I was lost to myself and carried with me an undercurrent of death. I am grateful to have been in such a beautiful place among such lovely, loving people while I endured the turmoil going on in me.

33

I felt without comfort because I no longer had Spirit to turn to, and I felt I was not in touch with myself as Spirit. But looking back, I now know that I *was* in touch with myself as Spirit. I just did not recognize it.

I wrote a lot in my journal about "my new Seeing". This was not seeing with the body's eyes, of course, but perceiving, intuiting, and sensing in my mind. I might *See* something unfolding in the material world, such as how I knew I was to go to Australia. But most of the time, *Seeing* referred to the Oneness I saw and felt all around as the Context I was in (the real world).

When I doubted Seeing, I feared it was a trick of ego, like some new fancy fantasizing. When I did trust it, I treated it like some new gift I would have to come to understand. I was still thinking like a person. I did not recognize that I was Seeing *as Spirit*.

In fact, for a lot of my time in Australia, I felt "I can't see that I can *See*." It felt like Spiritual Sight was *right here* and I was not able to access it. Now I realize I was telling myself that the Seeing I *had* was the Seeing I sought. If I had been capable of trusting it, it would have been my comfort.

I was aware I had only one problem, and that was ego. It was an *added thing* in my new State, and in an unpleasant way. It felt like something from my former experience tagging along where it did not belong.

I knew that ego's emphasis on the material changes in my life and on my new material life were a distraction. Although thoughts about those things filled my conscious awareness, what truly occupied my mind was the sense of upheaval in it since the shift in consciousness, and the dismantling and processing this caused.

I wanted to get to know my new State, but ego ran interference, so I could not access it fully. I was aware that my insights were distorted and limited by ego. I called them *bleed through*, and thought of them like sunlight shining imperfectly through a dirty window. I realized, in fact, that almost all spiritual understanding and teaching down through the ages has been bleed through.

Sometimes it felt like, where in my previous life Spirit was like a dream of a sunlit room, now I was awake in that room, but with my eyes shut, sunlight shining on my eyelids, hearing, smelling, and feeling the room around me, but not seeing all I would with my eyes open.

I certainly knew I was not seeing Hannah clearly. When I thought of her, she was a blurry place in my mind. Sometimes she was a black hole. Among all those people who were new to me, she was the only person with whom I had this experience. This was odd, because wasn't I in Australia to be with *her*?

Understanding the sources of the blurriness did not come until I was back in Las Vegas, and over a span of time watched structures of personal identity being dismantled. It was like seeing behind the curtain of ego defenses.

Sometimes the blurriness occurred because I was on the verge of Vision and seeing our Oneness. This was a kind of bleed through. But I discovered most of it was ego attempting to understand and justify my sense of Oneness with her *as people* as it cannot know Spirit.

Ego uses relationships to make whole. The wholeness is supposed to be supplied by special things in the other. These are aspects of the other person that remind one (usually unconsciously) of someone loved in their past or are to make up for someone in their past who neglected or hurt them. The *Course* points out that when two find this in each other, they feel that it is a "match made in Heaven." That is ego's "holy" relationship.

But I was not with Hannah because I saw in her something that would meet my psychological needs.

A holy relationship starts from a different premise. Each one has looked within and seen no lack. Accepting his completion, he would extend it by joining with another, whole as himself. (T-22.in.3)

This is not to say that ego did not get into our relationship. I projected onto Hannah much of ego's conflict with me, and in ego's resistance to her I often overlooked what she brought to the relationship. But the fact was, she was not ego's choice for making me whole, no matter I found much about her attractive.

So, I often felt ego probing for something in her. I deduced at the time that it was specialness, but I thought it was trying to make the relationship special. However, it would turn out that ego was looking for those special things that would justify my sense of Oneness with her. Not finding them, it could not understand the relationship.

I went to Australia having known Hannah for two years, as a mentor and a friend and, briefly, a romantic partner. So, I had a good general sense of her. But there were times when I felt surprised by what I did *not* find in her; ways that she did not line up with me. This was itself a surprise, because these were in areas where I *did* know about her and had not been expecting anything different. I had never experienced anything like it. It was not like unconscious expectations, because those tend to be in areas one has not given conscious thought. These expectations contradicted what I knew. It was like I carried a stranger's unmet expectations.

I was to discover that this sensation was ego's confusion because I experienced Oneness with someone who was so unlike the *person* of Liz. Here, though, I could see how ego can only see lack, because of course, like any two people, Liz and

Hannah have traits in common. Ego could have focused on those to justify my awareness of Oneness with her. Of course, that is not true Oneness, but it was an option ego could not even see.

Because it could not find in Hannah what it thought should justify my sense of Wholeness (Oneness), I watched it make an idealized version of her that did not line up with the reality of her. This was simply the flipside of being surprised that I did not find my twin person in her. This I *was* aware of at the time. I was familiar with this trick from when I was young and would realize after reconnecting with an infatuation after time apart that I had been *fantasizing*, not *thinking*, about her.

Coming from Wholeness, I was not experiencing *any* relationship as I used to. But ego cannot understand Wholeness. So, all it knew was I was not feeling or approaching my relationship with Hannah as it wanted. It projected this onto Hannah, blaming her for something lacking in the relationship, when I was the one not feeling what it wanted me to feel.

Sometimes, I caught sight of a passing horror and emptiness when thinking about Hannah. This was the darkest view of her, and did not fully surface until much later. Ego's attacks on her were very personal at that time because I persisted in my relationship with her despite the unique expression of her person being so different from my own, and not supplying the right specialness to justify my awareness of Oneness with her. This made ego aware that I was coming from Someplace Else in my relationship with her. As it had from the start, it saw its death in Hannah.

But ego's conflict was always with me, not with Hannah. And this was the cause of my conflicts with Hannah, no matter the shape they took.

As well as not seeing Hannah clearly and knowing it, my feelings for her were a jumbled mess of contradictions that try as I might I could not sort out. I loved her, I enjoyed her, and I was attracted to her. But I never felt the desire or possession or hurt or jealousy that ego wanted me to feel.

And despite my feelings for her, present with her I could not imagine us together as a couple. Sometimes, I wondered if I truly was attracted to her or if ego only wanted me to be, because there were times I felt no more than an older sister or friend to her.

Or was it only ego that could not envision us as a couple, because the Content of our coupledom could only be Spirit? In any case, this was a moot question, as she did not return my feelings. Repeatedly, I let her go because I did not want to be in an unrequited situation. I wanted to move on. But each time it would wash over me that I could not let her go any more than I could let go of my Self. So, I tried letting go of my romantic feelings for her, but they would not budge either. In fact, I felt it was not necessary to let them go.

As a part of me seemed perfectly okay with how things were unfolding, I was not always certain which of my material feelings were real or if they even mattered. I also felt there already *was* a Liz-and-Hannah, albeit unmanifested. Was this Seeing the future? Or just a metaphor for the Oneness I felt with her? Or was this the essence of us I had seen and felt before, the real world I was in now? I was not used to being conflicted and confused for such a length of time! After a while, I simply settled in for a long unfolding, sure that clarity would come some time.

34

When the shift in consciousness occurred, I felt not just that I did not recognize anything of myself, but also incredibly weak. Ego seemed to have the run, if not wholly of this mind, a good portion of my conscious awareness, as it had not in decades. And I could not stop it.

In the early days after the shift, I sometimes heard "Claim It!" and "Step up into It!" in my mind, and I felt I was being lifted. At the time I was not certain what I was to claim, but later I would feel it was my true Power.

Like immortality, *power* was not something I had given much thought to in my previous life. But suddenly here it was to be seen and felt and claimed. It was an idea and experience I was to revisit from time to time as Spirit emerged.

I did not know it at the time, but I started to claim my Power during The Mansion/shack Insights, just after Ginny died. I became aware I wanted ego only because I made it, signaling I was coming into myself as the Son of God, or Spirit. Four years later, I understood.

(Dialogue 20181128) "...I have to take complete responsibility for this whole thing. I don't mean in the blame way, but in the empowerment way. If I am Spirit and Spirit is the Wave I rode...then I am That Which, in emerging into this mind's consciousness, brought all of this about...

...it does seem like I am looking at things from every possible angle, like all those thoughts are in my mind, consciously or not...

... I want what happens because it is part of the Undoing, individually and macro-story. Of course I do. I wanted everything that has happened and I want what will happen, in this individual life as well as in the larger story. Thus I am willing.

Thus Jesus was willing to go to the cross. Not in sacrifice, but in recognition of its necessity in the Undoing, which is, in the end, just a story.

And it's why I have been and I am willing. My willingness is not individual, though that is how it plays out. I am learning I am more than the individual, anyway."

(Dialogue 20181129) "This taking responsibility seems essential to my feeling empowered. Nothing has happened to me against my will. Even now, any conflict I feel is because of a little will that tells a different story. The thing is, I do what I'm going to do willingly, so I wonder at the value of the little will...

...Just saw that the part of me that remains shocky about

the change and questions it, etc. does so not because of anything inherent in the past it claims to miss but simply to exert another will. Period. Because I'm beyond thinking any particular form matters..."

I did not just intellectually grasp but *felt* ego as an exertion of a *little will* or *will apart* opposed to my True Will. I felt that both were my will, and the little will was simply my will misdirected. I could feel I was opposed to me. *All* power was *my* Power.

Sometimes I felt I "conjured" Hannah. This was another example of The Author. I did not feel I manifested the person of her as a desired object of my personal choice. I understood I was experiencing Extension and had not conjured appearances. It was powerful to be in touch with Creation (Extension).

(Dialogue 20181212) *"OMG, is this what I've been facing around Hannah? My own power? Yes, this is what has left me breathless. There's more to this new world than just another way of seeing. There's this Power... It's Power Itself through me. It is the dropping of boundaries."*

The dropping of boundaries meant only one reality, Spirit, and that was powerful. *I just so happened* to feel this around my relationship with Hannah, as that was the new material life showing up.

I had taken a passive approach to ego and the dark fear, expecting that at this stage I should be on automatic pilot and not need to make any conscious effort. But this left ego unchecked, and it nearly overwhelmed me at times with clamoring thoughts and dark feelings. One night around Christmas 2018, when deeply sunk in darkness with ego attacks raging, I reached my limit and did not care if it was a mistake to get involved. I shouted "Enough!" and mentally grabbed myself by the collar and hauled myself out. I *refused* the attacks and dark thoughts and felt empowered in a way I had not for a very long time. This was the beginning of the end of feeling weak, and the start of a slow claiming of Power.

But I found, as weakness and darkness continued, that if I tried to make what I did that night into a practice, it had the opposite effect and empowered ego. What *was* automatic was knowing when I had to apply effort, and then it was always effective. It seemed to halt, or at least slow, the habitual running of the ego machinery for a while.

Months later, "Claim it!" rolled around another dark night. This time it had broader meaning as I understood I was not to resist ego but rather recognize that, although it was not me, I was the Power behind it. My fear of losing a part of me with ego had never been about losing ego after all, but about losing the Power I gave to it. And I saw I could never do that. It was impossible. I could misdirect my Power, but never lose It.

As I began to claim my Power, I sometimes felt I could hardly contain it and longed to express it. I went through a funny episode when I yearned to go out in any nearby paddock and *roar*. Hannah, laughing, encouraged me. But I didn't want to alarm the neighbors or the wildlife. Instead—giving warning—I roared around the house when Hannah was in the shower or played her music loud. Sometimes, without the urge to roar, I felt energy ripple across my arms and chest, and I flexed those muscles, bending inward, like a bodybuilder on display. I felt such Power that I was surprised my muscles didn't grow massive and tear through my clothes, like the Hulk's. My throat ached with the urge to express my Power, and whether I roared or not, no expression was adequate.

35

As I climbed into bed on New Year's Day 2019, I had the sense I was going to "receive a download" soon. As I had been processing so much already, I figured this meant something out of the ordinary. I dreaded a ton of new information hitting me. What if in my ongoing conflict and turmoil I was to write a book or something?

The next day I was on my usual morning walk in Elleker and stopped to look over a field of thriving rapeseed. I was thinking about my first holy relationship and my first Revelation and how since then I had only been coming to accept what they showed me...

And then I was Christ.

This was not a *Vision*. I did not *see* my Self; I *was* my Self. It was the most powerful, beautiful, and significant of all my spiritual experiences in consciousness because I was finally fully Me. I immediately wondered about my former experience of existence as a person and saw it was insignificant. This was not dismissive, but simply a fact.

Jesus was beside me the moment I was Christ. I understood this was symbolic, to be sure I understood we were equals (as though I needed confirmation!).

The *Course* says you cannot know your Self alone, by which it means as *one among many*, like a person. Christ is the One Self that *is*. There is no other beside Christ. It is interesting to note that until this moment I had always experienced my Self with another present or in my mind. The awareness of my Self extended as I saw past the appearance of two persons (me and another), and I knew I was *the Only* and not one among many. But this time, I did not experience extension. I did not See my Self in Jesus, as I had with Emily and Hannah. I simply knew I was Christ, as was Jesus, who has become a symbol of Christ.

I did not use the term *Christ* when I recorded *The Experience as My Self* in my Dialogues. I mentioned it in a vague, oblique manner, much as I had avoided writing directly about The Break when it happened. This time, though, it was not because the experience was frightening; it was simply impossible to capture in words.

About it the next day I wrote that I *"just slipped into Me."* But then this as well:

"This afternoon as I was raking grass I had a moment when I felt Myself and knew this was absolutely what Jesus was. Bringing to fruition the moment I had as a teenager that began it all..."

These moments faded, but not completely. The experience of it informed much of my processing for a while. And then a week and a half later:

(Dialogue 20190112) *"There's something I have avoided and not given thought to. It's what occurred in the moment when I was Me. It's what happened just before the experience faded away. It was my seeing I'm Christ. Really, truly experiencing and knowing this. I tell myself it's egotistical to go there. But perhaps it's egotistical to not go there. Perhaps it's egotistical to stay small. In fact, I know it is.*

...To truly be 'reborn in Christ' is not to simply know about Christ. It is to be Christ.

...I do not feel humble about this. I do not feel an overblown sense of my own importance. What I experienced was universal, not personal. I do feel a kind of relief, like I'm getting down to something...

...what am I really saying when I say I am Christ? I'm starting to have the horrid sense that I am to go into the world with this and be Christ and let...

Oh, shit. Oh, fuck. Is this the <u>download</u>? Nononononon- ono.

Am I seeing that I am not only going to just manifest Christ but that I'm going to acknowledge that's what I am and teach others this is what they are too? I mean—continue to break down Christianity as I have by teaching ACIM but, really and truly, directly, not just around the edges?

Nonononnnononnononooonnnoonononnonono.

This is patently ridiculous. This is...I can never say or write these words to anyone.

It's not enough to merely say Christ isn't what you think It is. It has to be demonstrated...

'What Jesus was, I am. What I am, you are too' is the message to be delivered. But it can't be from someone who is just teaching this. It has to be someone who is manifesting it.

And I thought I'd be attacked translating ACIM into plain language!

Actually, I'm not in the least concerned about attacks. I will be in an Invulnerable state. It's the patent absurdity of what I've just written that bothers me..."

This was one of those times that I consciously brought the machinery of ego to a halt. I allowed myself to rant only a bit longer before I decided to cut the melodrama. Later that day:

"...I didn't really see anything new today. It was just reframed using the 'Christ' word. I mean, I've known what's going on. I've known I'm rising in consciousness, and I've known to What. Was it phrased that way to bring forth my obstacles, which, as it turned out, weren't obstacles? The freakout was inappropriate and quickly seen as such. None of the concerns brought up were genuine."

That morning, Hannah had awoken in a rage and asked for a wide berth, which I granted. She spent the day reading Jan Frazier's (*When Fear Falls Away*) posts on the internet and they helped her shift. She wondered that evening if the shift was genuine, but I could see immediately it was. She was relaxed and grounded as I had never seen her. I told her this, but I did not tell her that in her new condition I recognized my "truest wife". I found her new groundedness very…appealing.

This was the shift when I felt some of the Hannah I had known online return. A few days later, I realized her shift happened the day I received The Download.

I found it amusing that what I had taught for so long about Christ being everyone's True Identity turned out to be true. Who knew? This almost made me suspicious of my experiences! *How could I have been right?* Feeling this question, I realized a part of me had never accepted what I taught. Well, what was that, but ego? I was deeply in touch with that doubter now. But this surprise and doubt only reinforced what I already knew—it had been Spirit teaching through me all along.

On one hand I knew and on the other I never accepted. That is the split-mind in a nutshell. (Just as Helen Schucman had said about the *Course*: She knew it was true, but she could not accept it.)

I had so many experiences, especially early on in Australia, when there was a flow of spiritual insight or fulfillment only to be followed, painfully, by an ebb. And it happened again here, perhaps most painfully as I had fully *been* my Self for a moment. But the experiences I had from The Golden onward were not like the higher miracles I had in my former life. Since The Break, they had been coming daily with an immediacy that revealed they were the ongoing Context I was in. And although they faded, they merely melted back into that Context and would come around again. Where formerly higher miracles were rare and buried in time in ego-consciousness, now the dying ego was simply blocking my sustained awareness of my new State the way a dirty window filters and distorts the light of the sun.

36

In March, I went to see an immigration specialist about staying in Australia. I had no family in Australia, and I was too old for a work visa, so my only way to stay was marriage or a *de facto partnership*. The Australian Supreme Court had determined that the latter did not have to be a sexual or romantic relationship, but the two involved did have to have a committed relationship, be exclusive, have their lives entwined domestically and financially, and intend to go forward with each other. In other words, to be family, whatever that meant for them. The immigration agent felt that the holy relationship I had with Hannah was exactly the kind of situation for which the de facto partnership was designed. She said the fact that it looked (even though I did not feel) like I left my former life for it showed how serious it was for me.

I was excited at first to have clarification and to see a way to stay, but I also quickly realized Hannah would never go for it. Soon after I arrived in Australia, she told me she did not want anyone depending on her. I felt this put the kibosh on any partnership of any kind with her, as to me *depending on each other* is the very definition of *partnership*, whether it be doubles partners in tennis, business partners, or life partners.

And I felt strongly that she was not someone I wanted to entwine my life with anyway. We were barely friends, much less family. We had different values in some ways that were important to me. My feelings for her were unclear. And I had discovered some things about her that I felt made it unwise to hitch my wagon to hers. But I also knew personal feelings were no longer my motivation for acting or not acting. (I did not fully realize yet they never had been.) I would ride The Wave wherever it took me and adjust to whatever situation I found myself in.

So, when I laid out to Hannah what the immigration specialist said, I was not surprised and I was a little relieved when she said, "I don't feel it." But I was also confused: *New love, new life, new land.* I had felt my life in the world had become a metaphor for the shift. Was this no longer true? I did not feel that. What I had seen from the start still held.

Something had felt off to me since Hannah's romantic feelings for me fell away and knowing now that I was to leave after a year, I felt this even more. I could only conclude *I* was off. My view of the situation had to be out of alignment with how things were. This was the adjustment I had to make.

For the rest of that spring and early summer, my journal is filled with a ton of processing. I revisited a lot that I had already gone through, had new insights, and glimpsed ideas and experiences that would come around again later. It reads to me now as a mind in the midst of a tremendous shift, but still largely thinking as it had been (a person) rather than as it was emerging (Spirit). The copious processing and journal writing was the release of a pressure valve.

Somewhere in this time, though, I experienced a turning point. It was like I reached a level of acceptance of the shift in consciousness as well as the slow winding down of ego. Things were no longer as difficult as they had been.

(Dialogue 20190610) *"Had a moment earlier where I was thinking about the dramatic shift in me. Not the outer life, or even in consciousness, but in my experience of myself; how I became a stranger to myself. And it washed over me that it had to be that way…I saw in that moment that it had to be a sudden, dramatic shift to break me away from who I thought I was. And I found this validating, because I've resisted my sense of strangerness to myself, as though it was somehow wrong for me to feel that way. This experience was like, 'Yes, you were correct to feel it was so dramatic and disorienting and difficult. It <u>was</u>.'"*

I wondered if I would ever "land" again, or if I had to acclimate to being "up in the air". At the time that I wrote about this, I was referring to my material life. I felt completely unmoored and adrift in the world. My former life was gone, and the life I had originally thought I was headed to with Hannah was not going to happen. I assumed at some point I would "land" again and have some sort of settled life in the world.

But another way to read "up in the air" is the way I used the term "in the ether" when I felt "in the ether" with Hannah and "on the ground" with Jessie. The fact was, no matter if a settled material life showed up, I would never again feel a part of the material world. I had left it long before when I felt a ghost in the world. I was Spirit now, feeling Elsewhere—or Everywhere or nowhere specific, if you will. My real frustration was not feeling able to settle into *this* yet.

(Dialogue 20190709) *"...Maybe I will not have a permanent home in the world again, and so no steady community, either. I will never be a 'part of' again. I can't imagine going back to LV and being a part of that family there, either. But, maybe, no matter where I go, and even if I do settle, I will 'play a part' and not be 'part of' so trying to see anything that way will not work."*

Whatever was to come in my material life, it would never be real to me again anyway.

(Dialogue 20190721) *"So I'm a little slow on the uptake. Talk about <u>not seeing</u>! Have I seen this at all before? Did I write something along these lines and forget? For Heaven's sake: <u>I am **living** none of this is real</u>! I am living forgiveness! That's why it feels like a character and a play! Because it <u>isn't</u> real."*

What were my new Context, Vision, and Seeing if not the awareness that Truth is unaffected by material appearances? It is here, beside the material world, whole and complete and untouched by it.

When I saw in The Experience as My Self that my former life was insignificant, I realized it meant my material life *now* was insignificant, too. But the winding down ego still took precedence day to day. Sometimes, I did get it, however:

(Dialogue 20190724) "...*I am not the Author of the unfolding story. My Being extends in this moment. It is What is. But I have to speak of the appearance of illusion because it is here, too, though nothing. In this moment there is my extension and an appearance. This is how the level of perception differs from Knowledge, as ACIM uses the terms. Knowledge is only Truth. In perception there is always an 'and': Truth and illusion. The highest perception is Truth as Truth and illusion as illusion.*

What appears is illusion. And this moment is perfect. Illusion is not perfect; it is nothing. But this moment is perfect because Perfection is present. This moment is loving because Love is present. This has nothing to do with appearances, not only as source, but also as extension. The appearance has no content. The content of this moment is Perfect Love...and there is an appearance, which is nothing.

The 'character' is part of the appearance. The content of this moment is Perfect Love and there is a character, with all her feelings, appearing. And she and her feelings are nothing.

This mind is split. It no longer thinks it is split between two realities. It sees Truth as Truth and illusion as illusion. In time, where it no longer resides, it will be made ready for Truth and will put illusion aside altogether...

I need to see this more."

I felt when I went to Australia that I was in transition and hoped I would become settled in myself there. Instead, I felt more up in the air than ever. As I made plans to return to the US when my visa was up in October, I accepted that this transition had a long way to go.

37

At the beginning of August, Hannah and I headed up to Katanning for her best friend's birthday and I had another significant experience that I call The True Unity Epiphany.

I was driving, and Hannah was beside me in the passenger seat. I was feeling how my year with her was just the start for us. It was a necessary period of getting to know each other. I still saw us together long-term in some form. I felt, as I had all along, that she would be a part of my life for the rest of my life. Hannah said she felt we would be in and out of each other's lives.

And then—how do I describe these moments? Words are so inadequate. This would turn out to be as important as The Experience as My Self, although it resembled The Break and The Minty Moment more.

(Dialogue 20190804) *"...I understood explicitly what 'truest wife' means. I saw with clarity and certainty that this applies to Who I am. I felt how our union was far beyond, and felt how it is far more satisfying, than any personal relationship. I don't know how it will show up in form, but it is very real. More real than what shows up in form. But I am sure we will always be, at minimum, in touch. I felt how our relationship 'lifts' me into myself. I speculated on how, since she can empathically feel me, my rising will lift her. I felt we are one and the same.*

...That our union is real is beyond doubt. How it will play out, I do not know."

I grasp for words after these experiences. Eventually I would realize *union* was not the most accurate word for what I saw and felt. It was *Unity*—Oneness. Oh, these words! Everyone forms their concepts of them, but the experience cannot be captured. What was most important to me in this experience was I was my Self—Christ—again for a moment. And I felt how wholly satisfying Oneness is and how no personal relationship can come close because *I am not a person.*

This began a shift in how I experienced my relationship with Hannah. It was one I had been waiting for, because I knew the mystical holy relationship expressed my new State. Our material relationship was an effect of that.

(Dialogue 20190808) *"...our union is not dependent on time, which I do feel. It is now. And since it is a fact, the unfolding story is irrelevant. It is not our union, but an expression of it. Our actual union is important to me, in itself, of course, but also because it is me, where what happens with Liz & Hannah is not. I accept how it unfolds, because that is our union now, however it looks."*

(Dialogue 20190813) *"...As* ACIM *says, I cannot look at myself alone and find myself because that is not what I am... I see Love, or Union, with Hannah. Seeking in myself alone and seeking in Hannah for Love are the same thing. Our Union is. If I look to It, I will find Hannah. But if I look to Hannah, I will not find Love. The Vision of our HR is the way to see myself."*

To be in touch with our True Unity was what I had wanted all along. Now that I had seen and experienced it clearly, it stayed with me, although resistance was undone in stages over the next year and a half.

I knew I was experiencing things Hannah had only glimpsed. It was difficult to discuss with her because she did not believe my experiences expressed my new State. In any discussion, it sounded like my mind was as split as it ever was. The difference was, in ego-consciousness I experienced Spirit and ego like two parts of me. Now, ego was floating suspended within me, and, yes, often eclipsed Spirit, but never wholly. It was in my mind like a chronic story of lack in the midst of

Wholeness. I could understand why Hannah couldn't see what I felt. There was no way to convey it, and ego was clearly on the surface. But it meant I could not share with her my lovely experiences of her.

I culled quotes from the *Course* about the holy relationship for Hannah, but I don't know if she ever read them. We discussed reading the *Course* together and I wanted to focus on the holy relationship. But somehow, we never got around to it.

In time I realized our conflicts had no effect on the process I was in. They neither helped nor hindered ego winding down or Spirit emerging. I felt these would have gone on wherever I was and no matter who I was with. I experienced the correct relationship of cause and effect. Spirit affected my material experience, but my material experience did not affect Spirit. This was forgiveness.

At least three times when in Australia I considered that what I saw of Hannah and I unfolding on the material level was maybe about someone other than Hannah, because insights of what was possible came spontaneously. The last one occurred a month before I left.

(Dialogue 20190904) *"What came in so beautifully, gently, and quietly was a clear vision of an expression of the holy relationship as a full, loving partnership between two who know they are One…I saw the beautiful expression that is not only possible but is what this is supposed to be about. But I also realized later that I could be using her to block this expression with someone else. It's beautiful either way, as it is the expression, not the person with whom it happens, that is the point."*

This came a month after The True Unity Epiphany, which was whole and satisfying and pulled me into my Self. I did not understand why I kept seeing a material relationship that expressed Oneness, because I did not feel one was necessary before and certainly not after the epiphany. Perhaps it was only a metaphor.

As my departure neared, Hannah and I processed our relationship. This is when she told me about having to restrain herself from coming to my bed in Perth when I first arrived. I was gobsmacked. I had felt very briefly when I first arrived that our relationship could go anywhere, and she told me she had felt the same.

I did feel that I heard about this at the right time. Earlier in my stay, I simply had too much going on. But ego had wound down enough as I was leaving for me to hear this without rancor. Besides, I was correct our first night alone in Elleker, when I felt it was not time to become emotionally involved. Our subsequent conflicts attested to that. I imagine they would have been worse if we had been involved.

Anyway, Spirit emerging as my Identity was most important to me. I was in transition the entire time I was there and not stable enough to have anything to offer anyone else.

Just as I was leaving, I began to feel I had arrived.

(Dialogue 20190914) *"...I feel I am now what I felt I came here to become. And this is who I said was Hannah's partner. I certainly feel that as far as the integration goes I have a way to go. But I have 'stepped up' into the fullness of that process..."*

I had more clarity than I had for most of my time in Australia. My sense of being lost and not recognizing myself was starting to dissipate. I sensed that when I returned to Las Vegas, the difficulty of the past year and a half would simply fall away from me.

I left saying to Hannah "let's just watch *how* we unfold." She said, "let's see *what* unfolds." This distinction would be key later.

As I was returning to live with my sister, C, with whom I had spent the last month before I left, I wondered if I would have occasion to wonder if Australia was all a dream! I told C to not get used to me, as I felt I was still in transition and my life was not settling soon. I did feel I would be back to Australia at some point. I felt, in fact, that I was returning to Las Vegas for closure, with ego, certainly, and maybe with the former life.

I had a vague idea of being in the US nine to twelve months at least to satisfy visa requirements, but no firm plans. But as it was, world events would put off any thoughts of returning for a while longer.

I still was not certain about income. In Australia, I met with clients in the US, Canada, and Europe (I could not invoice Australian clients, as I was not allowed to work there), wrote articles, and compiled articles into books. I expected to somehow kick-start life coaching and build on the smattering of clients I still had, and maybe go back to cleaning part time.

I spent an amazing year in Australia. I felt both lost and more awake than ever. Once, a predator got a parrot in Hannah's yard and left behind a spray of colorful feathers. Hannah said, "Beautiful carnage." Because of the darkness underlying my stay in Australia, which seemed to grow even as (or maybe because) I gained greater clarity, for a while I labeled that time *beautiful decay*. I thought an underlying sense of death and destruction would always tinge my memories of that year in Australia. But I was wrong. After The Dark Passage ended, I remembered great difficulty, but I could not recall the experience of dark fear.

Not long before I left it went through my mind, "I died here." But later I would feel I both died and was born there.

(Dialogue 20190901) *"It's not like I'm a person who has to give things up. That would be sacrifice. It's that I'm not a person so those things of a person don't fit anymore."*

F. CLOSURE

The closer you come to the foundation of the ego's thought system, the darker and more obscure becomes the way. Yet even the little spark in your mind is enough to lighten it. Bring this light fearlessly with you, and bravely hold it up to the foundation of the ego's thought system. Be willing to judge it with perfect honesty. Open the dark cornerstone of terror on which it rests, and bring it out into the light. There you will see that it rested on meaninglessness, and that everything of which you have been afraid was based on nothing. (T-11.in.3)

38

When I returned to Las Vegas, I felt the sensation that I was *Someplace Else* strongly again. I could not grant significance to the material world anymore. I had felt this for over a year, but the change in my material life seemed to highlight the feeling that I felt the same wherever I went.

(Dialogue 20191007) *"Elleker was quiet and gorgeous, but it was wasted on me as I feel no different here than there."*

I felt that my material experiences were happening in a vast Space, much like a scene is suspended in a snow globe. I compared this to being like Glenda the Good Witch in *The Wizard of Oz*, overlooking the snow globe-world, except I felt both the observer and a participant in the suspended world. I had tried to convey this to Hannah when I explained the new Context in which I experienced everything. Yes, I was manifesting ego, but I also felt it was just a role I was both playing and watching. More and more I was aware I did not need to take any of it seriously.

I read Bernadette Roberts's *The Path to No-Self*, which I found much easier to understand than *The Experience of No-Self*. She said it was a mistake to expect super-humanness or a sense of divinity when ego falls away. And, indeed, I felt the banality of my continued humanity. But I also had all those interesting new experiences as Spirit, including feeling immortal. And although the person was not me, for a while when I acted as the person, I felt more fully human, just as years before I felt I stepped into a maturity that was not simply what came with age and experience.

I would go on to read *What is Self?* in which Ms. Roberts would detail (beautifully) her experiences in a Christian context. Having read her and Jan Frazier (*When Fear Falls Away*) at this point, I was fascinated by how our traditions seem to signify how our individual awakening will unfold. For example, a student of *A Course in Miracles* will not go through the same process as a Christian contemplative, although there are similarities. We each understand our processes through our spiritual traditions, of course, and so we explain them in that context. But then our Universal Experience illuminates our paths in ways we did not expect, deepening our understanding of them as well. Ultimately, It takes us past our traditions.

Even before the shift in consciousness, readers told me my writing had changed. This probably began around The Barrenness and The Forgetting, but no one could characterize the difference for me. It seemed to be more tone than content. Now, as I referenced both Ms. Roberts and Ms. Frazier in my articles as I sorted out my own experiences, readers told me I sounded more like Ms. Roberts. They explained that, like Ms. Roberts, I didn't pull any punches and shared the darkness and difficulty I experienced. (Of course, Ms. Frazier had no darkness as she totally dropped ego literally overnight! Neither I nor Ms. Roberts had that same joy to share.)

Ms. Roberts's darker experiences reinforced my own

until one day I realized my mistake (to be explained later). But she also validated many of my other experiences.

(Dialogue 20191029) "I've found validation in some of BR's 'What is Self?' book. How the falling of the ego is discovered in retrospect. How the joining with the 'divine', which accompanies it, is not wholly joyous because it is shattering. How the acclimating (my word as well) takes years…

…She also refers to how everything else becomes superficial—my feeling of being in a play…

She mentions not being able to come from a self-centered position anymore. I don't know that she experienced any external shift, as I did. I don't think so. She mentions a new way of seeing and finding oneself in a new dimension, as I have. And she talks about how eventually you find Truth in the emptiness—how the barrenness slipped into Spaciousness for me.

She says eventually, as one acclimates, the new state becomes the new normal, which is something I have expected would happen.

Where we differ greatly is that she sees all this unfolding as purposeful where I have come to see it as the natural progression of Light in the dream."

Ms. Roberts felt the journey from ego to Spirit and Christ and onto God was the God-given journey meant for all. But I could feel God's indifference to me as a person, and even to the Atonement—an illusion. (She experienced that same indifference but interpreted it differently.)

I felt the drama I experienced was what occurs when Spirit breaks into a consciousness limited by ego. It was due to the limitations of my mind, not caused by Spirit, nor required by God. It is inevitable this will happen in some minds as the Atonement is expressed through them as the idea of not-God being undone. My life was never personal or individual, but part of a whole expression. My error, my illusion, was feeling it was ever mine alone. This was corrected when I came to experience myself as the Son of God, or Spirit.

When I was first a student of the *Course,* like many new students I felt disturbed when I found I was not emotionally charged in a situation that used to upset me. I did not want to be upset, of course, but I felt I lost something of me as my reactions changed. Now I was experiencing that same thing on a massive scale. I could not choose what parts of ego to release. The whole thing was going and, in its place, came an entirely new experience.

Material living did not change; I did. The usual things occurred in my material life, but I experienced them in new, often unrecognizable, ways. Sometimes I felt lighthearted and enjoyed even conflicts. But I could not always articulate in my journal my new experiences of familiar people, places, and events.

My new way of experiencing things meant for a while I made the mistake of granting significance to things that were not significant. Of course, I did that with the material life shift. But I also did this on a smaller scale. For example, I might have an experience of Light while doing something ordinary, like grocery shopping. I would then think there was something significant about that supermarket or the people I encountered there. Maybe I was to work there; maybe someone I saw was to be in my life in some way. But this was a false association. The Light experience and my being in the supermarket and around those people when I had it were coincidental.

Of course, this made me wonder several times if I was mistaken about Hannah, as I came to understand her being present or on my mind when I had experiences of Oneness was coincidental. Our relationship was not the source of my experiences of Oneness and Oneness was not the Source of our relationship. Yet, time and again I came out of resistance to her to see and feel she is to be in my life. It turns out I experience Oneness and *I happen to know* what is going to unfold in the material world. *Whatever* my material life is to be, I will have experiences of Light and Oneness in it, because I am Spirit.

Oneness is the Real Content of all relationships. (Really, of every moment. There is no reason to single out *relationships*.) When I came to understand this, it seemed as though the material world floated like so much debris on an ocean of deep peace.

This new experience of existence would have been *only* fascinating and would have taken *only* acclimating if ego were not around. Only ego made the experience uncomfortable as it judged everything as fearful. And yet, I forgave this.

(Dialogue 20191022) *"I saw it again: As I am Spirit, any manifestation of the ego in me…is of absolutely no consequence.*

This is, of course, forgiveness. And it's not new for me to see the insignificance of the ego…I see the echo (of ego) experiences as wholly out of the realm of Spirit. Those experiences have no relevance at all from the point of view of Spirit. It's like they are non sequiturs. Spirit speaks of how to make a pie and echo (of ego) speaks of how to drill for oil. So Spirit does not shrug it off as not important, as it would, say, the idea one should use both butter and lard for the crust rather than lard alone. It sees the echo (of ego) as completely irrelevant. It doesn't overlook sin; it doesn't see it…

It's as though I saw a continuum of sin to Innocence, but in fact sin and Innocence do not occur in the same place. Innocence does not see sin and dismiss it; It does not see sin, period."

Slowly, for the next year, I would acclimate to new experiences even as ego judged them. And this would help to silence its judgments.

39

I had lived for 26 years in Las Vegas before spending a year in Australia. It was my home; I knew it well. But now I had no emotional connection to it. I was a stranger in a city in which I just happened to know my way around. No place in the world will ever be home to me again. I live Elsewhere and watch the world pass by.

A few weeks after I returned, I met up with Jessie. She had lost sixty pounds, so she looked radically different. Not only was her Liz gone, but her Liz's Jessie appeared gone. The change in her physical appearance was another symbol to me that the former life had completely ceased.

She was doing well and said our breakup brought her closer to God. I told her I was happy about this, and she joked "the next time you have a lesson to teach me, maybe don't make it so hard."

Her friends were still more upset with me than she was. They said I left her for Hannah, and Jessie felt this way, too (and humiliated by it), but she simply told people I had left her. She did feel her Liz had died. She said a divorce was a kind of death anyway (words I had used in *A Good Woman* a year before I left her, never imagining the marriage I was in was coming to an end). We continue to be family, most of our contact over family or practical issues.

Given my different experience of existence, I had no reason to doubt a shift in consciousness occurred. But if I did, I would only have to think how completely Jessie's Liz is gone and remember how I felt when dismantling her life that I was taking apart the life of a stranger. How quickly and effortlessly I did that; how it flowed without logistical glitch. I call Jessie my ex-wife because that is expected, but I do not feel she was ever *my* wife. I have the memories of the former Liz, and sometimes her feelings, but they are not mine.

(Earlier, I used an episode of Star Trek: TNG to describe how I felt like I woke up to find I was living a different life. But eventually I felt another Star Trek-universe analogy is closer. I felt like a Trill symbiote transplanted into a new host, the person of Liz, whose memories and feelings I would now experience. The analogy stops there, however, as I will not blend with her and I do not bring the memories, skills, and feelings of past hosts.

While in Australia, Hannah and I watched Travelers on Netflix, which I found amazingly analogous to my situation. To alter the course of history, the Travelers, who were from the future, had their consciousnesses implanted in people in the present as they were about to die so they could take over their lives. They experienced the body and some thoughts and feelings of their new person, but they did not identify with or blend with them.)

On my return to Las Vegas, I felt I had another big shift up ahead. I did not expect anything on the level of The Break, but something more like The Golden or The Experience as My Self. I also experienced a period of several months of intermittent rough nights. I sensed some mornings that I thrashed about in my sleep or semi-sleep, expressing a restless, uncomfortable mind. My dreams and thoughts were tortured, if not remembered when I awoke. After a while I recognized a pattern: Within a few days of one of these nights, I would have an important insight or shift.

A major insight came as I continued to read Bernadette Roberts. As a contemplative, she found the union with God that she sought. Having read other contemplatives' experiences, she thought that was as far as she was to go. But after twenty years in what she called the *unitive state*, she discovered God is beyond consciousness, even consciousness of God. This is what the *Course* teaches, of course, and I discovered in Revelation. But she illuminated for me what I must have intuitively known but had never thought: The Spirit-consciousness (her *unitive state*) that follows the "death" of ego is *the end of consciousness*. This was logical and obvious, but it had never consciously occurred to me. When I read this in her book, I felt that when I hit the floor upon Hannah's Return it was not just in recognition that the existence and material life that I had known were over, but because I knew I was at the beginning of the end of consciousness. (I had glimpsed this as The Break approached. See the journal entry I quoted earlier [LII-B.10] from April 6, 2018. The leaving I felt was not going from ego-consciousness to Spirit-consciousness. I saw something beyond that. But as I recorded what I saw and felt, it began to slip away, and I didn't see it again until I read Ms. Roberts.)

That was a profound and significant insight. I was experiencing ego "death", the end of identifying with a person, and it was awful. I felt it was a "living death", as I still experienced the person as this occurred. And now I understood I was entering a State that would be a continuation of "dying."

The *Course* says:

Consciousness is correctly identified as the domain of the ego. (T-3.IV.2)

There are two ways to read this: Consciousness *belongs to* ego, so they are in essence the same thing; or ego *is found in* consciousness but is not the totality of consciousness. The latter is how I always interpreted it. So, while consciously I never set up Spirit-consciousness as a goal in itself because I knew God is beyond consciousness—so consciousness is not real in any case—ego must have done so for me to be thrown by discovering Spirit-consciousness is a passage rather than an ending. This shock was baffling, just as was the shock when I relearned feelings of expansion, peace, and love were effects. It must be that while I knew these things, ego never accepted them, as the end of consciousness means the end of ego altogether. But now the part of my mind that had been lost in ego was waking up.

Of course, at the time, the awareness that Spirit-consciousness heralded the end of consciousness only enhanced the darkness I was already experiencing. But I also knew my new State was to reflect Heaven and would not be a continuation of my current darkness. I knew that only to ego were its end, and the end of consciousness, bad things.

But as I was still more caught up with the ending of ego than I was having new experiences of Spirit, thoughts about the end of consciousness did not stick around. The darkness in my mind was increasing, and some of what Ms. Roberts wrote about her own harrowing experiences seemed to land right on it. (As awful as my Dark Passage was, it was not as bad as the experiences she shared in *The Experience of No-Self*. I do not know if that is because what she shared came at the end, rather than the beginning, of what she called the unitive state, and I was just entering it.)

(Dialogue 20191111) *"I know that in Truth I do not exist. I never wanted to look at that after Revelation. Revelation wipes out this experience. We rise in consciousness only to reach a point where we will be wiped out. In a way, I can accept that. Of course we are. That is the Ultimate Undoing."*

The language in this entry of my journal shows how deep I was still in The Forgetting. My sense that I would be "wiped out" by God was a classic ego-pout. I was in the dry, gray Barrenness still.

40

When I left Australia, I had the bare beginning of feeling I was finally arriving someplace solid within myself. From the start of this process, I had insights like this and then watched them unfold through several stages over several months. So, despite that sensation, for a while I still felt completely adrift.

Both ego and Spirit felt *other*, and I felt I was only an observer and recorder of experiences. I revisited and examined everything about consciousness: Truth/illusion, personal unconscious/Spirit as the Unconscious, the subconscious, and conscious awareness. What in my experience had ever been real?

(Dialogue 20191115) *"Here's the thing: I don't know who I am. I have automatic responses and ways of seeing myself that very quickly I realize are no longer true... But I have nothing to replace it. And if I did, it wouldn't be another of the same kind of identity.*

...I think of my former marriage and all the values I had then and then I feel a desire for that kind of thing again because 'that's me'—but then I realize it's not. And it's not that I am now someone who does not want marriage. Neither of those would be true. Really, I have no personal identity! But then what am I? Will that ever be answered? Or will I just drift without an identity? Will I just stop automatically falling into one?"

As much as Christ as my Self had come to my awareness, I was still in The Forgetting. I drifted without an identity for a while longer, lost in growing darkness, and strained to understand it.

(Dialogue 20191113) *"...I opened myself to Truth in what I called communion. I sought to be guided by the part of my mind that knows the Truth is true. I turned to It throughout the day. Always there was that dark block in my mind, of which I became more aware as time went on. My awareness went only so far.*

I guess until The Golden. And since...have I just been in that dark block?"

I could only conclude I was going through darkness because it was there to go through. I saw it as a membrane between ego-consciousness and Spirit-consciousness. It was the dark veil ego held up that looked like a solid block but was easily (if not comfortably) passed through. I felt and saw ego to its depths, but there was nothing for me to do with its feelings and thoughts but let them surface and pass.

I also had mistaken expectations about ego before my shift in consciousness which it corrected. Although the *Course* stated that consciousness was the domain of the ego, I felt there would come a time when ego would fall away from my consciousness. But my mind has been correctly reoriented regarding ego, and ego is not gone, and I see now never will be gone from my consciousness, until maybe the moment the real world (Spirit-consciousness) is perfected and God "takes the last step" and this mind is lifted out of consciousness to Knowledge.

Split is what consciousness *is*. And my seemingly individual consciousness is not separate from consciousness as a whole, so I cannot get away from the split. At minimum, ego will be in my consciousness as I perceive it in others, like Jan Frazier, who said she knew she would never experience fear (ego) again but continues to see it in others. She *could* experience fear again. It is there to be picked up or not. She just knows she will not.

I have an image of ego lying inert in my mind, like a deflated balloon. This is the proper position for the idea of not-God. Being All, God must contain the idea of Its opposite. But being All, God cannot have an opposite. The idea arose; it was immediately undone as it is impossible. So, it lies there, empty, meaningless, powerless—correctly perceived, but not "lost."

During The Mansion/shack Insights, I felt how I valued ego only because I made it. I felt I would lose me if I let it go. But I learned through my shift in consciousness that nothing is ever lost in consciousness, not even the false. I found a sense of wholeness in this awareness.

I had long thought (and taught) that ego is a *mistake*. But *this* was a mistake. Ego is *false*, not a mistake. It is, just as God is, but what it is, is nothing. The *mistake* was believing in it and taking it seriously—which is only done in ego!

You must perceive that what is strong enough to make a world can let it go... (T-21.II.4)

It was empowering to have my expectations about ego falling away corrected, just as it was to take responsibility for ego. This sense of responsibility was not *blame*, but the awareness I was the *source* of ego. Only then could it be put aside, but this was not a personal putting aside, because what I put aside with ego was any sense I had a will independent of the whole. I did it as the Atonement was expressed through this mind, and learned I am the Son of God. And *this* was the source of my empowerment.

41

During the December after my return, I felt I was about to go through a door that I was never to come back through again. At first, I felt this was just another case of feeling I had to *do* what had already occurred. But actually, the shift I felt up ahead when I returned to Las Vegas two months before was imminent.

I again felt steeped in the sense I had died. Reading through my journal, I find I did go through an actual grieving process besides experiencing the pseudo-grief that I realized was simply what ego feels like without covers. Every now and then, I still felt shocked about the shift. Mostly, I felt anger and depression. Now, I had my first glimmer of acceptance.

(Dialogue 20191205) *"Ah...it just washed over me again that this huge thing has really occurred. But in a way now that I can feel acceptance is possible. I feel as if I've been struggling to go on as I was, but that is winding down. It has taken so much effort, without me efforting! Habitual effort, I think...."*

Finally, I could see ego's winding down occurring.

Part of this was an episode I call *Face It*, in which I experienced bouts of an intense sense that I needed to look directly at something. Soon after I felt this, I would see an experience, thought, or belief head on, without filters, with the sensation it was *right in my face*. These were powerful moments, but what I faced was never new. Nor did it mean the experience, thought, or belief was over. But after facing it, it gradually diminished in power.

The first time this happened, I was driving south on I-15, passing The Strip. The feeling of death had been strong on me that day, and I felt close to seeing something to do with this experience. *What is this? What am I feeling?*

And then there it was, right in front of me: I fully, completely, and thoroughly faced the fact that I was grieving. Although I had known this all along, I felt I was seeing it for the first time. This would be characteristic of Face It moments.

I felt I was finally accepting that loss had occurred. Yet, the hardest part was still up ahead. The difference between this grief and grief I had experienced before was it was tinged with *horror* because I felt I was facing the worst thing ever; the thing I never wanted to see, much less face head on. It was worse than fear of death; it was ego's fear of nonexistence. So, after this Face It experience accepting the loss, the horror aspect of the grief became more pronounced. It felt like I was at the source of all fear I had ever felt.

But as I headed deeper into horror and darkness, I had glimmers of Light:

(Dialogue 20191213) *"...a shift I felt this morning. One I'm not sure will hold, but I think is where I'm headed if not. Back before Hannah I had an experience of myself that was strong and solid...I felt whole in myself. But when the holy relationship showed up I fell...Back into fear, essentially. I have actually felt weak. I knew my wholeness and strength were not gone, but I have* not been able to access them…until today. I don't remember what I was thinking, but I felt a shift back into that. I felt like myself again, strong and whole…"

This was another step in coming back into myself.

42

I had been writing a sequel to *Towing the Moon*. It was not going great, but it was something to do between my smattering of mentoring clients and cleaning jobs. And then I was moved to write about my experiences since Ginny's death.

(Dialogue 20191213) *"I've begun a book about my 'awakening', a word I do not like, but there it is. Did I write yesterday that the Ginny stuff led to me writing a…prologue?…I wasn't sure what that was, but I haven't felt this way since I translated* ACIM *into plain language. But without the tension and fear I had then! This has happened very quietly—and unexpectedly…"*

(Dialogue 20191214) *"Well, shit. The Christ crap keeps coming up. What I'm writing is basically a memoir and what goes through my mind for the preface is 'this is a story of Christ'. It already began with me talking about Christ. Well, it's not my memoir, is it? That's what it means.*
Well, fuck.
I can't say it's not mine. It doesn't feel accurate anymore. That separation is gone."

(Dialogue 20191220) *"As I work on the memoir, just at the very beginning, thinking how it all began, I feel 'this is what my whole life has been about'. And then I thought 'No; this is what the other life was about.' But then I realized that to Christ, that line* is not there. Yes, it is true that there has been a significant shift; a breakthrough. But to Christ, both lives belong to It, one unconscious, one conscious."

(Dialogue 20191227) "...I see how the memoir is forgiving, reframing that life as a life of Christ. There never was an actual split. A part of my mind believed there was, but that is all. And that's no sin, no matter how convinced it was...

...Now I look back and see it was My life—I was always there. The other stuff was insignificant.

How was I there? I was the Presence to child-Liz. I was the 'inner adult-therapist' to teenage-Liz. I was there at her coming out. I was her Teacher/Guide. I was the Holy Spirit Who taught through her. I was her Constant Companion. Until, finally, I am her Consciousness. Her life always was mine...

...The person of Liz was never real. This 'new' life is the only life I've ever had. It was all that was real in that other life. On any given day, at any given moment, only this Life within can be accorded any reality. The further back I go in her history, the further I go from awareness of Me...

...Ah! I thought I would be a person who woke up. But to wake up is to no longer be a person.

...This shift was a blow (to this mind). Christ was not unfamiliar to it. It glimpsed It on occasion. It recognized Christ. But, still, it thought it was a person and Christ was What it would become as a person, not that it would be such a huge shift in consciousness that its reality would be totally different. It's not something impossible to adjust to. But it does take adjusting to.

Suddenly I feel able to reclaim this mind. I feel like myself again. Not a person who has 'died' or who faces something unacceptable. But a mind that has experienced a significant change. But is still me and can learn What it is now."

This was the shift I felt up ahead when I returned to Las Vegas. This was the door I passed through, never to return.

Suddenly, I was using the terms *God* and *Christ* again,

language which in my former life was so loaded that I dismissed it for a couple of decades. But it felt natural and easy to use these terms again. They were without fearful connotations. They were normalized for me, not just conceptually, but experientially as well.

While I understood since picking up the *Course* that Christ was my reality, and not just an idealized and idolized man who lived two thousand years ago, this notion seemed distant. But now I experienced myself as Spirit and was comfortable saying so. What was the difference between Spirit and Christ?

The Holy Spirit is the Christ Mind which is aware of the knowledge that lies beyond perception. (T-5.I.5)

Home of the Holy Spirit, and at home in God alone, does Christ remain at peace within the Heaven of your holy mind. (W-pII.6.3)

The Holy Spirit reaches from the Christ in you to all your dreams, and bids them come to Him, to be translated into truth. (W-pII.6.4)

There is no real difference between Spirit and Christ, but, for me, experientially, it is a matter of degrees. I experience myself as Spirit in an ongoing way, in the real world, as I go about the material world. But Christ is a Blazing Light I experience as my Self, blinding me to any world. So, I feel Spirit is Christ's Extension in consciousness, the Bridge between ego and Christ, and Christ is the Bridge between consciousness and God.

I had been feeling "off" since my first holy relationship. Now I understood why.

(Dialogue 20200102) *"...after Emily I felt I was in 'plan B'. Over the years, the sense that I was supposed to be with Emily faded, but not the sense I was in plan B...Now I see what it was... With Emily, briefly, I was Christ. I would not have put it that way, but that is the Self I saw in her and so met in me...*

...I was Christ but stepped away from It. I cannot say it was wrong. It was clearly to be so. But the 'offness' I felt was I was not Myself, not that circumstances should be different."

The Vision in my holy relationship with Emily *revealed* my Self to me. The Vision in my holy relationship with Hannah *expresses* my Self.

(Dialogue 20200103) *"Now I know what I've been feeling all along. I don't want a relationship with any person. Because I am not a person...*

I want True Union. Yes, this means I will be in Myself in a way that is not with others as a person would be. Yes! 'Truest wife' was Myself; Christ, in me and in Hannah—and anyone else...my relationship will not be with the person of Hannah.

...Relationships of all kinds will show up, but they will not be my actual Relationship."

Later, I would make a distinction between *Unity* (True Union) and *relationship*, as the latter implies a perception of more than one. *Unity* is Christ, my Reality; a mystical holy *relationship* is a material expression of Unity between what seems like two persons who know they are One. So, *Unity* is with my Self; the mystical holy *relationship* is with Hannah.

As I sorted out my experience of Unity from my experience of material relationships, I sorted my Self out from the person of Liz. I had longed to do this since The Break.

(Dialogue 20200104) *"I think about my time in Australia and how...I couldn't get away from the person but knew it was not just being a new person...*

I am so clearly not what I was and not a different version of what I was. And seeing that this is true not just for now, but has always been so, is remarkable. It really is the ultimate 'coming out'!..."

The memoir, and particularly its angle, seemed to come to me out of the blue. I had returned in a moment to Christ as my Identity.

(Dialogue 20200104) *"It was another sharp corner to turn, this 'I have always been here'/Christ stuff, wasn't it? Really, when the memoir began, I was approaching it, I guess, with all the 'face myself' stuff, not really getting what it meant. I had to face what was in the way of my Face…*

I just never expected this journey through the past to see I have always been here as Christ…

…I am…confused by this turn to Christ as my True Existence. Not in the sense that I don't believe it, but because it does seem to be coming full circle and I'm dazed by yet another shift in a direction I didn't see coming."

43

As I came back to myself, I still felt like me, but different —not *gone*, as I had feared when I felt lost to myself. I was surprised by how much of me was still here, yet I no longer felt the boundaries of a person. My sense of existence expanded, and I felt immortal.

My only remaining issue was the dying ego. Every step of the way, I had to sort out my new experiences from ego's judgment on and distortions of them. Ego was no longer my context, but it was a warping insert between me and clear Seeing and understanding.

My journal is not filled with the persisting undercurrent of dark fear at this time, but it was there. I had no way to discuss it, as it was pervasive and there was nothing to single out to describe. I often felt what I could only call *anguish*, a generalized experience of the darkness.

Much that I felt during this time, good and bad, I felt intensely. In claiming my Power, I learned to not push any experience away. The *form* of the experience was not me, but I was the *Power* behind all of it, true or false. If I allowed it, it passed by quickly.

Both Bernadette Roberts and Jan Frazier wrote of feeling, after their shifts in consciousness, pain sharply and deeply before it passed relatively quickly.

(Dialogue 20200106) *"...And maybe even my anguish is a fullness of feeling. Beginning with Ginny...It's like 'living life to the fullest' is not going on adventures or living totally uninhibited, but rather feeling experiences to their fullest...*

...The difference now is I do not feel I am the feelings, but rather that I contain them. I hold those feelings. I observe them and I feel them, but they are not me. Like an expression—a painting or a role played. Or like when I wrote AGW. The <u>expressing</u> is me; the form is irrelevant. Even anguish. It is something I pass through. It is temporary, both in the sense it is passing and that it is an experience in time.

...It's an entirely different way of experiencing—everything! There's a different quality. Because I am different. I experience me in a whole new way...I feel I <u>contain</u> these experiences. I am more than them. They are acute, but temporary, and I am eternal. The Timeless holding time; an idea, a thought. But experiencing it fully."

Now I understood why I had felt Ginny's death so acutely. As I woke up to myself as the Son of God, I became fully conscious and in touch with my Power. Power cannot be limited to only parts of my mind, so extends even to the false. I had been nearly overwhelmed by feelings I could no longer repress.

As this process moved along, even ordinary experiences

could seem stark, as though exposed by a too-strong light. But everything passed quickly now, no matter how intensely felt.

Sometimes I despaired that I would ever get past the darker thoughts and feelings. At times they were convincing:

(Dialogue 20200113) *"...I really felt I would look directly into this stuff of the black box in the corner and find it was not valid. But instead it's the other way around."*

That was a bad moment, because I *was* looking directly at the darkness and finding it was not real. It's just that it didn't dissipate immediately, which is what I expected. I was in a process and seeing through illusion would occur more quickly as time went on.

While it was deeply uncomfortable to live with an undercurrent of darkness, death, and fear, I did have the sense that facing this was ultimately empowering.

(Dialogue 20200114) *"I think that something that has happened in the past couple of years is I have ceased to be afraid of fear.*

I wonder if that was what was in the black box in the corner after all: Fear of fear. Fear of myself, really. Fear of what I made. Fear of my own power to oppose myself.

...I don't think I understood the power behind the obstacle was me. I felt I made the obstacle, but I did not see I <u>empowered</u> the obstacle.

It has only ever been just me and me.

I just felt a 'stitching up'. The divide has always been in me. Love and fear have always been versions of me.

... When I just reread, 'Love and fear have always been versions of me' I felt I made the universe. I feel it now. Very matter-of-factly. I am responsible for it all."

I wondered earlier if the darkness I traversed was due to knowing I was at the beginning of the end of consciousness.

But the more I experienced Christ, the more I felt The Dark Passage was due to Christ breaking into my conscious awareness, as opposed to simply experiencing Spirit-consciousness. (My sense of this was reinforced by memories of an episode in childhood that I mentioned in the first part of, and will be shared later in, this book.) Maybe these are not different things, as I feel Christ bridges consciousness and God.

(Much later I would realize Christ Consciousness is not the *beginning of the end* of consciousness but, as the Bridge to Knowledge, must be the *End* of consciousness.)

As I still vacillated between Spirit and ego, as I had in ego-consciousness, I noticed how often my dark experiences were ego backlashes to an experience *as* Spirit. But no matter, because unlike how it had been in ego-consciousness, each swing back to ego resulted in it dissolving if I just sat with the horror and let it pass.

When I felt a ghost in the world, I was detached from the old world (ego's world), but I was not in touch with my new world (the real world). The Golden heralded the real world rising to conscious awareness and, ever since, I longed to get further into it, but I was caught up in the dying ego. Now, two and a half years after The Golden, I was finally moving—at a snail's pace—further into the real world even as I continued to deal with what had passed. Over several episodes, I visited the sensation of being in a new experience of existence, and each time deepened my awareness and acceptance of it.

(Dialogue 20200128) *"...It really, really is as though I died and have gone on to an immortal existence that I have yet to understand. I feel I am waking up in a new place. And I'm amazed by how I still feel so much like me. More intensely than ever. I guess I mean more alive than ever."*

This coincided with feeling in the new year that The Wave had set me down into a more normal, gentle current.

44

Dark, fearful experiences continued and were baffling. They often left me shaky.

(Dialogue 20200128) *"My only comfort in all this is that there has to be a limit to the hard stuff and when it's gone there's only Light and Love."*

I realized that after I got past the darkness, I would never be unhappy again. As I was in touch with my Immortality, I was Eternally Safe. This would never change back.

I began to question if the fear I felt was mine alone. My first thought was maybe it was Hannah's, but when I checked in with her, she was not fearful. One evening, I felt horrible fear come over me out of the blue, and as it peaked, it occurred to me it was not mine, and it quickly faded.

Sometimes I heard what I called a "cosmic shout" in my mind. I felt I was hearing universal fear itself, rather than just my own or any singular person's fear. And then I had an experience in which I felt and saw the "body of fear".

(Dialogue 20200123) *"...By which I think I mean the whole of that consciousness, not just someone's individual experience of it. It was like I was seeing that's what I experience at those times. It's not mine...it was like if I am at Christ, this is what I see or something. It's into the whole mind, not just mine..."*

As my mind expanded to the Son of God, it was not just open to the universal Christ, but to consciousness as a whole, which would include universal not-God (fear). In any case, I passed through this sense of tapping into universal fear in only a few weeks.

I was deeply struck by the contrast between Eternal Security and Immortality, and fear and mortality. I could only gape at the huge mistake it was to believe fear was real, but I also saw how the hugeness of the error validated God.

(Dialogue 20200129) *"Its depth and seeming-magnitude only attest to the Mind in Which it seems to occur. That's all. I have to remember I'm used to smallness. So when something seems huge, I grant it great significance. But the size of the error only attests to the Power of the Mind; it does not signify great meaning.*

Like the moment I was given my ontology: Your mistake is taking it seriously.

…The meaning of the error is in the correction of it. Maybe this is what I've been trying to grasp when I think how this error/correction thing gets to the nature of God. God is All. In God there is only God. Error/immediate correction/return to God. It's impossible.

In the meantime…here on the ground, as it were…in the correction…If the meaning of the error is in the correction of it, there is no error. The massive error I see…the Power of Mind…the only error is believing it is something real."

Despite these insights, which would unfold in my experience over time, I was frustrated by the persistence of fear in my immediate experience.

(Dialogue 20200202) *"I watch helplessly as I respond in ways I know are no longer authentic. The fear itself strikes me as inauthentic. The grief does not grab me anymore. I no longer have any sense that it is me. Yet, the fear…I just do not see why I cannot get past it, but it remains. Nothing I've seen; nothing I've done moves it. I can only hope it is truly unwinding, because I am at a loss as to what to do about it. It is so frustrating, because it is no longer me, but I can't seem to get past it. All I can do is recognize its distortions and sit through it…*

I'm not afraid of Love, but the closer I get to It, the closer I am to the juncture in my mind where fear hides Love. Apparently this is beyond me to release."

I was in the release! I still confused myself with what in my mind seemed to continue in a process—a process that was indeed winding down. So much of my discomfort was due to this habit of identification, even as I saw it was not me. But that habit was winding down, too. Eventually I trusted this; I trusted me.

(Dialogue 20200202) "'I am the correction now' goes through my mind. Whatever I felt I was before, I am this now."

It seemed the journey through the darker parts of my mind *was* to see that they were not real.

(Dialogue 20200203) "Today I've taken a different approach. Instead of addressing the thoughts alone, I am also getting directly into the feelings. I have been struck by the power or will behind them that has made them seem autonomous. But when I breathe through them I find no substance behind them. I do not believe in these thoughts and feelings anymore. They feel false. They are like something I put on or hold onto or contain, but they are not me and I do not believe they are. They are very familiar; I recognize that for a long time I believed they were me. But I also recognize that is gone.

… although I never thought in terms of empowerment (just as I never thought in terms of immortality), I seem to have to look right into the face of my resistance and acknowledge it. No passive acceptance (of resistance) here. I have to look at <u>every inch</u> of my resistance.

… It seems I am only coming into wholeness by seeing that which I gave over to lack. I am only coming to understand me, in totality, by seeing the darkness I made as well as the Light.

…I do feel that in seeing my darkness, as uncomfortable as it is, I gain myself as I would not otherwise. I gave part of myself over to that darkness; now I reclaim it."

I undid guilt in my previous life. However, that was for me alone.

(Dialogue 20200203) *"...This seems like so much more than just me. Like the fear-body experience. I have to accept this not just for a singular person—I did that in the past life. But, at the Son of God level, to accept Christ, I have to accept forgiveness <u>for the whole thing</u>.*

...Because I am not limited now to just a person. I say I cannot think like a person anymore. I feel it is <u>all</u> me. So that means I cannot accept the Light without acknowledging the darkness blocking it is about more than just a person's singular guilt. The fear I feel in the holy relationship is that I see the magnitude of the error. The flipside of the Vision of Oneness is this cosmic guilt.

Can this be correct? What I faced with the first holy relationship was a person's guilt and with this one, the Son of God's guilt? I am far more aware of the scope of the Light in this one, because I am aware of my Self as all instead of a singular person.

Can this be correct? I do not feel overwhelmed by this guilt. Nowhere near, actually. I feel I can get past this guilt and fear. I did so for a person. It's just about scale. My sense of existence has expanded, so is all that comes with it. And, again, it attests to my power.

And maybe this is all I see when I see the extent of the error. Maybe the wow-factor of it is my power.

... All of this helps me to perhaps begin to understand these past couple of years. If this is not a continuation of the past life then perhaps there's a way to see this time on another scale. I have often felt I'm thinking too small. And I do vacillate between these experiences of Hugeness-like episodes and then back into the mundane, ordinary, day-to-day slog with this mind. But maybe it's not 'this mind' as I've thought of it—singular; one among many. Maybe it's not that the boundary between my mind and Hannah's has dropped but that, through this one dropping, it has dropped between my mind and Mind. And it's not a collective. I do not have

to deal with individual darkness; it is just the darkness in Mind, which was reflected in what I thought of as mine alone as well as in all seemingly-individual minds."

I saw I confused power with fear, because I often confused power with *forcefulness* rather than *strength*. True Power is a strong but gentle Force, but It is not *forceful*. I recognized that the power of the fear and guilt I felt was Power Itself, simply misdirected or mis-creating. This was empowering to find, even if it was still occurring.

45

My experiences of fear were coming as something I described as *the awfuls*. It was undefined terribleness. But I also had strong feelings of *vitality* and things took on a vibrancy for me, as though I was feeling and seeing **Life** as I never had before.

(Dialogue 20200211) "There's something in my experiences lately, no matter how awful. And there have been awful moments. There has been no Love and very little peace. But…there's something, maybe since I realized the way to characterize the shift is this new experience of existence, that has been different about my experiences. An intensity or vitality. Like everything has a deep meaning in itself in the moment. Nothing is for anything else. It's all right here. It's like I am truly alive in a way I never was before. Forget the content of the moment, it is like the previous experience of existence was death and this is Life.

…I reach for relief from this time of awfulness, but I almost think it is because I feel I should. I feel the very thing that makes me feel so awful tells me I should seek relief from the awfulness. But I am vitally alive around it, through it, within it. Here's the thing: I *am immortal. I will outlast it.*

The death of death is what I experience. That is the juncture between ego-consciousness and Spirit.

What is God? <u>Life</u>. Light. Love. But, to me, the characteristic that stands out is vibrant, vital Life.

…Love, peace, joy, yes, but they rest on Life. God is Life.

…Life is the experience of God or Truth. Before, I was aware of Truth. Now I <u>experience</u> It as Life. Life Everlasting.

So in the moment of intense awfulness as, say, fear, there's Vitality behind it and around it that, in essence, <u>forgives it</u>…"

Face It experiences continued, but I found that sometimes I simply had a deep and clear focus on an issue, as though all the obscuring aspects were gone. These new experiences of my new State were refreshing and encouraging, but unfortunately infrequent and buried in unsettling darkness and fear. I did not know it at the time, but they were the light at the end of the tunnel. They hailed the end of the darkness.

With this memoir came a change in perspective I had glimpsed yet had been unable to fully access:

(Dialogue 20200226) *"The memoir reframes that life not as a person who then had a shift, but as Spirit unconscious to Itself. It mastered being a spiritualized-self, split against Itself, but coming to know Itself.*

That experience of existence did not lead to this one. I broke away from that experience in The Break. I mastered the spiritualized-self and had no further to go with it. This is not something that happened to a person. That was always the mistaken point of view, as it is now. This is the giant shift in perspective I have felt. This is why I felt I was 'thinking too small'. This was the ship I felt I was turning in a wide arc. This is a completely different view of me and what I am and what happened to me."

What came to mind was I was moving "from correction to Creation (Christ)". The *Course's* mind training in my previous life had been for correction and I saw I would unlearn that posture as I recognized there was nothing to correct. Ego was not *error* but was *not real*. So, the perception of a need for correction was an illusion, too. I was done with that experience of consciousness. It would only *seem* to continue as an aspect of ego winding down.

I felt that error/correction was the highest form of ego-consciousness. (The lowest would be wallowing in ego without Spirit.) I felt that I had "maxed out" that experience, and this brought it to its natural end, and that is why that material life ended.

(Dialogue 20200226) *"I have felt that life was complete. In that consciousness I mastered correction. There was no place to go with it. But that consciousness could never <u>become</u> this consciousness.*

Maybe that consciousness was the moment of the idea-of-not-God/the undoing-of-the-idea-of-not-God. I completed that. This consciousness is not a continuation of that. This one does not correct that one. That one was about correction. It was that moment.

...That whole experience of existence was false, both the perception of error and the correction. It could not 'lead to' this one because that was wholly false and this one is true. Here, there is no error so no need for correction. This is why it is a wholly different experience of existence!

That experience had no reality at all. Even the Correction was not real because the error never occurred. A perception of error and a perception of Correction."

Christ was real, but the need for Christ *as Correction* was false. That Christ corrects the perception of error is incidental, and not Its *purpose* any more than the purpose of sunshine is to make plants grow. Christ corrects the perception of error because It is Truth, the way the sun shines *and* plants grow.

The "dark corner of my mind" that I had felt for so long,

and knew I would have to one day face, did not hide some sinister belief yet to be undone. It was simply denial of Christ. The darkness I walked through was ego's defense against What I am. I truly was at the juncture where ego gives way to Christ.

46

Finally, my terrible experiences peaked. I had been approaching ego's fear of nonexistence, and one day found it front and center.

Because ego could not destroy me, or get me to destroy myself, it threatened me with insanity instead. Sometimes I felt that threat hovering in the background. Then twice I went to the extreme edge of fear of nonexistence. I knew if I stayed there, I would make myself ill or I would go insane. I stepped away. I could do so because ego did not have power over me.

I saw I *could* spend time in insanity, but it would not change anything. The Truth in me would be untouched, as always. At most, I would waste time and put off awakening. The only reason to do this was to exert a little will against my Will, just for the sake of doing so. Frankly, I could not find the will to do this.

But the center of ego, I found, was something else. I finally wholly went there and hit bottom with it:

(Dialogue 20200303) *"…This is my worst fear! My worst nightmare! Love has come and I don't want It. I don't say this lightly. I say it absolutely. This has been my vacillation all along. This has been what has hovered around all the Light experiences. I have always returned to this, because it is true and absolute. <u>I do not want Love</u>.*

Every experience of Love I have ever had, no matter how subtle, I have responded with this: I do not want It. This is the absolute me. More me than Love could ever be. I am not Love; I was never Love. I cannot be Love. All concepts aside. <u>This is the absolute truth</u>. This is what I have never wanted to face.

I am shaking from head to toe. I feel I am finally seeing myself as I really am. This is the real me…

Love will drive me crazy. It approaches and I grow closer to insane. I cannot force myself to accept Love. I cannot do it. It sends me into a panic. It always has.

…Called Hannah in a panic and laid all out. Shaking head to toe. Left her feeling helpless…"

Often, especially in Sorting Out, I felt deeply that I was ego and Love would cost me too much—my existence. But I had never gone to this depth of feeling as absolutely as I could with a false identity that it was me. I did not know at the time that this experience was the turning point, but that night I remembered something that indicated this was the case:

"I saw something when speaking with Hannah. Something along the lines that facing this is closure with the former experience of existence. I saw something whole."

I felt I came back to Las Vegas for closure with ego-consciousness and here it was. But I did not feel immediate relief. Only in hindsight did I see this was when I hit bottom and began to rise out of darkness. As with all my shifts, I watched it unfold in my mind and material life over the next months. Over a year later, I would feel I was at the beginning of the end of closure.

Immediately after this episode, I continued to have the sense I was facing my worst fear. I often woke up in the morning feeling *something terrible has happened*. I looked further into fear of nonexistence, but with great clarity. Ego told me that only material death could release me from guilt. I saw clearly that ego's attraction to material death was it at least made it seem that there *had been* a material life and therefore ego was real. But this "death" through a shift in consciousness revealed its nonexistence. For it, this was the equivalent of total annihilation.

I experienced all of this with horror. But the more clearly I saw and felt the horror, the more it diminished. I walked through ego's worst fears in their raw and unfiltered state, and I was untouched.

A significant shift followed when one day I remembered that besides reinforcing my darkness, Bernadette Roberts mentioned something I had forgotten about Revelation: The Glory of God.

How had I forgotten that God is Love???

Really, more than Love, as God's Glory surpasses not just human love but the Wholeness (Oneness) of Christ that we call Love. God is indescribably…What word could suffice? God is unlike any experience in consciousness. Yes, this is bad news to ego *but not in itself*. Each time I came out of Revelation I was shocked, and ego quivered in fear. But there was no fear *in* God, not even as an idea. *How had I forgotten this? Where had I gone?*

The Forgetting was over. I could only come back to myself from here. It would take The Dark Passage a few more months to fully subside, but in essence it was over, too.

It was like the part of this mind asleep under the dream of ego (ego-identifier) began to wake up years ago, became aware of the ego dream more than ever, seemed to get lost in it, but actually awoke through it, seeing its unreality as it did so, to join with the part of me that had always been awake.

Sometimes I wondered if the darkness and what I termed *the awfuls*—feeling generally terrible—were how I experienced dysthymia and panic disorder in the new consciousness. The darkness was not dysthymia, but I was onto something about the awfuls.

I observed that when I had a frightening thought, it was followed by the awfuls, and that if I let it be, it peaked and subsided. This was just how I had learned to handle panicky and dark thoughts and feelings during a panic attack. It turned out the awfuls were a milder response to adrenaline—perhaps the way I experienced it in my new State. Catching this was key to reducing my discomfort. It seemed this awareness came as an effect of my emergence from The Dark Passage.

While considering Bernadette Roberts's difficulties and mine, I discovered that in ego I was drawn to the endurance required to face ego. This was not new to me. Facing a challenge by flexing certain mental muscles and growing was often how I had developed the person. At times, I felt pride in this. In fact, pride in my strength was part of why I accepted *God-is-desolation* during The Forgetting without question.

But this time as I considered whether I wanted more difficulty up ahead to demonstrate my strength, I felt a gentle *no*.

(Dialogue 20200331) *"What I feel is that in ease I lose my 'character' (as in strength or integrity, etc.). By which I mean my identity boundaries, I think. Because ease is to be in the flow. Subsumed to the Greater Being. If ease is part of Love and Love is Oneness…in challenge, sacrifice, difficulty I am apart and distinct. I flex muscles, even if they are of God. In ease my boundaries blur into the flow and I don't know where one ends and the other begins.*

I choose Love. What do I need boundaries for?"

This gentle *no* signaled another turning point. There is no value in a hard path. The way of Christ is not *meant* to be difficult. I faced difficulty only because the false state I was in was so far off from What I am.

47

My former experience of existence was less than *insignificant*, as I had seen in The Experience as My Self. All that had ever been real was Christ. I felt this even as I wrote the first part of this memoir detailing that false experience.

I had the growing sense that my life before had not happened at all. It was no more than a dream. I began to see, too, that it had not been a dream of *attaining* an awakened dream, but Christ was *expressed* through the arc of Liz's spiritual path.

(Dialogue 20200311) *"Maybe it's like this: Let's say I go to sleep and dream and in that dream I become aware I'm dreaming. When I wake up, I do not think that awareness in the dream lead to my waking up, but rather my awareness of myself led to that awareness in the dream. I also do not feel that there is a connection between the dream and me awake, except that I was the dreamer. In other words, it did not define me. But my waking up does define the dream—<u>as a dream</u>."*

(Dialogue 20200408) *"It is like I dreamt I was walking toward chimes I could never reach only to wake up and find that chimes were playing and therefore I heard them in my dream. But walking toward the chimes in my dream did not lead to my waking, although the chimes themselves woke me up."*

Most importantly I saw:

(Dialogue 20200312) *"...all consciousness is dreaming. I am enlightened, because I am aware of dreaming, but I am not Awake, which would be beyond dreaming, or consciousness."*

As I now understood time is the expression of the Atonement and everything is unfolding perfectly, I no longer saw need for healing, correcting, or fixing. If I continued to teach, it would be without personal motivation.

(Dialogue 20200312) *"As to teaching…beyond correction to creation. I realize now that to know my Self is to 'teach' others about our Self. I represent their Self to them, without a word spoken. I do not even have to consider this myself. It is incidental, not intentional."*

(Dialogue 20200317) *"…When I envision going forward in Christ, I see a life of quiet simplicity. Joy and Love. It is not to correct the world. It is not to correct this mind. It is simply the effect of Truth."*

As I felt this movement into a new stage of teaching, I was suddenly getting a logo (*The Christ in You*), revamping my website, and reducing and streamlining my fees. I was surprised as a new service came to me, *Joining in Christ*. I had a Vision of a place in my mind that I called *The Golden Threshold*. On the other side of the Threshold was God; the Light pouring into my mind from the Threshold was Christ. I was to use this awareness of Christ to strengthen it in others in quiet joining (an inapt word, as it is a recognition of *Unity*) in a telephone or video call.

I continued working one-on-one with a smattering of clients, which still came quite naturally, but writing articles fell away. I felt no movement to write beyond this memoir and my journal.

Drama passed with The Dark Passage, except in my relationship with Hannah. I was to persist in acting stupid for several more months, but that wound down, too.

Since the shift in consciousness, I was aware of ego as something only tagging along. It did not add to or take anything away from the overall process I was in. It blocked clarity and caused doubt, but nothing else. It was nagging thoughts and feelings of lack in the midst of Wholeness. It had no real effects.

I realized after a while that I was going to act as I was moved, and the thoughts and feelings that filled my mind between movements were superfluous, ultimately even to me. They were unreal appearances and had no more significance than if I had watched television all day.

In this, I discovered ego is nothing more than a storyteller, making up motivations for action or inaction. What is going to happen is going to happen, and ego comes up with explanations or justifications to make a personal identity around occurrences. Even in my former life, ego never moved me to act or prevented an action. It either went along with the movement of the material unfolding, providing a story of motivation or justification, or resisted and made me uncomfortable as I acted or did not act as moved. I never had a will apart from the whole, only an illusion of a will apart.

My new relationship with time continued and I had several emerging experiences. Some of these seemed to have been temporary, and perhaps steps along the way. One I called the *twinkly swirl*, and it inspired my logo. Sometimes when I focused on someone or something, in the material world or in my mind, it was like looking at a swirl of twinkly lights. This was not physical sight, but in my mind, and I felt it was a touch of The Golden. Sometimes I experienced it with Love, but not often. At times I could apply it to uncomfortable thoughts and feelings, and they would dissolve. Later, it showed up when I focused in on a thought or problem.

My new Christ experiences signaled darkness ending as I moved further into Light. I see this only in hindsight, of course. In early April 2020, I wrote about feeling, finally, solid in myself again. I had come to be unsure anything like this would occur, so this was a great relief. It also did not feel temporary, but rather that the solidness I had always felt was Christ and now I knew it. Christ was the through-line in both experiences of existence.

48

The darkness of The Dark Passage—which was a dark feeling of fear I can only call *horror*—had a depth and quality like no other form of darkness or resistance I can remember. It was beyond the fear of death. It was certainly related to ego's fear—or, really, *awareness*—of its nonexistence. I would not say it was *evil*, but it was like it was the source of all dark feelings, so I think of it as *primary darkness*. I only seem to have experienced it in relation to my awareness that I am Christ. It began with The Break and accelerated after The Experience as My Self when I became aware that I am Christ.

And yet it was not unfamiliar. I had experienced it before, and it is because of this that I am sure I also knew at that time that I am Christ. (What follows was indicated in the first part of this memoir [LI-One.3] when I discussed experiences of Presence as a child, and in this second part [LII-F.43] when I noted the relationship between Christ and the darkness I experienced.)

In the spring of 2019, I wrote in my journal about feeling-memories of guilt in my childhood. I connected them to a sense of responsibility I did not want. They were vague and unspecific. But a year later, I felt a connection between the present and an episode when I was moving out of early childhood, perhaps when I was seven or eight years old. Throughout the spring of 2020, I flashed more and more on feeling-memories of this distinct darkness at that time. I had throughout my former life flashed on these feeling-memories on rare occasion, but I could never grasp them. I did not remember specific incidences, but rather a general time, and a general feeling of what I now call primary darkness.

It seems there were episodes at that time when I felt Spirit and/or the primary darkness I was to pass through at my shift in consciousness fifty years later. Sometimes, the darkness came alone; at other times, it seemed to follow Spirit. In fact, I became aware that I had a sense for a brief time as a child that Light and darkness were warring over me. I felt, though, that this was occurring outside of me and not in me. Of course, the world provided many stories of Light and dark (Good and evil) fighting over someone or something, so it would not have been a totally foreign idea to me. However, I have no sense I ever gave this thought at the time or later. First, I would not have known how to think about it. Second, I would have been too afraid to think about it. Just as with my experiences of Presence as a child, I would not remember it until an adult.

These vague flashes on Light-and-dark episodes in my childhood went on for several months. As time went on, they homed in on a specific period. The feeling-memory of this time grew, peaked in intensity, and then passed over a course of weeks, but even as I end this memoir, I occasionally flash on that time, usually indicating to me that a puff of ego's fear of nonexistence is hovering around.

I don't really know what to make of these memories, except that something to do with an awareness of me as Christ at that time seems to link up with this time. It was an interesting episode, because so intense for a brief time, and so, I share it here:

Around the time I was seven or eight, I was involved with a family that lived in a cul-de-sac down the street from my family home. (We called the cul-de-sac "the loop" so I refer to this episode as *The Loop Time*). I do not recall their family name, and only the first name of their eldest son, who I believe was my age and possibly in my class a few years after this event. I had a mom-crush on the mother of the family, a woman I now realize was likely to have been in her late twenties. I was obsessed with babies and she had one, a girl, I think. While I also played in her backyard with her other children and the neighborhood children who joined us, I was drawn to their house because the mom let me help with the baby.

I have always recalled certain vivid things about this

family when they came to mind, and with memories always came a tinge of primary darkness. Sometimes I thought it was because even as a child I felt there was something a little "off" about the family. The mom was friendly but seemed unstable and possibly overwhelmed. My home and the homes of my other friends were well kept, even when both parents worked. But her home was a disordered mess, despite her being a housewife. This is all I can remember of anything specific that indicated something off. My suspicion now is the young mother likely had a destabilizing mental illness.

A grandmother lived with them—I think the father's mother. I realize now that she was probably only middle aged, but she seemed ancient to me then. I only ever remember her in her own room, which I avoided as I was afraid of her. She smoked and had a green parrot and she reminded me of Bette Davis in her spooky older years.

The son who was my age was very tall and he was a bully. He had what I now realize was a physical disability and was mocked (including by me, but not to his face). I think his younger brother was a bully, too. I never liked them and would have had nothing to do with them if other kids were not also involved, or if I were not drawn to their mother and baby sister. All I remember of their father was he was very tall, and my sense is somewhat older than the mother. I have the sense he managed her. I did not see him much, but there was something in the boys' bullying attitude in him as well.

Eventually my time helping this young mother with her baby simply tapered off, I assume because I got bored or something more interesting came along.

I do not remember any bad event, nor do I suspect I have repressed one. At some point I characterized the darkness that I would feel whenever that family came to mind as guilt, and I had three theories about this. One was that I felt bad for my mom-crush when my own mother was just up the hill. The second was, in my codependency, I felt guilty for not being able to rescue the likely overwhelmed young mother. The third was that maybe my crush was more than a mom-crush and was a romantic crush as well. These burgeoning feelings probably would have confused me. (My first romantic crush was on Diana Rigg as Emma Peel in *The Avengers* when I was five.)

Of course, it was possibly all of these. I never felt, though, that these theories really explained the sense of primary darkness or significance I felt about The Loop Time. These were run-of-the-mill expressions of guilt, and primary darkness does not accompany any other guilty memory.

I also recall a home three or four houses away from theirs with white statues and a deep green lawn out back. I don't recall who lived there, just that, with the owner's permission, we neighborhood children were allowed to play in their yard on occasion. This place seems entwined with this episode, and sometimes I have felt that it was at this home that some spiritual event occurred, and it became associated in my memory with the entire Loop Time. I am not certain, though, as memories of that young family were always the trigger of sense-memories of Light-and-darkness.

I began flashing on that time strongly in March of 2020, and I became certain that I had some experience of Christ at The Loop Time; something more than my later experiences of Presence as a child. Whatever it was, it was so threatening to ego that I came to associate that time with primary darkness rather than Light.

This sense of connection between the primary darkness of these two times of life fifty years apart continued on and off for a few months. Then, in August, the sense of connection grew stronger, but as The Dark Passage had receded, I felt I was sensing the connection between the whole likely event, not just the darkness.

(Dialogue 20200827) *"...I feel strongly a huge shift occurring with regard to how I see Hannah or something. Again that sense of something breaking open and Light pouring out. And—so mysteriously—I find coming to mind again that time as a child of*

7 or 8 and that family in the loop...that sense again that there's something of this time linked with that time."

The sense of a link between The Loop Time and this time persisted the more I moved into myself as Christ. Did I see I am Christ at The Loop Time? Whatever I experienced, I also seemed to grasp ego's nonexistence, judging from how The Loop Time triggered whenever that came up as well. In any case, fifty years later I sensed something from The Loop Time coming to fruition.

I think it likely that I felt guilty for rejecting the Light because I did not want what I felt would be the responsibility that would come with knowing I am Christ. (I am sure I did not label it, but just *knew*.) Certainly, as a child in a Christian culture, even knowing little about religion, I would associate Spirit with sacrifice and even crucifixion. No doubt a dread of great responsibility was also behind my feeling "I am not so ambitious" when as a teenager I first consciously saw that I could be what Jesus was.

Of course, these are all just the shapes guilt and resistance take in ego. The real reason I rejected any notion that I am Christ is the threat it posed to ego.

I find it interesting that I felt primary darkness only in relation to the awareness that I am Christ. Bernadette Roberts, too, went through something harrowing, but not when ego fell away and she entered what she called the unitive state. She described that as shattering in its own way, but her difficult passage came much later, when she discovered God was beyond consciousness, and encountered Christ in a whole new way.

49

My resistance to Hannah and our holy relationship took many forms, most of which I recognized, whether direct (as an open attack) or indirect (as with projection). But I could not always discern ego's resistance from Spirit's movement. And, still sorting out a confusion of conflicting feelings about her, I was not certain which of my feelings were valid. I often went with feelings I would have felt valid in my previous life, but which I no longer felt were authentic, because I didn't know what else to do, and doing nothing didn't feel right, either. I may have come back into myself, but with regard to my relationship with Hannah, I was still at sea.

Sometimes, I was simply overwhelmed by resistance and expressed it in words and actions. Other times, I found it best to simply take time away from Hannah as ego's attacks on both of us were intense. A few times, I was convinced we were to part for good and made it so, only to come back around again in a few days.

This happened in a larger context of feeling as I had from the start that we were never going to part in any lasting way. Sometimes, I acted even when I felt this just to resist. Other times, it was completely obscured, but not for long. In a way, taking time away or even parting for good made this awareness clearer. Cutting her out of my life felt like swimming upstream, always the indication I was pushing against the way things were to unfold.

Of course, now I understand that if I acted, it was to be. My feelings and thoughts and behaviors were part of the material unfolding. I do not live in a vacuum. No action (or inaction) is ever just for me. The material unfolding is a complicated tapestry of interconnection.

When I read in the *Course's* description of the Period of Unsettling that I was to learn to put all judgment aside, I assumed it meant judgment of others, as well as making decisions for myself. I did not realize the degree to which it meant not judging the thoughts and feelings that cross this mind and their resultant effect on the behavior of this person. But in this period, I have learned I am not the person, that she is part of the material unfolding, and the material unfolding is the least significant aspect of consciousness. In fact, it is nothing. So, if I want peace, I must let the person go to do what she is to do, without judgment. (And, of course, whether I do or not is also part of the unfolding!)

When I left Australia, I had a vague sense that I might return in nine months to a year—long enough to justify another visitor's visa. But I had no set plans, and I expected to feel my way forward, waiting for movement to take me. In the early part of 2020, Hannah and I made plans for her to visit Las Vegas in June when my sister, C, was to take a vacation in the UK. But then the COVID-19 pandemic was declared, countries shut, and all travel plans were put off indefinitely. I rolled with this, as I had not felt clear about the future anyway.

In May, a significant reorientation of my mind that I call *The Paradigm Shift* began. It seemed on the surface to be about undoing a rigid way of looking at an aspect of my material life but was really the onset of understanding my new relationship to the material world.

I often had the squirming sense of aimlessness about my holy relationship with Hannah that the *Course* warns about. Sometimes I accepted it, but often it resulted in my trying to grasp at something recognizable in our relationship. So, I often projected this sense of aimlessness onto Hannah and blamed her for not being in the relationship. I understood the purpose of a holy relationship is to be an ongoing reminder of the experience of the holy instant, either through the Vision of Oneness, or, when unable to access that, remembering our Oneness when the peace of our relationship is disrupted. While obviously we did not have to be physically together for me to experience Vision, I did feel we were meant to be regularly connecting in some way as an expression of our Oneness.

As I left Australia, I took the approach of "let's see *how* we unfold" because I still saw a future with us together in some way. But Hannah said, "let's see *what* unfolds." But until this point, I did not realize we were not on the same page. I came to feel she treated me as a casual friend when she was much more to me. I accused her of being satisfied with our holy relationship as just a nice idea in our minds. We ended up in a kerfuffle over this, and parted ways.

What is interesting about this episode is my sister, C's, involvement. She precipitated it with a question to me about my relationship with Hannah that, the day after asking it, she revealed Jesus had told her to ask me. (C had returned to the Catholic Church after decades of searching, just as I had felt she should.) She was concerned about me, and had asked him to take care of me, and he said to not worry, he had me. And then he told her to ask me how long I was going to put up with things the way they were with Hannah, and everything went from there.

C only told me of Jesus's involvement because the next day he told her to tell me. She felt awkward revealing this to me, and I told her that I had known from Where her prompting came, whether she was conscious of it or not. I explained that this was all very natural to me; it is the way I live my life. But somehow, she never seemed to hear this, no matter how many times and ways I told her. (None of my family read my books or understand my work—or my life, which is the same thing.)

In following conversations with my sister, I confronted my set idea of what going back to Australia was to look like. She said, why not go back and forth? She had said something like this before, but I dismissed it as absurd. Who lives like that? Well, if I had tons of money…But discussing this with her I felt something in me breaking down. Certainly, a rigid, structured way of looking at my material life, but I felt this represented something more. I felt it wasn't really to do with what happened in my material life. Structures in my mind were breaking down as well.

I reconnected with Hannah. And through a series of insights it became clear to me that The Paradigm Shift was not about going back and forth to Australia. It was about accepting what I saw in The Experience as My Self: The insignificance of the material experience. *It is not my reality*. When I speak of my new *Context*, I mean my new reality, the real world.

This understanding evolved well into the next year. The material world was no longer being repurposed for me by Spirit, as in my previous experience of existence. As Spirit myself now, it is only an appearance, and nothing to take seriously.

50

In the August 27, 2020 Dialogue I quoted discussing The Loop Time, I recorded feeling a shift coming around how I saw Hannah, felt something crack open in my mind, and saw Light pour into my mind through the crack. Soon after this, I heard "rolling back the stone" a few times. I looked it up on the internet. It is a Biblical allusion to resurrection.

I had been aware, since I became aware of our singular expression of the holy relationship, that the habits of ego thinking distorted how I saw what Hannah was to me. I was attracted to her and I loved her, but as much as ego wanted me to believe I was making a special relationship with her, I was not. And one day this was firmly sorted out in a beautiful experience.

I was thinking of Hannah, and felt how I thoroughly enjoy the sights, sounds, and smells of her, like one does a lover. And suddenly I saw them as an insubstantial frame around a Blazing Light of Love. Ah! Now I understood why I felt those lover-like things but no longing. They did not replace for me our True Unity, which is so wholly satisfying that it blows away any emotional satisfaction I could find in any material relationship. I saw in that moment that there is *only* Wholeness (True Unity), and vividly understood that the emotional connection I had sought in material relationships was, in ego's view, meant to substitute for Wholeness.

It was as though I saw what really went on behind the veils ego threw over everything. Wholeness (Love) is always here. It is the real world. Correctly seen, the material experience becomes only an insubstantial frame around Wholeness. The forms that appear are incidental, whether they be people, places, or things. Hannah was *not* special to me. She just happens to be a form in the material experience appearing in the midst of Wholeness. Appearances are incidental to Wholeness.

But even after the beautiful and clarifying experience I just shared, events soon occurred that called our relationship into question.

I felt since we began that Hannah and I were to have a parting of some kind before we came back together to stay together. There were partings along the way that I sometimes thought might be it, but then came a parting that I *felt* was it. Hannah pulled away, from me and another friend she considers a spiritual partner. Based on Seeing, she had expectations for this time of her life that had not come to fruition. She needed time to grieve what she felt were fallen illusions.

Before leaving, she had expressed that in our time together, I had grown considerably, but she had not. This struck me with force as I realized it was true. If she had grown or shifted, it was not showing up in her material life. It was the same before, during, and after my year with her.

This made me aware that I had thought that we were to somehow grow together, and this had not occurred. So, just as I had felt when her romantic feelings fell away, and when I realized I was to leave Australia, I had to again adjust how I saw our relationship.

I did detail to Hannah what I had observed about her

and felt were the reasons she was not growing. These were not new. I had brought them up before. But, she felt, as she had before, that I was wrong, and that I did not see or understand her. I could only drop the topic.

Over the next weeks, Hannah did make casual contact occasionally. But I began to feel I was moving along on a current that was taking me past her. I shared this with her, but she did not express concern. As time went on, I felt I *was* past her. One day the thought came that I was "done with the part of me that was about Hannah." I found myself spontaneously putting away mementos of Australia. It felt like she and Australia were in my rearview mirror, and I let her know. She said she had nothing to give at that time, so I let her go.

As November began, I felt I was to move out of my sister's condo and into my own place. Within ten days of feeling this, I effortlessly found and moved into my preferred situation, a mother-in-law's apartment attached to a house in the middle of the city. It came mostly furnished, saving me a lot of money in that regard, as I was starting from scratch.

My sense that I had moved past Hannah did not feel like the usual ego tantrum pushing her away. That was always emotional, and this I felt with something more like wonder. Yet I found, as usual, that I could not wholly let her go. The sense she was a part of my life for the rest of my life persisted. I accepted this and figured it would work itself out in time.

But in the new year, I had the strong sense one evening that I had to speak with someone about being stuck in this. I felt right away that it was only Hannah who could help me sort this out. But as I formulated what to say to her, I realized I was to contact her, but not about this. We were simply to talk, but I did not know about what.

So, I sent her a message saying we need to talk, and she sent back that she was not ready yet. But this did not matter. I had another vivid experience of our Unity, and this one lifted me into my Self and left me There.

After nearly three years of feeling hoisted up to Spirit

now and then only to slide back down a bit each time, to my surprise this time I felt my feet firmly land on the new Level. And since this experience, our Unity has been real and fully established to me. This was the return after a serious parting that I had foreseen, and, whatever our relationship, I am not going to part from Hannah again.

Once again, I felt the meaning of *truest wife* driven home. I had touched on this in The True Unity Epiphany with Hannah in the car on the road to Katanning, and when I realized my lover-like feelings for her were only an insubstantial frame around our Unity. I could call it a mystical *marriage*, *union*, or *partnership*, but those words imply at least two. The best way to describe my experience is a *mystical Unity.* It is Wholeness; It is Christ.

> *Think what a holy relationship can teach! Here is belief in differences undone. Here is the faith in differences shifted to sameness. And here is sight of differences transformed to vision. Reason now can lead you and your brother to the logical conclusion of your union.* (T-22.in.4)

> *Beyond the body that you interposed between you and your brother, and shining in the golden light that reaches it from the bright, endless circle that extends forever, is your holy relationship, beloved of God Himself...For at its center Christ has been reborn, to light His home with vision that overlooks the world.* (T-22.II.12)

A couple of months later, I was meditating and saw how God "inflows" into Christ. I saw Their Unity. And it went through my mind, "This is what your marriage to Hannah is about."

> *The holy relationship reflects the true relationship the Son of God has with his Father in reality.* (T-20.VI.10)

> *...you will realize that your relationship is a reflection of the*

union of the Creator and His Son. (T-22.VI.14)

I was struck that there was no irony or air quotes around the word *marriage*. Later it occurred to me that ideas like *wife* and *marriage* were being reworked for me the way the *Course* redefined common and religious terms. As Spirit, what could be called *marriage* but Unity? What could be called *wife* but my Self? What fell away when I felt "done with the part of me that was about Hannah" was any emphasis on our material relationship. It was a furtherance of the The Paradigm Shift, the reorientation of my mind. The material world is only an effect, an expression of the Atonement, and has no consequence.

In The Minty Moment during The Terrible Week, I experienced the *essence* of us—Liz-Spirit and Hannah-Spirit, a Unity representing the Onlyness of God. Not long after I returned to the US, I had a future vision of myself walking across Hannah's kitchen to her electric teapot. She was in a room somewhere behind me and I had just come from a discussion with her. I was totally at peace—and I found her mind and communicating with her as difficult as ever. After this vision, I began to accept our material relationship will never be wholly easy or clearly defined. Whatever it will be, it will never manifest the Unity of our essence. We will in some way be in each other's lives, and that is all the material expression it will have.

Unity makes material relationships superfluous. Like all material appearances, they *just so happen to be here*. This is what I was telling myself when I heard in The Dismantling that I was to forget everything I learned about relationships going back to Mom. I thought this referred to *how* I related, but I was telling myself to *forget relationships*—I was already whole and did not need to make them or judge them. Just let them be as they are.

Unity alone is not a thing of dreams. And it is this God's teachers acknowledge as behind the dream, beyond all seeming and yet surely theirs. (M-12.6)

After *The Lift Into My Self*, I was able to access Seeing "beyond all seeming"—the real world. The only way to know my Self and my Wholeness is to look away from physical sight and ego's judgments to Unity instead. Finally, I was able to choose this when I felt ego stirring.

There is something in the mystical holy relationship for me that is beyond Spirit and goes to Christ. I experience my Self as Spirit as the Son of God; I experience my Self as Christ in the Unity revealed in a mystical holy relationship.

In this world, God's Son comes closest to himself in a holy relationship. (T-20.V.1)

Christ comes to what is like Himself; the same, not different. For He is always drawn unto Himself. What is as like Him as a holy relationship? And what draws you and your brother together draws Him to you. (T-22.I.11)

The Wholeness I experience in the corrected consciousness I call Spirit extends to Christ through a mystical holy relationship as I know my Self in a Unity where once the sight of bodies blocked this Vision. I am as God created me as the Golden Unity of the holy relationship wipes out sight of the world, and ego's judgments on it. This is still consciousness, but only just.

Both the Bible and the *Course* state that only through Christ Consciousness can a mind return to God. Christ corrects the authority problem—the question of *source*.

Ego death was not easy, but it was necessary for Christ to emerge in consciousness. It was the effect of Christ on this mind, as was the shape of the life that came before. It shattered the illusion that there ever was a me apart from the whole, and that was a painful correction. But Christ is not painful. On the contrary, It is Wholeness beyond anything ego can offer through human connection, or anything else it offers for fulfillment.

But this does not make human connection and personal

relationships *wrong*. They are part of the experience of consciousness. In fact, they are classrooms in which to learn of the Holy Spirit in a Spirit-centered life. But:

(Dialogue 20210319) *"Sometimes I marvel at how I don't miss the former life. I think of the home that I made and loved, but in the end, I found all that empty. Oh, but it was not the fault of those things. It was not the fault of the world. It is innocent. I did find, if not wholeness, a high degree of satisfaction in that life. No, it was the ego that let me down, because it told me I was a person. And no matter how satisfied the person, being a person could never satisfy me."*

As I maxed out that life, I had the nagging feeling there was something more—the "black box in the corner" of my mind—to overcome. It turned out to be my denial of myself as Christ.

There are a great many details I have not shared in these pages, both dark and Light. *The Grand Tour of Ego* validated everything the *Course* said about ego. I saw behind the curtain, as it were, and peered into its machinery as I had never done before. But I have nothing to add to what has already been written about ego through millennia, except to emphasize what the *Course* says: No matter how vivid, intense, and compelling, it is not real. In the end, that is the only thing anyone needs to know about it.

It is increasingly difficult to discuss my lovely new experiences as I See more and more. I know how others will hear what I have to say, as I used to, and will think they understand, as I used to. What I understood about Spirit in ego-consciousness was incomplete and warped by concepts. Now, any attempt to conceptualize Spirit is like trying to grasp air.

This material life appears like any other life, but I do not experience it as I did in my previous experience of existence. Then, I lived in the appearance. Now, appearances are like debris floating on the surface of a vast ocean of Peace.

As Christ, I am limitless, whole, and free.

AFTERWORD: THE PATH TO (SIX) ACHIEVEMENT

And finally, there is "a period of achievement." It is here that learning is consolidated. Now what was seen as merely shadows before become solid gains, to be counted on in all "emergencies" as well as tranquil times. Indeed, the tranquility is their result; the outcome of honest learning, consistency of thought and full transfer. This is the stage of real peace, for here is Heaven's state fully reflected. From here, the way to Heaven is open and easy. In fact, it is here. Who would "go" anywhere, if peace of mind is already complete? And who would seek to change tranquility for something more desirable? What could be more desirable than this? (M-4.I.A.8)

1

I was used to writing books when it was time to consolidate my learning and move past their topic. So, the first part of this book flowed out as I felt I was putting the former life behind me. But the second part was challenging. Rather than consolidating, I was still coming into understanding, and writing this book became a part of that process. This slowed my writing considerably. And by the end, it became difficult for another reason: A memoir by its very nature is written in personal terms, and the person was falling further and further behind me. The more I emerged as Spirit, the harder it was to recall my material experience and grant it significance.

A Course in Miracles meets you where you are. It uses illusion—the material experience—to lead you back to Truth. For me, this happened almost immediately. I experienced the maximal holy instant—Revelation—and the miracle of the mystical holy relationship. This mind became an embodiment of the *Course*. I did not know, until I began to teach, that I was a manifest instrument of the Atonement.

Consciousness began for me as ego. But once I had those mystical experiences, I had an ever-growing awareness of myself as a split-mind. The dichotomy between God and the material experience—Truth and illusion—crystallized for me over decades. I went forward in this contrast, using Truth to see into and mitigate the discomfort of illusion. I taught Truth to learn of It, which was the Atonement being expressed through this mind.

When I shifted to Spirit-consciousness, my mind was no longer split. It took me almost three years to understand that feeling I no longer had boundaries between inner and outer and higher and lower meant I experienced only one Reality now, God. But for a while I was confused by the changes in my material life, particularly my holy relationship with Hannah. I wondered if there was some reality to the material world after all, but that did not last as I came to understand the material experience as an expression of the Atonement that occurs in minds. The shift in my material life was an effect of the shift in consciousness, like a tidal wave after an earthquake. Some life would show up, and it was inevitable that, as Spirit, I would experience Vision, and this would be expressed as a holy relationship somewhere in it. From my point of view, it could have been any life; it could have been anyone. The form was dictated by the expression of the Atonement.

I could not get comfortable with the material shift for so long because its foreignness is where both ego and Spirit dovetailed. It is not the material life ego thought it shaped and, as Spirit, my life is not in the material world anymore.

There is no narrative in this mind for the person in Spirit-consciousness as there had been in ego-consciousness. But there is a material setting, and that setting is just an appearance. I cannot separate out the setting in which I go forward in Spirit-consciousness from the Spirit-consciousness in which I go forward. They are associated, but not One. So, I feel, first, that Spirit is the remainder of my experience in consciousness and, second, Hannah is in my material life for the rest of my material life. There is no cause and effect here, in either direction. It is only coincidence, but it is coincidence that, as Spirit, I foresee.

I am post-Atonement now. I have no need for correction, and I see no need for it, as I stand at its end. But I continue to see it and play a part that must mean something in it, but no longer to me. The thoughts, feelings, and actions attendant to it are just appearances.

Ego is part of the appearance for me still, but it is no part of my reality. Where in ego-consciousness I felt split between two realities, now ego is suspended in Spirit, and an ever-diminishing part of my experience. No appearance has reality for me, no matter how lovely or how ugly.

Deep into the transition from person to Spirit, as I filled page after page in my journal, I sometimes felt I was simply an experiencer and recorder. Those were moments of true insight. I am consciousness thinking, feeling, observing, and sometimes recording. As far as the material world goes, without ego there is nothing more to do than that.

As far as God goes, however, I am more than consciousness thinking, feeling, observing, and sometimes recording experiences of the material world. I See, and what I see is the real world, a perception that reflects the Wholeness of Heaven. Beyond Seeing, I have Vision, and this Vision is Christ, God's Extension. In Vision, the Seer, the Seeing, and the Seen are Christ. And for me, Christ is a blazing Golden Light and experience of Love, or God's Abundant Wholeness. Christ is the Unity that occurs where once I seemed to see another.

Certainly, the long discomfort and darkness I walked through was the boundary between ego and the rest of consciousness. As ego is about individuality, it was undone. What "died" was my identification with it. *Ego death* was *it dying to me.*

I went through three interrelated things simultaneously: The *emergence of Christ* as my Self, which caused *ego death* and a unique, horrible *Dark Passage* that was not a depression nor a dark night of the soul. I never lost sight of God, but I lost sight of anything I felt was me, Spirit, ego, or person. As I came out of The Dark Passage and ego continued to wind down, I found my Self as Christ.

One morning, after an evening when I had again watched a form of fear rise up and identified it simply as the lack at the heart of ego, I awoke to the thought that in The Grand Tour of Ego and The Dark Passage I brought illusions to Truth to watch them be dispelled. I was lost for so long because I seemed to be revisiting thoughts and feelings I felt long past. I often felt I had regressed. But I was correct that I was past those things. I no longer valued or believed in them. They were like empty buildings, no longer useful or used, but still standing. Yet I had to see them *as constructs*—appearances, illusions. I was correct that the reason I walked through them was *because they were there to be walked through*. They were the stuff of my former thought system.

I was also correct that I would not remember how bad it was. I know I felt it was terrible at the time, but I cannot recall the *experience* of the darkness.

I had expected that I would come to see illusion as illusion. What I had not expected was that this would occur for me in detail in slow motion over years.

I am not in the Period of Achievement yet. Consistency will take time and more gentle unfolding. Ego continues to wind down and I continue to see through constructs. I understand the material experience is only an appearance that, at most, is an insubstantial framework in which I experience Wholeness. My glorious new world grows in my awareness, and I slowly acclimate to new Seeing and existing. Increasingly, I am aware I am Home. These are the "mere shadows" that are yet to become "solid gains."

I used to think it odd that Achievement was referred to in the *Course* as a *period* when it seemed to be the end, as the word implies. But of course, no state of consciousness is the End. That is God. Yet, as the description indicates, *Achievement* fully reflects Heaven. The *Course* indicates one will appear to remain in the Atonement until their part is over and "God takes the last step."

2

There is a way of living in the world that is not here, although it seems to be. You do not change appearance, though you smile more frequently. Your forehead is serene; your eyes are quiet. And the ones who walk the world as you do recognize their own. Yet those who have not yet perceived the way will recognize you also, and believe that you are like them, as you were before. (W-155.1)

Clients, readers, and friends often want to know how my experience is different. If I say, "I no longer live in the world" they may say, "Then why are you still here?" Of course, I have just told them I am not! They are caught up in the appearance with which I no longer identify.

So, I have thought of a way to put others in my shoes:

Imagine you somehow find yourself back in your ten-year-old body and surroundings. Everyone sees a ten-year-old, but you know you are an adult. You are expected to do what a ten-year-old does. You go to school, do your chores, play with other kids, and follow the rules that your family and society have set for a ten-year-old. It's not hard. Having been ten before, and having much more knowledge and confidence now, you can go through the motions with ease. It's just…it's not your world anymore.

At first, you may feel wonder. You look around your old primary school and reminisce, for example. How different it looks from an adult perspective! What a different experience it is to be in that place with an adult's knowledge and experience and self-awareness. But the contrast fades in time.

You do not respond to things like a ten-year-old, so other kids think you are odd. Your wisdom is alien among them. You enjoy some of their world, and sometimes you get caught up in its pains, but both experiences pass. You are detached from most of it most of the time. Of course, you know the kids do not need to take their childhood troubles so seriously, but if you say that to them, they feel slighted. You hold back a great deal. You must pick your moments to impart your wisdom—with a child's words, of course.

Obviously, if you try to explain your situation, others think you are nuts or strange.

Even those kids who know of adults who regress to their ten-year-old body, and maybe even aspire to this experience themselves one day, are baffled. They've read about this. They've seen YouTube videos. But still, you do not show up the way they expected. Why do you look like a kid, dress like a kid, have the gestures of a kid, and talk about kids' things if you are an adult?

They seem to forget that you are an adult *within*. This whole experience is about what is within, not appearances. You appear to be a child, but you *see* as an adult.

And what else would you talk to kids about but kids' stuff?

They are not so certain now that you *are* an adult in a child's body. Maybe you're a phony; a ten-year-old kid just acting as you think a body-regressed adult would act.

You are far past a world that suits a ten-year-old, so you happily spend a lot of time alone with your adult thoughts and interests. You are not missing anything, because *you* know what you are, despite functioning in a world that only fits your body now—a body you do not identify with anymore.

3

(Dialogue 20210504) *"What am I seeing?*

Just a moment ago I was making notes for (a work of fiction) and it was in the back of my mind how Liz's life now is really no more to me than a book I'm writing. This is the kind of thing I've seen and as fascinating as it is, it is also uncomfortable to think it's real!

And then I returned to editing the memoir and was reading over the first experiences of catching on to living through my own 'death' and I kept having this thing come over me, like a kind of laughter, and sense of how all that darkness and death stuff I went through was just dramatic play and not real or serious. But I wasn't feeling this with lightness. It was in a way more solid than that. I've not felt this before. It has a whiff of world-shift around it. And I'm not even sure what that means! But, like, something I have not done yet…Another step in seeing the unreality of ego and maybe consciousness altogether, but in a new way, like a part of mind I have not accessed yet…It has a feeling of waking up further. And there's something to it that is familiar, as in recognizing myself, from outside "the dream". Yes, being more awake. And so being more about Self than dreamer. This makes me see I'm still very much in the dreamer…I have a joyous-giggle feeling, like Self is laughing…really, in a way, laughing at me, which means laughing at itself. Not in a cruel way, but…yes, joyful. Happy to see me waking—itself waking. But, yes, there is a tinge of laughing at me dreaming, like, how silly. And I sense how I will not feel even as I am now. I will be so different, because my Self is so different from what I thought I was.

Transition-Liz is really the dreamer, isn't she? The Son of God, yes, but the dreaming aspect. So, I went from thinking I was a dream-figure to dreamer of the dream. And it seems the next step will be Self awakening, so being less about the dream I've left and more about…well, God. Christ bridges consciousness and God by looking toward God, leaving consciousness behind."

ONTOLOGY OF A COURSE IN MIRACLES

One day I hit a wall in my study of *A Course in Miracles*. The *Course's* aim is what it calls the *Atonement*, or correction of the perception that you are separate from God. Yet, if God is All and Perfect, as it assures us God is, how could God have even an imperfect thought that needed correcting? I could not go forward until I had an answer and told this to Spirit.

The first thing Spirit said to me was that I was taking it too seriously. This, too, is said in the *Course*. And I got it. Yes, I was, and I could feel that. Yet...that was not enough. I had to have an answer.

What follows is what was given to me that day and the elaboration that came over years. I do not remember when the initial explanation occurred, only that it was referred to as "long ago" by Spirit in my first Dialogues (journal) entry in August of 2005. In time, I came to see that everything in this ontology, or theory of existence, can be found in the *Course*, just not in one place.

Often, Spirit gave me answers that suited my understanding at the time. Some ideas were modified or fell away as I advanced. However, this ontology not only stood up to every question that followed from me or students who came to me, but spiritual insights only continued to illuminate it, up to and into writing this memoir.

Here I share it and what it means about you.

The Ontology

God, being All, must contain the idea of Its Own opposite. But being All, God cannot have an opposite. So, as soon as the idea of not-God arises in God's Mind, it is undone by God's All-encompassing nature. It is only ever an impossible idea.

As God is Formless, Timeless (eternal), One (the Only, whole, the same throughout), and Infinite, the idea of not-God is time-bound, diverse, imperfect, limited form. So, *within the idea* of not-God—but not in God— *time* makes it seem like the idea of not-God arose long ago and will be undone in some indefinite future. Time is that instant of the-idea-of-not-God/the-undoing-of-the-idea-of-not-God unfolding as a "story". Time is the illusion of not-God on which all other illusions of not-God rests.

As God *is*, the idea of not-God just is, too—or would be if it could be at all. So, not-God is not intentional, it has no purpose, it is not a sin, nor is it a mistake. As an impossible idea over as soon as it was thought, it is a *false* experience. It is an illusion.

The place in God's Mind where this idea seems to have occurred and been undone is called the *Son of God* in *A Course in Miracles*. The Son of God is always a part of God, so it is split between God and the idea of not-God. The part of the Son of God that never left God is called *Christ*. The idea of not-God in the Son of God's mind is called *perception* (the *Course's* preferred term), *consciousness* (used here), or *awareness*. The Son of God projects an appearance of a universe of form as the material of consciousness. Into this pseudo-reality, the Son of God projects itself as billions of *Sons of God*, each a mind seemingly split between an awareness of God (Christ/Spirit) and not-God (ego).

The material universe is neutral—it has no meaning in itself. This includes persons (bodies and personalities). The conflicts that play out in the material universe reflect the conflicts in the minds (seemingly individual consciousnesses) of the Sons of God.

As time is the expression of that moment of the-idea-of-not-God/the-undoing-of-the-idea-of-not-God, what began as an impossible expression of fear (not-God) was instantly transformed into an expression of Love. So, from the start, time has belonged to *Spirit*, Christ's Extension in consciousness, and been an expression of the *Atonement* (correction). Because that moment was over as soon as it occurred, the Atonement is complete, and the outcome of time as the completed expression of the undoing of the idea of not-God, is inevitable.

Therefore, time does not *bring the Atonement* about, rather it *expresses the already complete Atonement*. So, every moment in time, no matter how it looks, manifests the Atonement's completion. It has never been necessary to take time, and all that happens in it, seriously.

As only one mind seems to project not-God, only one mind seems to be corrected in the Atonement. Each seemingly individual mind, as part of that one mind, manifests that correction, no matter how they appear, or their level of awareness of God. So, everyone, every moment, is playing their part in the Atonement perfectly. This does not mean that every mind will awaken and manifest an awareness of God. It means all awaken simultaneously as each perfectly fulfills their part, just as each piece in a jigsaw puzzle of a castle is necessary to make the picture whole, even if it is not a piece of the castle.

The Atonement occurs in *minds*, so you find it in Spirit within you and, through Spirit's Vision and Seeing, in other minds. The Atonement is any moment of awareness of Truth and is perfect in that moment. It is not a progression, although its effects can be seen in the material unfolding through time, both in individual minds and all minds collectively. As the final expression of what occurs in minds, what unfolds in the material world is the least significant aspect of consciousness. It is only meaningless effect; it has no consequence of its own.

So, you will not find the Atonement in the arc of human history, although you can see the effect of the awareness of God on minds in the arc of human history (as in the world's evolving spiritual understanding through its philosophies, religions, sciences, etc. and their effect on human society, etc.). Because it takes time for correction to show up, the material world will disappear from the Son of God's Mind before the Atonement fully manifests in the material world.

The *Course* points out that there has been no significant awakening yet, but the Atonement can be completed in any single mind or in every mind at any moment. As with everything else in time, the time for the Atonement's completion is predetermined as it is already over.

What This Means About You

In Christ in your mind, you are One with God. Your experience as a person in a world apart from God is an illusion.

Your mind and your life in the world are an *expression* of the Atonement; they do not bring it about. So, any sense of purpose you may have is your sense of the "part" you play in the *expression* of the Atonement. As the Atonement is complete and simply unfolds as the story of time, everything that happens in your mind and material life is predetermined.

While your experience as a person is false, it is not *wrong*. Neither is your experience of ego, which is your identification with the person, with all its attendant fears and willfulness. Whatever is in your mind and plays out in your material life, in every moment it expresses the Atonement. To whatever degree you are aware of God as Reality, it is the Atonement being expressed through you. It is your part in the expression of the Atonement.

You cannot step wrong. You cannot deviate from a predetermined path. Every thought, feeling, and action you take is part of the Atonement. Live as you always have done, as your mind and material life have always been part of the Atonement. Your thoughts, feelings, will, desires, motivations, and actions, while sometimes ego, have always manifested the Atonement. If it is your part to play, you may sort out with Spirit when these are attuned to how things will unfold and when they are ego pulling in its own direction away from the whole unfolding.

Ego cannot prevent the Atonement and at no time is it

an obstacle to the Atonement, although it likes to think it is. In fact, ego (not-God) is the manifest reason *for* the Atonement (correction) *in* the Atonement! Whether you put ego aside, and the timing if you do, is the Atonement.

Some minds manifest the Atonement *overtly* in that in their seeming individuality they are aware of God to some degree. This may be anything from a vague sense of God that they do not pursue, all the way to their fully manifesting Christ Consciousness. But even those who have no conscious awareness of God are part of the Atonement, as no mind can be apart from it. They simply represent the idea of not-God yet to be brought to correction.

Think of it this way: You are watching a movie called "The Atonement". If you do not know that it has a happy ending, you worry for the protagonist over every painful scene. But if you know that it has a happy ending, you understand that the protagonist's pain is only temporary, and you relax and watch with curiosity to see how the happy ending comes about.

You may not find this comforting, as the one Son of God is the protagonist in "The Atonement", and your seemingly individual life represents the Son of God's mind in the middle of the story, not the end. The Atonement does not guarantee that *each* Son of God gets a happy life. But it is not an accident that you are reading this. It is the expression of the Atonement. If you did not before, you now manifest the Atonement in your awareness of it, and you have Comfort and Guidance in Spirit within you. To what degree you are aware of this Comfort is the Atonement manifesting through your mind.

GLOSSARY OF TERMS
(Alphabetical. Underlined words are also in this glossary.)

Atonement
Correction of the perception of separation from God. The moment of the-idea-of-not-God arising and being undone in God's Mind, expressed in time in seemingly individual minds. Ego-consciousness is the condition requiring the Atonement. Spirit is the Source of the correction that is the Atonement.

Authority Problem
Ego-consciousness. The denial of God as your Source; the denial of Christ as your Identity.

Awake (upper case)
God. Knowledge.

Awake/Awakened dream/(an) Awakening (all lower-case)
The state of Spirit-consciousness, when one is aware of God's Onlyness and that consciousness is illusion.

Awareness
Consciousness.

Christ
God's Extension. (As sunlight is the sun's extension.) As the Aspect of God that reaches into consciousness as Spirit, Christ bridges consciousness and God. Christ (Spirit) is all that is real in any consciousness.

Christ Consciousness
Spirit-consciousness. The real world. A joyful, peaceful, loving consciousness of God's transcendent and absolute Onlyness and awareness that consciousness is an illusion. The ultimate manifestation of the Atonement.
As God's Extension, Christ is Eternal, but the *Consciousness* of Christ is an illusion that falls away as consciousness gives way to Knowledge. (I experience Christ as a blazing Golden Light of Love I recognize as my Self. That which experiences, recognizes, and identifies with Christ is the *Consciousness* of Christ

that falls away at Knowledge.)

Consciousness
Existence, experience, being, mind, perception, awareness, relativity. As only God is real, consciousness is an illusion, even the highest consciousness, Consciousness of Christ.

Creation
God's Extension, Christ.

Dream
A metaphor for consciousness as illusion where Spirit-consciousness is an awakened dream and only God can be said to be Awake.

Ego
An individual experience of not-God. One's identification with a person and denial of their True Self, Christ.

Ego-consciousness
Not-God. The denial of God.

Ego-identifier
A label given to a part of my mind that seemed to have over-learned ego, and so has been the last part to enter awakening. I slowly got lost in it as ego "died", but as I emerged from The Forgetting and The Dark Passage, I returned to myself, bringing it with me, unifying my mind. It is the part of my mind in which the habits of ego thinking are strongest.

Enlightenment
Awakened dreaming.

God
The Transcendent, Absolute, and Only Reality. God is formless, limitless, timeless, and unlike anything in consciousness.

God's Onlyness
God's transcendence and absoluteness. The fact that only God is real.

Heaven
God.

Higher Awareness
Spirit's Seeing; the real world.

Higher Miracle
A miracle in which one temporarily shifts consciousness to Spirit and experiences Truth as true or illusion as illusion or both. This comes as a mystical experience rather than intellectual insight.

Holy Relationship
A relationship in which one allows Spirit to lead the way, in essence making Spirit the relationship. A holy relationship is *mystical* if one experiences Unity as the Content of the relationship. In a mystical holy relationship, the relationship is an expression of the awareness of Unity.

Illusion
Consciousness, as only God (Knowledge) is real.

Jesus
A very misunderstood man who lived in the material world two thousand years ago, became aware that Christ is his Identity, manifested Christ Consciousness, and taught that Christ is everyone's True Identity.

Knowledge
God.

Love (upper case)
The transcendent experience of God's Wholeness.

Material Experience
Consciousness. One's experience of oneself as a person in a body in a material world.

Material Unfolding
The Atonement's effect manifesting in the material world as the story of time.

Material World
The physical world perceived by the body's eyes.

Mind
The source of Creation or consciousness. In upper case, Christ Consciousness (Creation) or Knowledge (God), depending on context. In lower case, consciousness.

Miracle
An experience of Truth. This can be anything from an answer from Spirit up to a mystical experience in consciousness, or Higher Miracle.

Mystical
Transcendent, otherworldly; nonmaterial.

Not-God
The aspect of consciousness that denies God, manifesting as ego in seemingly individual minds.

Oneness
The Wholeness of Christ and God. Unity.

Perception
Consciousness.

Person
The body and personality of an individual experience of consciousness.

Pseudo-grief
The strong sense of grief that I thought at first was true grief, then felt was ego's resistance, and finally recognized was simply the experience of ego without covers.

Real World
Spirit-consciousness; nonmaterial Seeing.

Reality
God.

Revelation
A direct experience of God. Knowledge. A Revelation is outside of consciousness.

Seeing
Spirit's nonmaterial perception. I use this to refer to the real world as well as Spirit's awareness of the material unfolding.

Self (upper case)
Christ.

Son of God
The Part of God's Mind that seems to be split between the idea of not-God and Christ, resulting in consciousness. The Split-mind. *A* Son of God is a seemingly individual consciousness. *The* Son of God is consciousness as a whole.

Spirit (Holy Spirit)
Christ's Extension in consciousness. The Source of the Atonement. The Answer to not-God and ego. The replacement thought system for ego. The Bridge between ego and Christ and, as Part of Christ, consciousness and God.

Spirit-consciousness
Christ Consciousness. The real world. A joyous, peaceful, loving consciousness of God's transcendent and absolute Onlyness and the awareness that consciousness is an illusion. The manifestation of the Atonement.

Split-mind
Son of God. Consciousness.

Truth
God or Christ, depending on context.

Unity
The Wholeness of God and Christ. Oneness.

Vision
When lower case, an insight or Seeing. In upper case, a perception of Christ or Christ's Perception. For me, a blazing Golden Light of Love. When I see this but do not identify with it, it is a Vision *of* Christ. When I see this and know it is my Self, it is *Christ's Vision*. *Vision* also refers to recognizing my Self, or Unity, where once I saw another.

World
Depending on context, material world or one's consciousness (ego or Spirit). Ego makes no distinction between the material world and its thoughts about it, but, really, in ego-consciousness you live in ego's thoughts, and this makes up your *world*. Spirit's *world*—the real world—is nonmaterial Seeing.

GLOSSARY OF SIGNIFICANT EVENTS IN LIZ'S EXPERIENCE

(Roughly chronological.)

The Young Golden Time
A period on the edge of Spirit-consciousness after my first Revelation and holy relationship.

Plan B
My sense after experiencing Revelation and the mystical holy relationship that I was not living the life I was meant to. Originally attributed to Emily's leaving my life, but later understood to be because I am Christ and no material life is my real life.

The Hiatus
The approximately 2-year organically occurring break from all things spiritual that I took between the Periods of Sorting Out and Relinquishment.

The Mansion/shack Insights
That I valued ego *only* because I made it.

Ghost in the World
My earliest, unrecognized experiences of myself as Spirit, when I felt unlocalized and no longer a part of the material world.

The Forgetting
The long period between The Mansion/shack Insights and the end of The Dark Passage when I seemed to forget God's Glory and Love and my Identity in Christ.

The Barrenness
A dry, empty place within me that accompanied The Forgetting.

The Spaciousness
A delicious sense of my mind as a vast Space that came be-

tween The Barrenness and The Golden.

The Golden
The Light of Christ that came into the Spaciousness and heralded the shift to Christ Consciousness.

The Author
Early (misunderstood) experiences of Oneness in which I felt I was the Author and everyone and everything was my beloved creation.

The Terrible Conflict
The irreconcilability of my former experience of existence as a person and my new experience of existence as Spirit.

The Hugeness
The feeling of a huge Presence over and around me as I shifted consciousness. I later recognized it as the entirety of my mind.

The Terrible Friday
The day Hannah seemed to leave our relationship before The Break.

The Terrible Week
The conflicted week that followed The Terrible Friday.

The Minty Moment
Two conflated experiences of Hannah during The Terrible Week, in one of which she told me she would be back.

Hannah's Return
When Hannah returned at the end of The Terrible Week and I hit the floor in recognition that existence as I knew it was over, and the end of consciousness had begun.

The Break
The moment my identification with the person of Liz fell away, I saw Hannah is my "truest wife", and felt hurled upward in consciousness and outward toward Australia.

The Wave
The feeling after The Break that I was lifted and carried along

on a strong current I could not resist.

The Dismantling
The undoing of the former Liz's material life.

The One Dark Night
The night I went into a hot red rage of doubt and denial of God after Hannah told me her romantic feelings for me had fallen away. The beginning of The Dark Passage.

The Dark Passage
A year and a half with an undercurrent of death and grief and horror-tinged fear, beginning with One Dark Night and ending with going to the extreme edge of the fear of nonexistence, the threat of insanity, and ego's total denial of Love.

The Grand Tour of Ego
Seeing into every corner of, and the inner workings of, ego, over the course of several years.

The Author
My sense of myself as the Source of my experience of Wholeness, manifesting as shallow material feelings and a lighthearted sense of material life as a play.

The Time of the Daggers
When Hannah was going through a rough patch soon after I arrived, and I felt as if daggers were flying at me through the air.

The Experience as My Self
The moment in Elleker, Western Australia when I knew my Self as Christ.

The Epiphany of True Unity
The moment I experienced the Unity behind my holy relationship with Hannah and felt it as wholly satisfying beyond any emotional connection I could experience as a person, pulling me up into my Self.

Face It
The experience of facing full on thoughts, beliefs, and feelings

that heralded the beginning of the end of them having power over me.

The Golden Threshold
The place in my mind beyond which is God. The Light pouring from the Threshold into my mind is Christ. I first discerned this around the time I was moved to offer Joining in Christ sessions.

The Loop Time
An episode as a child in which I seemed to know myself as Christ and experienced a corresponding dark horror that seemed to link up with the shift in consciousness fifty years later.

The Paradigm Shift
The awareness of the insignificance of the material experience.

The Lift into My Self
The Unity experience with Hannah that lifted me fully into my Self and resulted in acceptance that the form of our material relationship is insignificant.

ACKNOWLEDGMENTS

Thank you to my prereaders, Deb, Ed, Jean, Joan, Kathy, Mike, and Mindy for their proofreading, feedback, and suggestions.

I am solely responsible for any errors that remain.

Made in the USA
Coppell, TX
13 April 2022